Living Is for Living: A Caregiver's Story

Terry Perkins Mitman

Terry's writing always touches my heart. There were many times on my caregiving journey with my mother, who had vascular dementia, that I recalled Terry's words and experiences. I was comforted to know that I was not alone in my fears, doubts, humor, and joy.

—Mary Ann Hill, Massachusetts

My Dad had Lewy Body dementia when he died in 2017 and my Mom has other issues that often bring me to the same edge Terry describes…out here in the wide world it's good to know other people share our struggles.

—Susie Knuth Miller, Wisconsin

I returned to Terry's words over and over again and found so much peace and guidance. While her elderly mother with her memory loss over years and my young, college athlete son with a sudden terminal diagnosis seem so different on the surface, the message I took away and that comforted me the most from her writing was the celebration of a life well lived, no matter the circumstances of death.

—Christy Hale McKenna, Pennsylvania

Comments posted on Terry's blog, thejoyofcaring.com

Living Is for Living

Mom, 1949

A Caregiver's Story

Terry Perkins Mitman

Walk With Me, LLC

Living Is for Living: A Caregiver's Story
© 2022 by Terry Perkins Mitman
ISBN 979-8-9859370-0-8

On the cover: Mom at camp by Terry Perkins Mitman
Edited by Karen Thompson and Genie Daley
Cover and text design and layout by Lindy Gifford, ManifestIdentity.com
Publisher: Walk With Me, LLC, www.walkwithme.site
Printed in the United States of America

Mom, 2019

*This one's for Mom,
Laures Terry Perkins,
and all the rest,
who remind us how to live
even when, especially when,
Alzheimer's disease and other dementias
meddle with our minds.*

ACKNOWLEDGMENTS

I'd like to give thanks to all who read the reflections I blogged,
providing a community that fueled me as I cared for Mom;

to my tutoring colleague, Darlene, and Mom's longtime friend Ann,
who encouraged me to offer these reflections in book form;

to my cousin Margie, who knows me through and through
and is always there to give me a pep talk and make me laugh;

to all Mom's caregivers, who met her where she was,
with friendship and humor, giving me time and space to write;

to my creative coach, Lindy, who helped me share, more broadly,
what I learned before, during, and after our Alzheimer's stretch;

to my faculty adviser, Lisa, at the Chaplaincy Institute of Maine, who so
generously shared her wisdom about book publishing and other things;

and to my copyeditors, Karen and Genie, who carefully reviewed
my every word and gave me confidence to pass this on.

CONTENTS

PREFACE

Here's why I took what felt like a leap of faith and decided to blog. As we cared for eighty-four-year-old Mom, diagnosed a year prior with Alzheimer's disease, I realized what a gift to her and to us were the scrapbooks she'd kept and the memoirs she'd penned, from which I'd made a memory book that she perused daily. I wanted to create my own version of her efforts, woven together with what I'd learned, as mother and daughter, to offer others as they walk their own caregiving paths.

The toughest part of this decision was letting go of the anonymity I'd found so reassuring in the fourteen years I'd attended Twelve Step meetings, which had meant I could share my experience, admit my mistakes, and seek solutions privately. That freedom had allowed me to be honest and get healthy. With practice, I'd made peace with my story and found comfort in sharing it with family and friends. Still, I wondered how I could share our experience caring for Mom on a broader level, while respecting her and others' privacy. In an effort to honor Mom's spirit, I decided to focus on the positive, thus the name of the blog: thejoyofcaring.com.

When I started blogging, eager to help others, the feedback I got actually helped me. Caregiving can feel isolating, especially as needs increase. It can stress even the best of relationships. Early on, my sister-in-law Nancy offered the airline advice to put on my own oxygen mask first, before assisting others. Sharing my caregiving journey was one of the ways I did that. Quite literally, it helped me to breathe, while I helped Mom keep breathing, too.

Later, as a student at the Chaplaincy Institute of Maine, I recognized that this sharing, in addition to caregiving, is one of the ways I am called to serve. Sitting here today, I acknowledge the privilege that supported us in caring for Mom in our pre-pandemic home, as well as the many ways COVID-19 has since intensified and complicated caregiving concerns. I also mourn with those who live in war-torn places, like the Ukraine, whose elder care, in addition to so much else, has been brutally interrupted. I write with deep appreciation that we were able to care for Mom right here, and with profound respect for all who are doing their best to give care in these uncertain and exigent times.

Caring for Mom allowed moments when I sat quietly at her side, looking back at things I'd written before as I reflected on what I was experiencing in the present. Now that Mom is no longer with us, the time has come to connect the dots from this side of our journey together. The reflections that follow, gathered over a twenty-year span as I parented and daughtered—and revisited in a time-travel sort of way—saw me through the twists and turns, the highs and lows, and speak to our efforts to walk with Mom, the best we could, all the way through. I offer them in the order they became relevant in Mom's care, except where it took me longer to find the words, like the decision to help Mom get a DNR (Do Not Resuscitate order).

I've heard it said that Alzheimer's disease and other dementias do not advance in a linear way. Change is not constant and in one direction; it is fast and slow, up and down, and all around. It reminded me of parenting when I'd struggle, find my way, gain confidence, and something new would happen—a developmental milestone, an illness, another pregnancy, a job, world events, a move, a death, the list goes on—I'd stumble and take what I knew, add my research, and carry on the best I could. The same can be said for caregiving. When I began to blog about it, wanting to be authentic and true, I wrote in real time about the experience of caring for Mom as Alzheimer's took its course. Sometimes I was feeling scared, sometimes hopeful, sometimes grateful, sometimes overwhelmed. When it came to shaping these moments into book form, I considered reorganizing, streamlining, supplementing, and omitting.

The thing is, recently ordained an interfaith minister, during a worldwide pandemic, with improved racial awareness, three adult kids raised and launched, and Mom laid to rest, I am not the same person I was when we brought her in, in hopes of keeping her safe from the winter's ice. I thought my job then was to offer an arm as I helped her to the car, to read a book at her side, to help her laugh, to make sure her dog, Cinnamon, was fed. I simply had no idea where each moment would fit in with whatever would come next. I only knew I wanted to be at Mom's side. The reflections in this book, each with its own title, describe different moments in the journey we took together. Looking back now, I can see how the dots connect. I resist pushing them into a line with what I've learned since, and I let them be, connecting them, instead, more like a constellation than a line. What follows reflects what I experienced in real time, with what I knew at the time. I did change tense to reflect the passage of time since and to allow for additional reflection in the present. I realize this format may not be helpful to everybody; however, I hope it will offer solace, connection, and hope to some who, too, are trying to navigate the ups, downs, all arounds, the constellation that is caregiving.

I found Alzheimer's disease, like alcoholism, baffling. Call it denial, survival, or some mix of both, my perception of what was happening to Mom's brain lagged behind what was actually occurring. Much like they guided me in living with others' drinking, even after I'd stopped attending Al-Anon meetings, the Twelve Steps of Alcoholics Anonymous (hereafter, AA) helped me to navigate Mom's dementia. At age twenty-seven, I had no idea how I would come to rely on the relationship I would develop with a *Higher Power*, language I heard at my very first meeting that I could substitute in AA's Twelve Steps for the words *God* and *He*, which, for a variety of reasons, had distanced me from the sacred. And, too, although I was raised to pray in private, my recent chaplaincy studies helped me to appreciate the healing power of shared prayer; in that spirit I also include prayers that lifted me when I faced my own limitations. When it came to organizing all this, the seasons came to mind, not because Mom's time with us folded neatly into the calendar's four quarters, but because of how the nature of her care evolved during the four years she lived with us—from Wintering, to Springing, to Summering, and finally to Falling.

In Wintering, Springing, and Summering, I was anchored in Mom's care, relying on family, friends, caregivers, health professionals, and life before caregiving to help me through. Falling is so different; even now it's hard for me to read the words I wrote. When Mom died, it felt like I ran full speed into a wall as she slipped through the window. While others had veered off, in one way or another, along the way, I hit the wall full force. Falling is my effort to share what I experienced walking through the pain that followed, sober. I finally got why Mom's alcohol use had escalated in her fifties when her mother died of lung cancer. If I were a drinker, my drinking would have escalated, too. I'm grateful for all the ways writing has helped me through instead.

The words that follow describe just one constellation of experiences in the many that made up Mom's life. As I reworked the last drafts of this manuscript, I wrestled again with how to share my story while respecting the privacy of others who were present, too, each with their own stories to tell. The last thing I want is for my sharing to come at another's expense. Raised not to discuss that which causes us pain, I wondered if this whole undertaking was a fool's errand; I considered shutting myself up and putting my experiences on a safe shelf. Thanks to years of hard work, supported by those who continue to welcome my experience, I realized that perhaps instead my fear indicated more work to be done, conversations to be had with those I'd named. The exchanges that followed, so full of blessings and encouragement, were healing, too. I took what I heard, and tweaked where needed, so that I can offer what follows with confidence.

This is not a scholarly look at caregiving.[1] Instead, I offer up how I scrounged around, looking for places to grasp, to get through, to where I stand today, ready for what's next. It's not that I have anything figured out; it's just that I have a whole lot of reflections I wrote along the way that I hope might help others on their own caregiving paths. I am in no way a medical expert; however, I do offer up information that helped me through, some of which has no doubt changed, as we know medical advice can. At book's end, I also include what I gathered in caring for Mom, in a more practical way: Communication Tools used to convey helpful information to health care providers and caregivers and to track Mom's care; a Topic List linked to my reflections to help locate information on specific caregiving topics; and Notes with links to the literature and organizations that helped me make sense of what was happening.

In offering this book, *Living Is for Living*, which Mom liked to say when I asked her about her wishes for end-of-life care, I take what feels like another leap of faith. To quote her as she sat down to write her memoirs years ago: "So here goes."

INTRODUCTION

Mom died two years ago, in our home, me and the animals at her side. We had several years together before that, as Alzheimer's disease took its toll. The nest empty for the first time in nearly three decades, I finally have stretches of time for what I've itched to do: write. Wondering how to proceed, I open a document on my desktop labeled "Mom Memories," which includes odds and ends from before, during, and after her time with us:

- ~ A memory Carol, widowed Mom's travel buddy, shared after Mom died, of the time they missed a connecting flight to Treasure Cay, Bahamas, and Mom marched her down to a separate hangar where she secured two seats on a cargo plane headed their way.
- ~ The strolls Mom and I took around our Wisconsin neighborhood, she in her wheelchair with her dog, Cinnamon, on her lap, asking questions of all sorts: "What happens to the trees in the winter?" "How does the sky get so blue?" "Where have all the birds gone?" "Why aren't there more people out and about?"
- ~ Our first winter back in Maine, when I was prepping frantically to leave for a vacation with my spouse, Doug, and the kids, and Samantha, who'd come from Wisconsin to stand in for me, asked, having pored through scrapbooks with Mom, "What do you want your photo album to look like?"
- ~ Then, upon our return, when the customs agent inquired, "What do you do for employment?" and I answered, "I'm a caregiver," to which he replied, "Keep up the good work."
- ~ There was the Christmas Eve, Mom's last, when we took her to a

service and, the church full, we were seated right up front, behind the podium and beside the manger, and Mom, a twinkle in her eye, whispered to our youngest, Garrett, as the minister came down the aisle, "Did you bring your wallet?" before thoroughly enjoying the caroling—singing the first verses, humming the later ones, and dancing the last ones.

~ And the time I took Mom to the doctor to check the hives across her back. To sweeten the deal, I offered to take her for a picnic at the nearby park or to get ice cream cones and take a leisurely drive afterward, to which she responded, "Why don't we do both?"

~ Also, there was the night when I asked her what I (age fifty-five) should be when I grew up and she offered, "You'd be good working with people...getting together and making things right." Another time, sitting at the table with caregiver Karly, Mom asked me, "Who are you?" and when my "Who do you think I am?" left her blank, I tried instead, "If you could name me anything, what would you choose?" to which she answered, with a smile, "Beautiful girl."

Even when she didn't know it, she was still Mom, pumping me up... except for that time she leaned over to another caregiver, Diane, and whispered, nodding at me, just back from a 160-mile bike trip, "Did she gain weight while she was away?"

Several days before Mom's birthday, the first since she'd died, I dreamed she was sitting at a table, crying. When I asked her why, she said she was sad about how she'd changed and all she'd lost. She stood up, took a step, and fell right on her face. I'm grateful that, in reality, Mom didn't grasp the ways she was changing as a result of Alzheimer's disease. While the rest of us had to figure out how to grieve the losses and still show up, she remained largely unaware.

Journalist Tara Bahrampour describes "a growing camp of people determined to approach dementia care differently, coming at it with a sense of openness, playfulness, and even wonder....It involves a lot of flexibility and willingness to expand one's ideas of how things are supposed to be—even, crazy though it might sound, to see Alzheimer's as a kind of gift."[2] While I'm not sure I'd call it a gift, Alzheimer's did allow Mom the least worried phase of her life, easing memories of loss that had previously weighed her down.

Gregg Levoy, in his book *Callings*, writes that "after working with thousands of patients, the psychologist Arnold Mindell, founder of Process Oriented Psychology, believes that symptoms are often dreams trying to come true and, furthermore, that the medicine is inherent in the symptom."[3] I am convinced that what Mom needed most during her last stretch, in addition to physical care and pain relief, was to let go of the past. Even as we sometimes floundered to make sense of her ever-changing medical needs, we did our best to keep her company and love her through, celebrating the joy of caring for her in the present.

As Lisa Steele-Maley, my faculty adviser at the Chaplaincy Institute of Maine, put it, "When I fell into step with my dad's journey with dementia, I did not have any idea where we were going, how we would get there, or what we would encounter. But we would travel together with attention to the moments that would arise along the way."[4] I am blown away to read Lisa's words today, two years after Mom's death—to think we had walked such similar paths before they crossed. I hope that, in its sharing, our caregiving journey with Mom somehow eases yours, whatever its details, and, at the very least, it helps you to know you do not walk it alone.

WINTERING

Little did we know that the weather would be the least of the natural elements we'd face when we brought Mom from her home in Maine to our home in Wisconsin in a well-intentioned effort to keep her safe and sound. We'd worried, the winter before, that Mom would slip on the ice collecting the mail or get stuck outside in the cold chasing after her dog, Cinnamon. What a relief when the pair came to winter with us.

Finding our way after their arrival, as Mom's physical health began to unravel, we appreciated the help we received from friends, health care professionals, and other resources, like the Alzheimer's Association.[5] I took heart in how words I'd tucked away before about parenting would resurface, reminding me to be positive, playful, and present, even when I felt unsure. When we realized the agitation Mom felt when I stepped away, we discovered that a reminder on the whiteboard—*Mom, I'm tutoring. I'll be home for lunch. Enjoy your book with Cinnamon and Samantha, here to keep you company*—provided a security blanket, keeping her snug until my return.

Wintering Mom meant bringing our hardy Maine chickadee in from her natural habitat, hunkering down, weathering the unexpected, and keeping faith that spring lay ahead.

Dear Higher Power,
Please help me to trust my intuition,
my experience,
my research,
those who know me best.
It's all I can do.
Please help me to stay in this day—
to live it as fully as I can,
to love those around me
as I give myself a little love, too.
Thank you for this opportunity to care…
Please help me to find balance,
handle the stress,
find relief—
so that I may fully live.
Please help me to act in faith.
Thy will be done.
Amen

❧

The Baddest Thing I Ever Did: a parenting flashback

You ask me,
"What was the baddest thing you ever did?"
Your seven-year-old innocence hanging there,
between us in the air.
At first, I shrug,
where do I begin?
Someday maybe I'll share…
the baddest thing I ever did:
I said "yes" when I wish I'd said "no"…
loss of me, loss of health, loss of time for myself.
Too ashamed to write down the details here,
after all this time, still filled with fear.
Fear you'll love me less, if you only knew.
True love of me—a cliché, I know, and one that is true.
Too much, too deep, too painful to pass along—

even after all this time,
so I hold it all in and I answer you back,
"Oh, I did my share,
but the baddest thing I ever did
was not be honest to others,
to say 'yes' when I wish I'd said 'no.'"
Then I ask you back,
"What was the baddest thing you ever did?"
You shrug.
Why didn't I stick with that?

I wrote this poem in 2005 for Garrett, now twenty-three. I'm grateful that, over the years, I learned to share my experience with our kids, even when it meant admitting *the baddest thing (I) ever did*. What a relief to discover that, instead of causing the disappointment I once feared, admitting shortcomings and missteps actually eases the pressure kids feel to get everything right and even helps them process their own regrets. Little did I know how I would lean on this sort of open and honest communication when it came time to care for Mom. Or that, sometimes, "the baddest thing you ever did" can turn out to be the goodest.

～

The Joy of Caring

Before we go any further, I want to acknowledge that caring for others, particularly when they are facing challenges, isn't easy. I state the obvious because I want to make sure that my words do not minimize the difficult reality of watching a loved one decline. After struggling through the first eight months of Mom's care in our home, trying to get a handle on her medical condition and memory changes, facing formidable decisions like moving her out of her own home, retiring her car keys, changing her doctors, and explaining, over and over, the significance of the DNR bracelet she wore, I was exhausted.

Then I had an epiphany. In the midst of all the answers I didn't have, there were three things I knew, because she'd told me so: Mom didn't want to live in assisted care, she did want to be with her dog, Cinnamon, and she didn't want to be, in her words, "a burden." To honor her wishes, my family and I needed to consider: Could we care for her and

Cinnamon in our home without letting them become "a burden"? That didn't mean we'd deny the hard parts; it meant we'd face the challenges, doing our best to retain balance, optimism, and resilience. That's what Mom would want for us.

And so I did my best to shift my perspective from one of incessant worry to one of gratitude: It was an honor to care for Mom in our home during this stage of her life, even with the challenges. That shift changed everything: It raised me up, eased my fears, and returned me, again and again, to inspiration over desperation.

We all need a place to share what hurts, to get support and encouragement; we all need a reminder to feel joy, especially in our most difficult moments. This was one of my motivations for blogging about our experience caring for Mom. In calling the blog, with our elder son Matt's encouragement, thejoyofcaring.com, I committed myself to approaching Mom's care in a way that would help me stay healthy, sane, and balanced, so that I could be present for her in a way that she'd have been comfortable with, in a way that would benefit Doug, and our kids, too—in a way that would let me feel joy along with the other emotions that would inevitably arise in our journey with Alzheimer's disease.

When Did Forever Start? another parenting flashback

So many questions
asked along the way:
"When did forever start?"
Who can say?
"Do soldiers have God?"
I sure hope so.
"Will you ever stop loving me?"
Never, no.

When the kids were little, some of their questions were easy to answer, others not so much. I'm grateful that, as they grew and their questions became more complex, they continued to ask. And, too, I'm thankful that, these days, I can ask them questions of my own when I'm trying to figure things out myself. I owe them some toughies!

Celebrating International Women's Day with a Mental Status Reassessment

While people the world over were honoring International Women's Day 2017 in a variety of ways, Mom and I spent the afternoon at the neuropsychologist's office repeating the mental status assessment she'd undergone a year before. As she was being evaluated, I filled out a questionnaire and met with the doctor to share my observations and learn more from his expertise. He explained that Alzheimer's disease typically affects short-term memory first because it begins in the part of the brain where learning occurs. A progressive disease, it then moves to other areas of the brain, leading to more severe symptoms.[6] The testing Mom was undergoing would help us better understand how Alzheimer's was spreading in her brain, which would help us to care for her. Needless to say, I ended up back in the waiting room with plenty to think about and not in good humor.

"How long was I in there?" Mom grimaced as we walked to the elevator afterward.

"Over two hours," I answered (it'd been closer to three).

"There were two of them," she said, "and they took turns while I was in there the whole time."

"You're a trooper, Mom." I gave her a hug. "What did they do with you?"

"Asked me lots of questions to try and figure out what's going on inside my head." She paused as she looked at me and then smiled wryly. "No wonder it took so long."

Mom's intact sense of humor left me laughing as I retrieved the car. When she was all buckled in, riding shotgun again, she said she was hungry and I asked what she'd like.

"Something special," she answered, so off we went for milkshakes.

Speaking of honoring women, what a blessing was Mom's strength, resilience, and good humor—it changed everything. I couldn't begin to imagine a day without her at my side.

The Infinity Between Now and Then

There are infinite numbers between 0 and 1. There's .1 and .12 and .112 and an infinite collection of others. Of course, there is a bigger infinite set of numbers between 0 and 2, or between 0 and a million....There are days, many of them, when I resent the size of my unbounded set....I cannot tell you how thankful I am for our little infinity. I wouldn't trade it for the world. You gave me a forever within the numbered days, and I'm grateful.
—Hazel's eulogy to Gus in John Green's *The Fault in Our Stars*[7]

One time, my cousin Margie mentioned her realization that, living far away from her parents, there was a finite number of times she would see them: two to three times a year multiplied by the number of remaining years of their lives. It was a sobering thought, which thereafter came to mind each time I left my parents in Maine to return to Wisconsin. That changed when Mom left her sweet home on Red Poll Drive to come live with us.

One of the many blessings of caring for Mom in our home was the infinity between now and then. For over thirty years of living thousands of miles apart, each *hello* had started a countdown to *goodbye*. With her living in our home, we had countless moments at each other's side. I'd never expected this, and although it could be challenging and I wished her memory were healthy and well, I was infinitely grateful for this phase in which we got to share a meal, enjoy the birds, watch a movie, look through scrapbooks, cheer our favorite sports teams, and help each other out without a suitcase anywhere in sight.

When I shared this post with Matt, a college senior living twelve hundred miles away, he texted back: "One of the problems in my computer science algorithms course that I did today was to prove that the number of real numbers existing between 0 and 1 is equal to the number of real numbers between negative infinity and infinity so in reality every infinity is just as meaningful as the next :) unless, of course, you compare the number of real numbers to the number of rational numbers. That's an entirely different story."

I am grateful for the promise that, even when time here on earth with our loved ones feels finite, we can still share infinite moments together—and Matt can do the math to prove it!

Note to Self
This is not the time
to doubt
what you're
capable of—
this is the time
to believe.
(Written on a scrap of paper and stuck in a book somewhere along the way)

Our Game

Shortly after Mom returned from a summer visit to Maine, I took her to the doctor for a checkup. In discussing whether it was time to try a medication to slow memory loss, she denied any concerns. A sweet conversation ensued in which the doctor tried to understand her better. She told him that she was quiet by nature so didn't need much talk and that she liked to read. When he asked her what else she liked to do, she replied, "I like to help out where I can…to play Terry's game." When he squinted his eyes quizzically at her, she explained, "You know, to help her in her life."

Years prior, when I'd been a caseworker at a foster care agency in Boston, my adviser had taught me the importance of *reframing*: looking at a situation from a different angle. More recently, a friend whose mom was dying from dementia at age sixty-eight had told me about the technique of *pivoting* (not the political kind): When we find ourselves overthinking, we stop and ask, "What do I want?" over and over until we break the cycle of negativity and find clarity.

Sitting there beside Mom in the doctor's office, I suddenly saw things differently. I thought I had been playing *Mom's* game, helping her with her life, when what she wanted was to help me with mine. So that afternoon as we pulled up to the hairdresser's and she said, "I don't remember why we're here or what's going to happen," I gently explained that we were going to get our hair trimmed, adding, "It's okay, Mom, I help you and you help me. That's what we do; we help each other out."

After that, I quit feeling guilty when Mom folded the laundry or washed the dishes. I realized that her help not only lightened my load, it brought her joy. I even asked her to make me the occasional PB and J (she made the best). At night, in addition to the regular "Good night, Mom, I love you," I added, "Thank you for all your help, it really makes my day easier." That put a smile on her face, which put a smile on mine.

When I asked myself, "What do I want?" the answer was loud and clear: I wanted to keep my balance, I wanted to have fun and appreciate each day, I wanted peace and closeness with my family and friends, I wanted to be healthy. I wanted a world where people treat each other with kindness. I wanted to look to my Higher Power as a source of infinite love and grace. I wanted to be real. I wanted to play this game—*our game*—with Mom.

#marchmadness pivot, aka I'm okay

Stay or go?
I don't know.
Them or her?
I'm not sure.
Where to be?
Don't ask me.
Either way,
I'm okay.

Speaking of *pivoting*, this poem, written on a family vacation in March 2007 when I was torn whether to go fishing with Doug and the kids or stay back and keep Mom company, describes the tension I felt and the commitment I made to handle it, for myself and my loved ones. Later, after Mom moved in, I sometimes faced that same internal tug-of-war. I still didn't want to let anyone down or miss any of the fun. Mom wouldn't want to hold me back, so I tried to embrace this challenge by grabbing the moments I could with each family member, accepting that there would be moments I'd miss in my caregiving role.

In that spirit, one night as Doug and the kids headed downtown to celebrate March Madness by attending the college games being played in Milwaukee, I curled up on the couch with Mom, the dogs, and Lawrence Welk. It helped that that afternoon, while Mom had napped, the family and I had cheered on number-eight Wisconsin as we defeated number-one Villanova to move on to the Sweet Sixteen. On, Wisconsin!

⌒ℯ⌒

In My Defense (Why I Write)

There I was, at age twenty-five, wearing the gray-and-white-houndstooth suit Mom had bought me, sitting across the desk from the partner assigned to interview me for a summer job, explaining how all my years working with kids had led me to law school to become a better advocate. When she dryly replied, "I can't imagine anything less intellectually stimulating than working with children," I was flummoxed. There were many things I could have said, which came to me later, once I realized she may have been looking for me to state my case and show some spine (after all, her firm specialized in litigation). Instead, I awkwardly explained why working with kids in foster care actually did challenge me intellectually. When I got a callback several days later, it was an easy "No thanks."

Still, in my defense:

1. I did not work with kids for the intellectual challenge. I worked with kids because (a) they're awesome; (b) they need nurturing; and (c) they deserve a voice.

Several years later, when I took time off from working outside the home to have our first child and move overseas for Doug's job, a law school classmate predicted I'd never return to my legal career. At a college reunion two years later, another classmate, also an attorney, asked me how educated women like me (still breastfeeding our second) could walk away from a career to raise kids. I sat there, my body aching, literally, for our kids, whom we'd left with the in-laws, unable to find the words to explain. These women were not trying to grill me; they spoke instead out of authentic concern. In both instances, I quietly took in their words and, because they were my friends, felt a bit hurt and misunderstood. I didn't question their choices regarding family and career. Why would they question mine?

2. Different people face different circumstances and make different choices. I never expected to do things the way I did, still (a) it all made sense in hindsight; (b) I had no regrets; and (c) I'd found other ways to help the world outside our home.

These experiences comforted me as I faced the challenges that came with the blessings of caring for Mom. When the kids were little, I'd decided to throw myself into their stages rather than drag them at my own pace (that of a somewhat compulsive individual with a knack for long to-do lists) or obsess about what might come next (shout-out to the Twelve Steps of AA and the meetings that helped me with this). One time, well before I had kids, I'd been walking home from law school listening to a tape by author John Bradshaw.[8] He said something to the effect that learning to live with boredom is key to mental health. That crisp sunshiny autumn moment still stands out. I'd always avoided boredom, as that was when my thoughts raced in directions I didn't want them to go. The notion of accepting boredom rather than fleeing it helped me repeatedly, over the years since that fall day, to notice when I was bored and how I react, to let that boredom be part of my experience, and to find outlets, like writing, to help me see it through.

3. This is why I write: It helps me be proactive rather than reactive by (a) providing a place to express, brainstorm, and race at my naturally unfettered pace; (b) allowing me to take an intellectual perspective on the daily grind; (c) giving me room to realize how fortunate I am, for this time, here and now; and (d) offering a way for me to share what I've learned, in the hope it may ease someone else's way.

Today, not only do I chuckle as I recall the self-assured interviewer in her corner office with the view of Boston Common, I also smile as I remember my friends whose questions have motivated me to pay attention to the choices I make. And I'm grateful for all the resources I discovered along the way, in addition to the Twelve Steps of AA, that offered encouragement and guidance as I pursued a healthy way of life.[9]

I'm thankful that over the years I found time to write and to express, an outlet that helped me through this last stretch caring for Mom. As she sat beside me, reading her book, I sat beside her, pecking away at my computer, thinking, strategizing, and having fun. Shout-out to my high school teachers Mr. Mullins and Mr. Conroy, who taught me how to write, and to my legal mentor, Justice Paul J. Yesawich Jr., who showed me how to write.[10]

Memory Loss in the Movies

One night, after watching *Sabrina* (1954), Mom turned to me and said, "That was a fun night."

I agreed, and referring to the love triangle between Audrey Hepburn and two (much older) brothers, one of them Humphrey Bogart, I asked, "Is that how romance was in your day?"

"I can't remember," she shot back playfully.

I must admit, what was going on in Mom's brain was a mystery to me. No wonder, as scientists are still trying to figure that out. One moment she seemed clear as a bell, the next she was calling for me to ask about the divot on her head (the skin doctor's handiwork), on which I'd spread antibiotic cream just moments before. There were times she recalled specific events from way back when, and others when she forgot whole chunks of time. In some ways, she seemed better than a year earlier when she'd moved in with us and we were trying to get a handle on her health. Her sense of humor and personality were intact, and she was content with her daily routine, Cinnamon nearby. At the same time, it was becoming increasingly difficult for her to follow conversations. Sometimes she couldn't find the words; she'd been reading the same book for months; and she had little ability to advocate for herself when it came to health concerns.

As we awaited the results of her mental status reassessment, my mind on memory, I watched two movies that were instructive, not in terms of the science behind Alzheimer's, but in terms of the experience of memory loss (I won't give too much away in case you want to watch):

Memento (2000), recommended by Mom's neuropsychologist, is so effective at conveying the confusion that comes with short-term memory loss that I still wasn't exactly sure what went down. Two stories run side by side: one in black-and-white moving forward in time, the other in color moving backward. Both show the efforts of Leonard, who has anterograde amnesia, to find his wife's attackers; it's unclear what happened to her, as Leonard has no memory of anything after his run-in with them. Leonard's intelligence and personality are intact so that, in each moment, he tries to make sense of what's going on around him; in the absence of short-term memory, he has to rely on notes he leaves himself (on photos, scraps of paper, even tattoos) and people, some trustworthy, some not. It reminded me of how we relied on the whiteboard on the kitchen counter, scrapbooks on the kitchen table, and caregivers who stood in to provide context for Mom when we stepped away, and how susceptible she was to those who might take advantage, like the guy who'd stolen from her when she was still living alone while he'd been "checking the furnace" (code for filling his toolbox with her valuables), as she'd stood by making polite conversation. *Memento* shows how a person with short-term memory loss can be totally engaged in the moment, using other cognitive abilities, and at the same time be completely vulnerable.

In the second movie, it's not short-term memory that is lost; it's long-term memory that is recovered. *Lion* (2016) tells the true story of Saroo, who was adopted from Calcutta by a family in Tasmania. After being left to sleep at a train station while his brother went to find work, Saroo awakes hours later, a thousand miles from his rural hometown. It's not memory loss that makes him vulnerable, it's his youth and his inability to speak Bengali. Over twenty years later, in school for hotel management, Saroo tastes an Indian delicacy, which sparks a flashback. Like Leonard in *Memento*, Saroo tries to reconnect the dots, relying on friends who encourage him to use Google Earth, as well as a map pinned to the wall with tacks and yarn, to find his way back. Even then, his search is challenging, as his long-term memories are anchored in what he experienced as a little boy, so some of the information, like the name of his hometown, is inaccurate. In the end, *Lion* conveys how long-term memory can sometimes be recovered with prompts, support, time, and space.

Obviously, Mom's story differed from those of Leonard and Saroo. Still, their experiences of confusion, frustration, perseverance, resourcefulness, and resilience were instructive. Not only did they put Mom's challenges in context, they affirmed the importance of providing safe space, reliable routine, patient reminders, and respectful boundaries. Just because a person can't remember doesn't mean they can't be fully present in the moment—trying to make sense of the world around them. I'm grateful Mom was near, where we could help.

Rereading this today, in fall of 2021, I lay my hand on my heart as I consider—in addition to memory loss, victims of violence and missing kids—those whose caregiving has been impacted by the COVID-19 pandemic, the ways it has kept families apart, and the blessing of those who have stepped in, where able, to help provide care in such uncertain times.

The Bottom Line

"What's the Bottom Line?"
Dad's catchphrase,
the one he came back to, used to bug me.
I fought its simplicity,
was irritated by his repetitiveness,
preferred the complications.
The Bottom Line:
Dad died almost ten years ago.
He was uncomfortable with difficult emotions.
He worked right up to the end.
He drank too much.
He was imperfect.
The Bottom Line:
Dad was funny.
He was insightful.
He was devoted to Mom, his clients, and his family.
He is still with me.
He was and is my Dad.
(Written in 2012)

As I cared for Mom, I often wondered what Dad would advise. He'd been crystal clear that, when it was his time to die, he hoped we'd "load [his] dinghy up with gin and push [him] out to sea." That's basically what we'd done when we heeded his health care directive and disconnected him from the machine keeping him alive. After my maternal grandmother, "Gum," had died almost two decades earlier, Dad had confided that he was unprepared for the way that losing her had impacted Mom, and he asked me for help. He loved Mom so dearly and, above all else, wanted her to be happy.

Bits of Dad's wisdom floated back to me now, like his words on my wedding day as we prepared to walk down the hill to the lake, me in a long dress and fancy shoes: "Spread your feet for balance and keep your eyes up to see; I'll make sure you don't fall." Not exactly the fatherly wisdom I'd hoped for, that practical advice actually comforted me as I tried my best to care for Mom, her memory giving way. I just needed to spread my feet for balance and keep my eyes up to see, and trust we wouldn't fall. I felt Dad's love and support every step of the way.

The Bottom Line:
I love you, Dad.
I miss you, Dad.
I carry you with me every day.
I know you trust me to take care of Mom.
I will do my best to protect her happiness, health,
and independence without sacrificing my own.
(Added in 2017)

Tuesday's Conversation—On Having a Stroke in the Eye

"How was your morning?" Mom asked as we raced to the ER at the advice of the nurse who'd called us back from the doctor's office.

A moment earlier, Mom had been studying her eyes in the visor mirror, closing one, then the other, trying to make sense: "My eye is open, but it feels like my eyelid is closed."

So far that morning, I'd dropped a stool sample at the vet, gone to a coffee shop to write, tutored seventh graders in math, and spent two hours at a technology store (I thought that would be the trying part of my day). I returned home to find Mom at the table with her PB and J, saying she'd slept funny on her face during her nap and couldn't see out of her right eye.

"Don't let me stay here," Mom said from the wheelchair as we waited in the ER.

"I'll make sure they take good care of you, Mom," I reassured, unsure what was ahead.

"She is on Stroke Alert; things will happen fast," the intake nurse said. I explained to Mom loudly (one hearing aid in the shop) that a lot of people would be coming into her room to help figure out what was going on with her eye.

Mom looked at me, blinked, gathered herself, and said, "The more the merrier."

"I have to ask," said the nurse before the rest arrived. "Do you feel safe in your home?"

"Yes," Mom replied, without hesitation, no confusion there. Thank you for that.

"You been outside?" Mom asked the technician with cold hands attaching her EKG.

"Warm heart," the tech replied in good humor.

"Ouch," said Mom to the prick of another's trying, unsuccessfully, to draw blood.

As Mom was wheeled out for the CAT scan, she looked at me, her jaw set.

"I'll be here when you get back," I promised, realizing I'd been biting the inside of my lip since I'd heard the word *stroke*. I started to scribble notes in my day planner, giving myself something to do in between texting Doug and the kids, drawing on their endless support.

"When are you going?" Mom, freshly CAT-scanned, asked the guy putting in her IV (I hoped he'd have better luck finding a vein than the last one). When Mom told him she was from Maine, he'd replied that he was headed to honeymoon in "Beer Harbor" (aka Bar Harbor). He told Mom he was going in the fall, to which she answered, "Oh, the colors are pretty then."

In between the comings and goings, Mom told me, again and again, "I can't see out of my right eye." Then, when the doctor began his exam, she, already planning her escape, told him, "I can see fine." I asked her to cover her left eye and tell him what she saw, and she modified her response, "I can see some light and your outline, I just can't see the details..."

When he left the room and I explained that he planned to admit her overnight for more tests, Mom looked at me intently and asked, "Is that really necessary?"

It turned out it wasn't. After checking with a nearby eye specialist, the ER doc changed course: Mom's "loss of vision without pain" had given him pause—her EKG, CAT scan, eye pressure, and other vitals were fine, so Mom was discharged. As we drove to the ophthalmologist, Mom, relieved to be sprung, was confused about where we were headed next.

When asked by the ophthalmologist's assistant what was going on, Mom answered, "My ear isn't working," then looked at me. "Or my eye?" Then she added, "My ear, my eye—at this point I don't know the difference." True, it had been a long afternoon.

An in-depth assessment revealed that Mom had suffered a central retinal artery occlusion (CRAO).[11] Who knows what blocked the central artery supplying blood to her right eye (testing in the coming week would, we hoped, figure that out). The sad truth was that, whatever the cause, just ninety minutes of decreased blood supply to the retina, the light-sensitive tissue at the back of the eye, could lead to permanent damage.

I'd never heard of such a thing when our caregiver Hannah had texted me: "Your mom says her right eye is being weird. She can make out my outline but it won't focus and she says this has never happened before. No pain or anything." I'd advised eye drops and monitoring, as recommended by Mom's doc in the past when her eyes bothered. As the morning had progressed, Hannah and I had texted back and forth. While Mom's change in vision had continued, she'd said it wasn't bothering her and had lain down on her favorite couch to read and take her morning nap.

Beginning to question myself for not reacting sooner, I now asked the ophthalmologist whether there was anything we could have done differently to prevent permanent damage. He replied, "Although there are various techniques that can be tried within the first ninety minutes of diminished blood supply, there's no guarantee they would have helped.... These clots usually happen during the night, while a person sleeps and blood pressure drops. By morning, the damage is done." Ugh.

"How are you feeling, Mom?" I asked on the way home afterward. "Fine," she answered, "How about you? That must have been boring for you." I could only wish.

We got home, Mom set about feeding her dog dinner, and I ran out to give an award at the girls' basketball banquet. Afterward, I went for frozen custard with our twenty-three-year-old daughter, Siena, and cried into my turtle sundae. She reminded me that Mom regularly shared her health concerns with me, and that I was constantly assessing, responding, doing my best—trying to figure out what she needed, whether eye drops, Tylenol, the heating pad, simple reassurance, a visit to the doctor—when she could not do so for herself because, thanks to dementia, she couldn't remember the changes in her health.

I thought back through the day: Even once I had called our family physician and described Mom's symptoms to the nurse, it took time for her to check with him and call us back, more time to get Mom to the ER, more time for the Stroke Alert protocol, and more time to get a diagnosis. I couldn't see how that could have happened within ninety minutes, even if we'd known from the start Mom's eye needed medical attention. I mention this here in the hope it might help others get medical care more quickly, in a case like this, in the absence of pain.

I came back to the knowledge that Mom didn't want to be a burden, so I needed to accept that, in my role as her caregiver, there would be things that went wrong in spite of my best efforts, and I needed to go easy on myself. We were doing the best we could, we had incredible support, and Mom was, for the most part, content.

When I got home that Tuesday night, the day Mom had a stroke in her eye likely leaving her sight permanently impaired, I went in to say sweet dreams. After I gave her her nightly medicine, including the long-taken baby aspirin to reduce risk of stroke and the newly prescribed drops to reduce pressure in her injured eye, Mom looked at me and said, "We had a nice afternoon, didn't we?"

"Yes, Mom, we had a nice afternoon." I hugged her, adding, "Thank you for showing me how it's done."

Step Three: Midair Challenge

Step Three: Made a decision to turn our will and our lives over to the care of God as we understood Him [hereafter a Higher Power].
                    —Al-Anon's Twelve Steps & Twelve Traditions[12]

I wrote the following in 2002, when our kids were nine, seven, and four:

Step Three simply asks us to make a decision. Having never belonged to a spiritual community and having grown up skeptical of religion because of the ways I had seen it lead to pain, I found making and sticking with Step Three's decision the single most difficult part of practicing the Twelve Steps.

After attending Al-Anon meetings for seven years, I went to a silent retreat for women in AA, ACOA, and Al-Anon, and I realized that I was right in the lap of Step Three. Making the decision to attend the retreat—to leave my young family for three nights and to open myself up to whatever the retreat would bring—was a stretch. I spent my time alternately wanting to snuggle in and stay a while in that lap, and wanting to jump down and run away.

At the retreat, the leader, a Jesuit minister and recovering alcoholic, called Step Three "a turning point step." He said we prove we've "made a decision to turn our will and our lives over to the care of God *as we understood Him*" by working the rest of the Steps. He also described Step Three as "the surrender step"— the one where we surrender to a Higher Power. He said that fear is a natural part of taking a risk and that we need courage to push on—like a trapeze artist flipping from one trapeze to another, there's a moment when we're suspended in midair. He added that the process of growth involves risk and change; we cannot progress if we stay anchored in the past. Turning "our will and our lives over to the care of a Higher Power" means letting go of our attachment to things and ideas, daily.

I attended that retreat over six years ago. Since then, each time I recommitted myself to finishing the book I'd been working on, I'd been interrupted by life. One morning, before the rest had awoken, or so I thought, I sat down to write. Just as I finished the words *today, five years later, I'm still in midair, still deciding daily,* our early-bird youngest, age four, crept up behind me, snuggled in beside me, and asked me about the war (in Afghanistan), followed by the all-important "What color are your boogers? Are they sometimes pink?" I realized parenting young children in these times constantly stretches and challenges me in ways nothing else ever has. I am so grateful for my developing faith and for this decision to trust something out there greater than me. Something I can grab onto. What a scary and thrilling ride!

Fourteen years later, with all that was going on in the world, and as Siena prepared to head east to graduate school, Matt boarded a plane to return to college for senior spring, and Garrett packed his bag for gap time in the Caribbean, I needed these lessons more than ever. Add in the daily concerns regarding Mom's well-being, and it was key that I turn over my worries, pray for guidance, and trust the intuition that came in return from a Higher Power—to me, the incredible healing power of love. I was grateful for the fourteen years of practice I'd had since journaling the above, letting go of the trapeze, surviving the midair challenges, and grabbing hold on the other side. When Mom told me, for the sixth morning in a row, that she couldn't see out of her right eye and asked, "How can we keep this from happening in my other eye?" I felt a rise of uncertainty, a shortness of breath, a hint of panic, as I calmly reexplained the stroke in her eye, the eye drops and prednisone meant to prevent another clot, and the tests ahead to gather more information.

Like the kids when they were young, Mom trusted me so completely it was sobering. It helped to know I was not alone. I took comfort in the daily joys, like sitting at the kitchen table as she ate her Rice Krispies, banana on top, the kids preparing for the day ahead. I am so grateful for the incredible support we received in these midair moments and for the Step Three reminder to choose faith over despair. As Pastor Sweeting, our son's mentor in Turks and Caicos, liked to say, "We are blessed."

Tuesday's Conversation, a Week Later—On Having a Stroke in the Eye

"Where are we going?" Mom asked on our return trip to the ophthalmologist. When I reexplained, mentioning our afternoon in the ER a week earlier, she had no recollection.

As we sat in the busy waiting room, Mom remarked in a not-so-hushed whisper, "Look at all the old ladies with canes." I looked at her, with her blind eye, her missing hearing aid, her bum hip, and the necessary crutch, and, in spite of the stare she was receiving from one of the other "old ladies," I had to chuckle.

A week earlier, I couldn't even pronounce the word *ophthalmologist*, and I had certainly never heard of a central retinal artery occlusion (CRAO). Since then, I'd done enough research to understand that Mom's sight was not coming back.

"In the past week, I've wondered how we could have gotten Mom help in the brief window between the stroke and the permanent damage," I confided, again, in the doctor.

"It's rare that people get the necessary help the first time they experience this sort of vision loss," he said, "so instead we focus on figuring out the cause and preventing a second clot." In that effort, Mom had a blood test to check her erythrocyte sedimentation rate (sed rate)[13] and an ultrasound to check her carotid arteries (fine). Next, she saw a rheumatologist to consider potential autoimmune disorders and determine whether temporal arteritis (inflammation of the arteries) might be the culprit. In the meantime, in addition to her regular baby aspirin and newly pre-scribed eye drops, Mom was taking prednisone to reduce inflammation. Except for her pink cheeks, she seemed to be weathering the high dose; I was relieved to hear that prednisone could be, over short periods, a "wonder drug."

"What do we do if the vision shifts in the other eye?" I'd asked a week earlier. The eye doctor had advised that, at the first sign of vision change, we were to call him. As an immediate step, we could try gently massag-ing the eyelid and eye underneath to move the clot. Thereafter, if we responded quickly, there were various medical interventions that might help, like drawing fluid out of the eye with a needle to lower pressure, taking a clot-busting drug, or going into a decompression chamber. It was hard to imagine Mom undergoing any of these treatments.

"Is her other eye at increased risk?" I'd asked, and he said that over the first week, yes, hence the prednisone; however, he had many patients who had retained vision in the second eye after a CRAO.

"How do we keep her injured eye healthy?" I'd asked. He advised us to watch for signs of ninety-day glaucoma, which could follow an eye stroke—any pain (in the eye, brow, or head) or redness to the eye, and he wanted to hear from us.

"I feel fine," Mom said, and believe me, I asked her frequently. Each time she rediscovered the loss of vision in her right eye, she said she hoped it didn't happen to the left and accepted my reassurance based on the strategy described above to keep that from happening.

That night, a week later, after I relayed all that we'd learned to Siena so that she, too, was prepared for what the future might bring, Mom stood up to go to bed and thanked me for another nice afternoon. Then she looked at me with her one good eye, smiled, and said, "Thank you for helping me to…to try to stay alive."

Not morbid, not dramatic, just straightforward and true—that was Mom.

Making Time for the One I Chose First

In the midst of all this, Doug and I fell out: He called me bonkers and I called him mean. I received a timely message the next morning at Orange Theory Fitness, when our coach said, as we did our timed row, "Today I will not trade in my children, my spouse, my job…" In other words, if we persevere through pain, we will gain strength. That hit home and provided a much-needed mantra: "Today I will not trade in my spouse."

After time to reflect, I better understood my part in the rift. With Mom, kids, pets, housework, tutoring, exercise, and Doug's work and other-related absence, there was plenty to keep me busy. The fact that I loved this wild mix didn't mean it came without stress, long hours, and unexpected twists and turns. I must admit, time with Doug, when he had my full attention, was rare.

Twenty-one years before, when Doug's job had brought us to the Midwest, far from the place I'd considered home, I decided I wasn't going to dwell on moving back to Maine, as I didn't want that to define our children's family life. Again, this winter, as we'd settled into caring for Mom in our Midwest home, far from where she'd lived the last eighty-four years, I'd pledged to stay positive. Still, that didn't mean having her with us came without new stress: to her, to me, and to others. Even as I wanted to prolong this phase, I realized it brought new challenges and less uninterrupted time for me and Doug.

Citing statistics that reflected the strain caregiving can put on marriage and other relationships, Paula Spencer Scott, author of *Surviving Alzheimer's: Practical Tips and Soul-Saving Wisdom for Caregivers*,[14] recommends "a mental patrol of the important people in [our lives].… Simply knowing to pay attention can help [us] avoid missing crisis situations with those quiet loved ones currently lower down the totem pole."[15] I'm not sure I'd describe Doug as *quiet*; still, he could be when it came to voicing his needs. When I looked back at recent run-ins, I realized that, while they differed in detail, both occurred the day after I'd returned from taking Siena to graduate school interviews while he'd held down the fort. Returning directly into our busy home, I'd misread his cues.

Scott also advises that, when time together is short, it's important to have shared rituals, as "they concentrate [our] togetherness in meaningful ways." Specifically, she recommends creating "small events for various loved ones that [we] can both look forward to." I realized I spent time with others in this way, rebounding the basketball for Garrett, exercising with Siena, hanging out with Mom, texting with Matt, walking the dogs, and breakfasting with friends, yet my regular time with Doug had diminished. Our morning coffee was often cut short, our date nights were infrequent, and even our family dinners had changed.

I saw that we could benefit from a new ritual of our own: When one of us got back from time away, we could give each other our undivided attention to check back in—whether a cup of coffee, a walk, or whatever. I needed to make this a priority; I'd think of it as a reconnection ritual. It turned out it was not my spouse I needed to trade in; it was the stress of being out of sync with him that I needed to address. With our ever-changing lives, some of the rituals we'd set up together along the way, and perhaps taken for granted, had gotten lost in the shuffle. It was time to make an effort to find new rituals that worked—making time for the one I chose first.

Windows Down, Music Up

That summer, when Samantha had brought Mom back to Wisconsin after spending three weeks with her in Maine, I'd asked her what she was most looking forward to doing when she got home. Samantha, easygoing and adventurous, had answered simply: "Driving my car, windows down, music up."

After the neuropsychologist confirmed that Mom's Alzheimer's had moved to the front of her brain, where problem-solving, reasoning, motivation, and emotions are housed, he cautioned me about *caregiver burden*. He advised me to monitor myself, to be aware of how I was doing and to make self-care a priority. Later, when I was talking with Siena about caring for Mom, particularly with respect to the recent vision loss, she told me I'd come a long way from a year ago, when Mom was first with us, in terms of finding balance and being healthy. Her perspective helped me resist the temptation to hunker back down at Mom's side for fear of another eye stroke; that wouldn't work—it wouldn't be good for anybody. Which led to the tremendous gratitude I felt for those who helped us care for Mom so I could care for me.

There was Samantha, who did whatever we needed and whose presence Mom enjoyed, so much so that she'd invited her back to Maine again the next summer. And there was Hannah, Siena's dear friend, who had played on a middle school softball team I'd coached. I'd never foreseen how she would help us, in her patient and upbeat way. There was also my reliable neighbor and friend Jen, who filled in at a moment's notice (like the day after Mom had the stroke in her eye and Garrett needed to go to the ER for a sprained ankle). Samantha, Hannah, and Jen all treated Mom with kindness and respect; they'd become her friends, a blessing that set me free.[16]

I was Mom's primary caregiver and, so far, I was doing fine. I could do this. In fact, I loved doing this, even when it was hard, thanks to Mom's amazing attitude and the incredible support we received so that I could step away to drive "windows down, music up." Yee-haw!

Aren't We Lucky?

"That's a low blow, isn't it?" Mom had said a year earlier, when the neuropsychologist stepped out of the room moments after diagnosing her with "*mild* dementia likely of the Alzheimer's type." The year since had been filled with moments of adapting to that notion and finding joy in the balance.

Fresh off the stroke to her eye, we'd missed the follow-up appointment to her mental reassessment, to see whether and how things had changed over the past year. It was too much to drag Mom to the neuro-psychologist for a conversation she wouldn't recall, so instead, I spoke with the doctor on the phone, taking these notes:

1. Mom is doing well in our home. Her intellectual skills are stable. Her basic attention is superior.

2. Her short-term memory is equally as poor as last year.

3. Mom's naming abilities and executive function skills, like complex reasoning and problem solving, have decreased, making it tough for her to jump from one thing to another, which might lead to behavior that seems rigid.

4. She is now considered impaired on a measure of home health and safety behavior.

Based on these outcomes, the neuropsychologist confirmed the significance of following a daily routine and balancing independence with safety. He explained the importance of *use it or lose it* as dementia progresses, as well as mental stimulation, of which she gets plenty in our busy home. Overall, he said, Mom was doing great here with us; she just needed me to be her decision-maker, and when I was not available, we needed to use the whiteboard to remind her of daily plans and to support whoever was standing in to keep her company.

I had plenty of questions, prompting these replies:

1. *What was happening when Mom's face went blank and she seemed stuck?* The Alzheimer's had moved to the front of her brain, the location of executive functions, motivation, multitasking, and planning. The speed of her thinking had slowed. When Mom seemed stuck, it was because she couldn't reason her way through.

2. *Was the part of Mom's brain that controls necessary functions at risk?* He was not worried about vital things like breathing and swallowing, and Mom's basic cognitive skills were still strong. In a situation like ours, it was not dementia that led to death, it was other health concerns.

3. *Were there medications that we should consider?* Mom's emotional regulation could be affected by the Alzheimer's as it progressed, meaning increased irritability. The doctor advised watching for triggers, like my absence, changes in routine, situations with a lot of people. He said there are antidepressant and antianxiety medications that might help if the emotional toll got too high, though he cautioned that medicines could be tough on the elderly, particularly where there's dementia.[17] When I asked him about Namenda, a medicine I'd heard was sometimes used to treat more advanced Alzheimer's disease, he said that, since Mom was doing so well and Namenda's long-term benefits were minimal, it was best not to rock the boat.

"Wait and see," he said.

4. *What else could we do to care for Mom?* He recommended we pursue medical care to minimize cardiovascular health factors that could affect the health of her brain, as well as provide a healthy diet, regular exercise, and engagement in cognitive and social activities.

Before we hung up, the doctor cautioned me, again, about *caregiver burden* and urged me to take care of myself, as caring for a person with dementia could lead to depression and other health tolls, particularly as decisions got more difficult, like whether having the loved one in the home was still appropriate. (We were a long way from that, I hoped.)

I realized, in retrospect, how fortunate we were that we'd sorted through so many difficult changes, like retiring the car keys, managing finances, overseeing medications, and moving her out of the home where she lived alone, so that Mom could adjust to new challenges, like vision loss, in a safe and consistent environment, with health care and other supports we knew and trusted.

Let me be clear: Mom—a college athlete (who excelled in three varsity sports), a Fulbright scholar (who opted out of a year in Denmark so she could stay close to Dad), and a working mom (who left education to run a small business)—was still Mom. She was adapting to each new change with such resilience and optimism that we were inspired, even as we grieved.

Bottom line? Mom still kicked ass, even with her new diagnosis—"*moderate* dementia of the Alzheimer's type"—as I witnessed at night when I went in to tell her I loved her and she said: "Aren't we lucky?"

Use It or Lose It: **an Invite a Day**

Mom had traveled the world and adapted to heartbreaking losses, all the while retaining her sense of adventure and curiosity. As a toddler, she'd survived a life-threatening infection. As a schoolgirl, she'd loved to compete with the boys on the playground across the street. In her teens, she'd lost her beloved father. In her twenties, she'd ridden her bike through Europe. In her thirties, she'd raised a family while counseling kids at school and then, in her forties, she'd left education to run a box factory. Her fifties had brought the loss of her mother to lung cancer, her sixties the loss of her husband (my dad) to a staph infection. In her seventies, Mom had moved out of our childhood home to a retirement community, where she'd cofounded WAGS (Women Alone Group). Mom's eighties had brought her to us in the Midwest.

When the neuropsychologist advised *use it or lose it* to slow dementia's advance, I understood what that meant with respect to daily activity and self-care. We tried not to overstep, helping where needed while not doing things that Mom could do for herself. In the context of our home, with family and helpers near, Mom was content making her breakfast and lunch, snuggling with her dog, reading her books, folding the laundry, keeping the kitchen clean, and watching the birds outside the window. Who cared if she put chocolate milk on her Rice Krispies? When I asked, she said she was happy, like it hadn't occurred to her not to be.

Still, the doctor's advice gave me pause. At the same time that routine was important in keeping Mom balanced, conversation was slowing, which led me to wonder how we could provide stimulation of the *use it or lose it* variety when it came to her sense of adventure and curiosity. We didn't want her to lose that![18]

Sometimes in the busyness of life, I wondered if I was making the most of our moments together. Sometimes I missed the twice-daily phone calls I'd made to Mom when she'd lived in Maine and we'd share the details of our lives. Sometimes I missed visiting her in her home or taking her on a trip when we'd give each other our undivided attention. With her in our home, I needed to spread my attention, keep myself healthy, while doing my best to keep her healthy, too, which entailed regular outings to various doctors. While we spent lots of time side by side, in parallel play, interactive play was getting trickier. When we sat and talked, Mom often didn't recall it later, so we had a lot of similar conversations; this was particularly challenging when the topics were sad, like the passing of Uncle Bill. It was hard for Mom to process grief when she just couldn't remember. Even with all the time we spent together, I sometimes felt like I wasn't doing enough to provide mental stimulation.

One day, while I was working out, the trainer encouraged the class to "move with purpose," which inspired me to set the goal of making Mom one invitation a day, to provide variety in our daily routine. That afternoon, I invited her upstairs to visit Edith, our newest addition, sequestered from the rest of our animals while she healed. With Mom's bum hip, we usually avoided the stairs. However, with me there to spot her, I hoped the climb might do her good. In the half hour that followed, I gave Mom my undivided attention as she petted this sweet little kitten and we talked about how Edith had arrived after getting stuck in a fence in the December freeze, being brought to the humane society, surviving surgery to remove her frostbitten leg and tail, and being adopted by Siena, who cared for her when the prognosis was poor and named her after one of the first female explorers of Antarctica, another curious and adventurous soul. That visit was a nice little escape for all three of us, no pun intended.

The reality of having Mom with us, with the kind of cognitive change she was experiencing, was that time together did not need to be complex—in fact, the simpler, the better. Routine was paramount and, at the same time, the goal of one invitation a day, in addition to all our regular overlaps, ensured that I was making time for something special each day, which fostered Mom's curiosity and sense of adventure so that, hopefully, she wouldn't lose them.

One morning, I sat at the kitchen table while Mom made me toast with margarine and peanut butter on top. We ate it together while we watched the birds outside the window. It was delicious. It may sound a wee bit self-serving; still, "inviting" Mom to make me a snack and enjoying it together, Edith darting to and fro, was a *use it or lose it* that nurtured me, too.

Step Four: Looking Inward with Love

Step Four: Made a searching and fearless moral inventory of ourselves.
                                —Al-Anon's Twelve Steps & Twelve Traditions[19]

It was day three of our spring break in the Dominican Republic. While Garrett hung out with friends and Doug golfed, I got some much-needed time to reflect. I knew I needed to relax and regroup; still, I found myself fretting: Was I doing enough to care for Mom? I thought I'd found balance, then along came her sudden vision loss and the results of her neuropsychological reassessment and, although I'd kept my worry in check in her presence, now that I had a free moment, I questioned myself. Friday, just before we left town, I'd seen the doctor for numbness in my leg; he suspected compartment syndrome (not serious). Ironic, as compartmentalizing was exactly what I'd needed to do as I'd handed over the reins to my brothers, who would take care of Mom in my absence. Then along came this Step Four reflection I'd scheduled to post today:

> Step Four scared me at first. I didn't need another excuse to
> beat myself up. The word *searching* indicated this was not just a
> surface look. Who knew what I'd find if I dug deep? I persisted
> because I knew I needed a new strategy, and others had found
> relief in this way. There are many guides to this process. The first

time I used *Alateen's 4th Step Inventory*,[20] the next Melody Beattie's *Codependent No More*,[21] and another time Hazelden's *Step Four: Getting Honest*.[22] At the silent retreat I attended, we were advised to write our autobiographies on the left side of a spiral notebook and then fill in missing pieces, themes, and patterns on the right side. These days, Step Four is part of my daily life, trying to be mindful of the choices I make and how they impact myself and others.

I still feel anxious when I look within—what will I find, what will I feel, and what changes will the process bring? The word *fearless* reminds me to go back to Steps One, Two, and Three: I know my life has become unmanageable, I believe a power greater than myself can restore me to sanity, and I make a decision to turn my will and life over to that Higher Power. When I feel afraid, I need to look to the first three steps and find courage in the growth and peace they offer. A Higher Power, which for me is the Power of Love, is there for me, no matter what I find.

I remember Mom teaching me about morals when I was a kid—I'd felt inspired and afraid, glad to have her standards to help me navigate and frightened that I might fall short. I believe Step Four asks us to consider our morals and how they fit our actions and to do so in a moral way, meaning with honesty: We look at the places where the two are consistent, as well as where they are not. This is markedly different from the way I used to critique myself, where I'd focus all my energy on how my actions fell short of the morals I'd been taught, without appreciating all the places where I was making good decisions. As a dear red-haired Al-Anon friend, nearing eighty, would explain to newcomers: "The bad news is that we can't change anybody else; the good news is that we can change ourselves." Step Four helps us along this path; by becoming aware of what's working and what's not, we can consciously choose how we live.

I was grateful for the gentle, healing opportunity AA's Step Four provides to look inward with love. I trusted it would help me step away from my role caring for Mom, to treat myself gently as I processed our last few months, so that I could unwind, reenergize, and get ready to pick the reins back up, bringing joy, when we returned. I felt better already—just in time to have breakfast with the other moms.

The Power of Love

In the midst of this unsettled spell, I got an email from someone I hadn't seen in years:

> Hi, Terry. Your entries are beautifully written, and my heart swells each time I see a new post. You are inviting us in to the specialness of the mother-daughter relationship while allowing us to witness the joys and the challenges of being the caregiver to someone you love so much. There is nothing that prepares us for that role: It is definitely a learn-as-you-go opportunity and responsibility. If anyone can do it with love, commitment, dedication, and an open heart, it is you. Keep enjoying the simple moments with your mom and every little adventure, for they will live in every fiber of your being as your mother's light dims…
>
> Fondly, Andrea

Blogging about my experience caring for Mom not only brought me out of the isolation I sometimes felt, it also provided much-needed fuel to keep at it. My high school coach's message found me when I needed it most—what a clear and undeniable affirmation of the Power of Love.

Thought Bubble Reset

I'm not gonna lie. Despite how thoughtfully I tried to tell our story in the hope that someone else might find help in the words, my real-time approach was not always so coherent, optimistic, or joyful. In reality, I sometimes had crunchy days when, despite my best intentions, I found myself dragged down into painful feelings of loss. I'd been holding a lot in, and there's nothing like free time to wreak havoc on a carefully constructed approach. Here I was, in the Dominican Republic, fifteen hundred miles from home, and I was still worried about my mother, as noted by Doug—apparently I wasn't the only one who needed a break. If you could have seen the thought bubble over my head as we sat and drank our morning coffee, it was filled with anything but vacationing; to the contrary, it was swollen with turbulent thoughts and feelings. Trust me, before the coffee even had a chance to perk me up, that bubble burst.

It wasn't pretty. Until then, I'd shed a few tears, only to rein them back in so I could meet the other needs at hand; this time, I could not quiet myself. I threw my stuff in my bag and, if not for the large body of water between me and Mom, I'd have started walking.

Thanks to the incredible support of my cousin and kids (well worth the ten dollars I paid for the international cellular day pass), I rallied by early afternoon to join our group of twenty-two high school seniors and their parents for an afternoon boat ride to the reef. When we arrived at the beach, the sky was cloudy and gray, the ocean rough though turquoise blue, and there was no sign of clearing overhead. As the first group boarded the skiff to careen through the waves to the party boat, several people opted out. I considered that choice; then, remembering Dad's love of the ocean, even with bad weather and seasickness, I felt comforted.

It started to rain as we boarded the boat after our own bumpy approach. I went to the bow, knowing from experience that, even with Dramamine (sounds like "drama queen") in my system, I would likely be the first to toss my cookies. Up front, face to the wind, was the best place for me when it came to rough seas. While we bounced toward the reef, Doug at my side, I had the nicest conversation with another mom. By the time we reached our destination, it was pouring. We were drenched. No end in sight, the group decided to reschedule. As we made it back to the beach and ran for our hotel, something inside me had shifted—the reset button had been pushed. During that thirty minutes at sea, I'd felt happy, comfortable, and free.

I do realize that the weather didn't revolve around me and my ups and downs as I worked my way through my caring roles; nonetheless, during that brief time on the ocean in wild weather, I'd gotten what I needed—like Dad was taking care of me from above, dumping water on my head, changing things up, and reminding me what it felt like to accept that I'm not in control, to ride it out, and to let myself have some spontaneous fun.

Afterward, my thought bubble was ever so much lighter and calmer—less ominous and fearful, more composed and hopeful—less like a spiral of upset words, more like this reflection—still a lot going on in there, and more orderly and cohesive, too. What a relief!

Vacation Defined: The Dictionaries and Me
Vacation (noun)
(vā-kā'shən) time devoted to pleasure, rest, or relaxation..."
(thefreedictionary.com)
...the sun on the horizon,
the wind in the palms,
the waves on the beach,
my family in their beds asleep, and
Mom at home safe and sound...
"...a period spent away from home or business in travel or recreation..."
(merriam-webster.com)
...exploring new places,
reading a book just for fun,
closing my eyes—sun on my hat, sand under my feet,
enjoying new foods prepared by another,
talking and laughing, together, apart...
"...the time during which a person temporarily ceases regular duties of
any kind and performs other activities...typically used for rest, travel, or
recreation, but may be used for any purpose..."
(webster-dictionary.org)
...I step away,
I unravel,
I rejuvenate,
I rediscover, and
I look forward to returning home to Mom.

The Way That Redeems
Maybe for worriers, it's a blessing to forget—
what we cannot remember, we cannot fret.
Somewhere in the middle, we may get stuck—
then we're totally, shit out of luck.
Unless we have someone, standing right there—
to give us a smile and offer us care.
Being the one to get it done—

can be a bit much and sometimes not fun.
Being a part of a bigger team—
that is the way, the way that redeems.

Memory Dog Goes to the Hospital

It was 4:30 a.m., my second morning waking up on the cot at the foot of Mom's hospital bed, three days after returning from spring break. Apparently, my thought bubble wasn't the only thing that had burst while we were away. I was grateful that Mom and her ruptured diverticulitis were sleeping peacefully. Her mind needed to rest; her body needed to heal. After our first moments in the ER, I'd known Mom needed me at her side. In the two days since, several people had kindly encouraged me to take care of myself, too. I was grateful for the knowledge I'd gained about what helped when I was under stress. Just then, a good night's sleep, exercise, and time with family and friends were elusive. Still, nothing kept me from praying and writing. So rather than just lie there in the dark, my thoughts whirling, I tried what I knew brought relief: I wrote.

A year earlier, I'd taken Mom for a bone marrow biopsy, which would show she did *not* have bone cancer. It was the first time I'd signed a consent form for a procedure on her behalf. Her questions as the medical team had prepped her had made clear she had no memory of why she was there, despite our many conversations, the most recent in the waiting room. I was touched by Mom's trust in me and felt profoundly the responsibility of making decisions on her behalf. While waiting in the room next door, I realized I was like a Seeing Eye dog, only my job was to be Mom's short-term memory where she had none. Mom was totally confused in the recovery room afterward, so I just sat beside her stretcher and explained, over and over, where we were and why. She told me she was glad I was there to help.

"Where's your tail?" Mom asked groggily when I told her I was happy to be her memory dog. Even in her confusion and discomfort, she made me laugh.

Mom had been through so much in the past five weeks, including the sight loss. While the prednisone prescribed afterward may have helped prevent another clot, it sounded like it might have also lessened her ability to fight infection taking root in her belly, masking symptoms that could have given us a heads-up. That Sunday, which marked fifteen years since Dad died, Mom had asked me who I was and how to get to her bedroom: two firsts. The next morning, I took her to the doctor to share my concerns about the changes I saw, as Mom shook her head in disbelief.

"I feel fine," she told the doctor, though she flinched when he touched her abdomen. The next day when he stopped in on her at the hospital, he admitted that, given Mom's initial demeanor and denial of pain, he hadn't expected the abdominal scan he'd expedited to reveal such severe diverticulitis. We were fortunate that the procedure to drain the abscesses in her gut had gone well, and so we waited and hoped the IV antibiotics would address the sepsis.

It came as no surprise that Mom was deeply confused about where she was, what she was doing there, and why her side hurt. Each time someone came in to do something new, she needed help sorting it through. Sometimes, when she seemed the clearest, she also seemed the most confused. Not having had much sleep or time to just *be*, and feeling the tension of what Mom was going through, I wondered how I could take care of me when her need for help was so vast. Then I came across this prayer I'd written when I stepped into my role as Mom's memory dog the year before:

Dear Higher Power, please help me to trust my instincts and intuition.
Please help me to be a good and confident advocate.
Help me to listen, witness, remind, care, and love.
Help me to remember that in this way I can give Mom the best possible life,
and the most possible independence.
Thank you for giving me care as I give her care.
Amen.

I saw how far we'd come. I'd found the support and balance I needed to help me in my caregiving role. As new challenges emerged, I was grateful for the tools we'd developed to help us adapt. It wasn't in my nature to say "I need help"—I wonder where I got that?—so I appreciated when others reminded me to take care of myself. I would continue to do what I knew helped me help Mom: I felt the love (from family and friends who'd come sleep by Mom if I asked, to the wonderful medical caregivers helping her get better, to a Higher Power who was always right there).

I ate good food (thanks to my family for making sure I got that). I took time to exercise. I prayed and I wrote.

Even a memory dog needs a break. As I lay at the foot of Mom's bed—6:50 a.m.—I reread the texts I'd gotten from Garrett the night before when I shared I was feeling low: "Wanna know what my advice is?... Sometimes in life you just gotta take a deep breath and watch some shitty TV." Truth be told, that advice has been helping this memory dog ever since.

↶↷

Homesick

homesick *(adj): longing for home and family while absent from them*
— www.merriam-webster.com

first thing this morning, Mom suddenly sits up in bed. i stop her before she rips out the tube in her side, to wait for a nurse's help to get to the restroom.

when i hand Mom her hearing aid a little later, she tries to put it in her mouth.

as i sit here in her hospital room, day four, i miss home—my family, the animals, the peace, and the fun.

last night, i lay on my cot listening to a deep-voiced man yelling angrily for help and then woke up to the young woman next door banging loudly on her bed. i listened to her swear as the nurse tried to settle her.

"it hurts," says Mom as she refuses the Rice Krispies she usually enjoys, sending me to the nurses' station to communicate the pain.

the nurse, busily preparing another patient for surgery, says she will ask someone else to help. i go back to her a little later, when no one appears, and ask again for pain relief.

when the nurse comes in herself to ask Mom if she has pain, Mom looks at her, confused, and says, "no, why would I have pain?"

i am befuddled. i am afraid. i don't want to miss another sign of something brewing inside.

when the aide brings Tylenol, Mom spits it out. when the aide crushes it up and puts it in food, Mom will not swallow. she won't even take it from me, another first.

until now, Mom has trusted me—if i urged her to do something, she would. i don't know how i will care for her if she stops letting me do so.

i take a walk, cry, gather myself, and return to Mom, who is nibbling a piece of toast.

i am so deeply grateful for my family and friends—last night the kids stole me away to eat while my husband kept Mom company. i have received several supportive emails and texts. today my friend Jen will sit with Mom so i can get home for a bit to take a walk with the dogs, shower, regroup.

until now, because of their support and Mom's willingness to trust me, taking care of her in our home has been doable. now i am unsure and afraid.

i will keep doing my best and, in the meantime, try to learn from the medical staff here. when the PT stops in and Mom doesn't want to get up, the PT doesn't force it. i will do the same.

i sit nearby quietly writing, giving Mom space, in this place where she has so little. she rouses and i offer her orange juice, which she sips. when the aide comes to help her clean up, Mom looks at me unsure, and when I explain that it will feel good to get clean, she closes her eyes and accepts the aide's help. afterward she says it felt good.

if i long for home and family while i am absent from them, i can only imagine what Mom feels inside, if she could find the words.

i think it's time for this memory dog to step aside and call in the BIG dog.

The BIG Dog

What an incredible thing that the hospital allowed dogs to visit— Cinnamon put a big smile on Mom's face, and for that we were grateful. Note to self: Next time they take Mom for an X-ray, or anything else, keep better tabs on the BIG dog so she doesn't run into the room next door looking for her! #learningfrommistakes.

There's Still Joy

This period was more challenging than anything yet, and still there were moments of joy:

~ The silly dance for Mom, which made her laugh as she sucked down the barium for the unexpected abdominal scan and broke my bra so

I had to keep my arms crossed thereafter;
~ The beautiful view from Mom's hospital window, discovered day two when I opened the blinds;
~ Mom's general practitioner stopping in to say hello, in contrast to when Dad was hospitalized for a fatal infection and his doctor couldn't visit because he hadn't been admitted at that hospital, which had traumatized Mom, long after;
~ Mom's visits in the hospital with the BIG dog, Cinnamon;
~ The way the kids showed up, with flowers, balloons, and even jokes, to lighten our days;
~ The various friends who lifted me up with nice texts and funny Lucille Ball clips;
~ The kind message from my mother-in-law, Millie, offering support, and a phone call with one of Mom's longtime friends giving encouragement;
~ Returning from an evening walk to Mom smiling as Doug described places in Maine and, the next day, when he came running from work, coffee in hand, when I lost my composure via text; and
~ The way Mom lit up when my sister-in-law called her on the telephone.

That night, after a tough day, when I roused Mom for her nighttime medicine and then told her how much I loved her, she smiled and said, "I love you, too; thank you for helping me." That moment of clarity was just what I needed to fuel me for another day.

⁓

Around We Go

Shortly after Mom retired in 2006, she had started writing her memoirs for our family. I'd since used them to make a photo book for her. Given the diverticulitis and abscesses that had landed her in the hospital, this section was particularly interesting:

My Ill Health and Recovered Energy
A defining event of my life occurred when I was 1½ years old. I was lucky to survive. A quadruple whammy of diseases coincided—pyolitis, erysipelas, scarlet fever, and a strep infection.

Fortunately, the infection localized in my abdomen and was surgically removed.

Many times I heard Mom's accounts of how state motorcycle cops relayed a new drug from Boston to my hospital one stormy night, of how the only food I would eat was bananas, and of how I had to re-learn to walk after being so weakened!

However, recover I did, and transformed from "a bag of bones and a hank of hair," as Mom so graphically described me, to a tyke highly charged with energy. Over time, my tendency was to run to and from any neighborhood scene—football, softball, ice hockey—where I was typically the only girl....I am thankful that I recovered strength and energy to develop athleticism, which has provided such fun times and lasting friendships.

I hoped that this time around, at almost eighty-five, Mom would recover her strength and energy, without surgery. However, we'd cross that bridge when and if the time came. In the meantime, the doctor said the drain and antibiotics were helping, and if Mom could transition from IV meds to pills, we could take her home. We were determined to get Mom back to our neighborhood for more "fun times and lasting friendships"—we just had to convince her to take her medicine. In the meantime, when Jen arrived to keep Mom company, I'd put the windows down, music up, and go get the BIG dog for another visit.

The Manipulation and Essence of Caring

I started to blog in the middle of the story. So much had led up to that point, from our first glimpse that something was amiss in Mom's memory, to the period of little adaptations hoping it was just normal aging, to the realization that it was something more, requiring us to step up and take care of her in bigger ways. My siblings and I and our families had arrived at this realization with differing perspectives at different points, and Mom simply didn't perceive her need for our help. It had been a road of bumps with sleepless nights, difficult conversations, and limiting freedoms in an effort to prolong Mom's independence as best we could.

Not only is it just plain sad to see a loved one lose memory and other cognitive abilities, it is hard to know, when it isn't requested, how to help in a way that is respectful, responsible, and kind. How many talks would we have about *retiring* the car keys to keep Mom and others safe before we'd just take 'em?

Along the way, I'd struggled with feeling manipulative in caring for Mom. We had so many heart-to-hearts about driving, medicines, finances, health care, visiting caregivers, and living alone, where we'd try to be gentle yet truthful; it was hard for her to understand our concerns because she didn't see what we did. Sometimes she got angry at what felt like a loss of autonomy. She might agree to accept help only to forget, requiring another talk about the topic at hand. It was not unusual for Mom to be out when the helpers we'd hired stopped in for planned visits. With concerns mounting, including the oncoming winter weather and various unattended health issues, we'd flown her to Wisconsin so that she could get medical care there and stay on for a prolonged visit until going back to Maine for the summer. In her clear moments, she'd look me in the eye and ask when she was going home. I'd re-explain and she'd acquiesce and thank me for caring for her; still, I felt bad about what had felt like manipulation.

When I shared my discomfort with Matt, away at college, along came this reply: "Yeah, I get that, the whole situation is clearly difficult for obvious and not-so-obvious reasons. All I can say is if one day you start to lose your memory, I promise to manipulate you to get you the best care and living situation possible even if you can't understand why. And I love you." Sigh.

That text had gotten me through a lot of uncomfortable moments. Since then, Mom's needs had amplified, particularly over the past five weeks with her vision loss and abdominal woes. After our five-night stay, the doctor managing Mom's care (the hospitalist) decided that, given Mom's medical progress and cognitive regress, it was time for discharge. I was grateful when he said there was no question that the best place for her was back in our home and that we needed to trust our instincts when it came to her care. I was concerned regarding her resistance to accepting help, even from me, and relieved when the clinical nurse leader told me she expected this new behavior to abate once Mom got back to her normal surroundings and routine. She explained that cognitive decline while in the hospital is common for patients with dementia, and it would have been worse without my constant presence and the plentiful visits of family, friends, and, of course, Cinnamon. I felt empowered by the promise of an in-home nurse, physical therapy (PT), and occupational therapy (OT) visits to help us meet Mom's new medical needs, like caring for the drain in her side and regaining her mobility.

What had felt a year earlier like *the manipulation of caring* felt now like *the essence of caring*. Mom needed us to make evolving adjustments to provide her care as Alzheimer's disease progressed and her physical health declined. Even as I felt exhausted from our hospital stay, I was eager to get home and find a new groove in the hope that Mom would bounce back. I was ever grateful for the love and support we were receiving from near and far.

Online History During Hospital Stay

Stuff I learned while googling from my cot at the foot of Mom's hospital bed:

Sunday, day before hospitalization: "Who are you?" asked Mom from the rocking chair.

Can prednisone make Alzheimer's worse?—Apparently, this varies patient to patient.[23]

Is it okay to chew prednisone? (Mom had started to chew her pills)—According to webmd.com, "Swallow this medication whole. Do not crush, chew, or break the tablet. Doing so can release all of the drug at once, increasing the risk of side effects."[24]

Monday, day one of hospital stay: "I'm fine," Mom told the doctor, wincing at his touch.

What is diverticulitis and how is it treated?—Diverticulitis happens when pouches in the wall of the colon get inflamed or infected, and can be very painful....Surgery's recommended when it doesn't improve with diet modification or antibiotics, or when there's chronic pain, obstruction, fistula, or abscess.[25] Thanks, webmd.

Chocolate-chip-cookie ice cream sandwich—Because I'm a stress eater and looking at photos was the best I could do on night one of our first hospital stay.

Tuesday, day two of hospital stay: Putting in the drain, IV antibiotics under way.

How to treat an abscess in the abdomen?—Webmd.com reassured me that sometimes the doctor can do so without surgery by using computer tomography (CT) to guide a needle into the inflamed pouch and place a temporary plastic drain.

What is a haiku?—Because Darlene, my tutoring colleague, suggested I write one.

Wednesday, day three of hospital stay: Weaning off prednisone and worsening of dementia.

Prednisone and infection—More from webmd.com, "This medication may mask signs of infection. It can make you more likely to get infections or may worsen any current infections."[26]

Bed alarms for people with dementia—Ideas on keeping Mom safe at night once she gets home.

Thursday, day four of hospital stay: "I hurt so much and you won't help me," Mom said to me after telling the nurses repeatedly that she had no pain. Fortunately, they overheard.

Pain and Alzheimer's disease—It's right there in Daniel J. DeNoon's subtitle: "Undertreated pain plagues Alzheimer's patients who hurt, but can't tell."[27]

Herb Alpert—Trying to get Mom's mind in a better place, and last time, he got her dancing.

Friday, day five of hospital stay: Medical progress at the cost of cognitive decline.

Dementia and hospital—"Hospitalized patients with dementia are at a higher risk for falls, dehydration, inadequate nutrition, untreated pain, and developing delirium," Carole B. Larkin confirms.[28]

Treatment of pain for people with dementia—According to Wilco P. Achterberg, et al., "The evidence presented in this review on pain management in people with dementia demonstrates the severe lack of effective assessment and treatment across the range of clinical settings. Pain is common among the elderly due to the increased prevalence of age-related conditions like osteoporosis, arthritis, and cardiovascular disease, and this is also true for people with dementia. These individuals appear to experience the intensity and affective component of pain differently than their cognitively intact counterparts do. In addition, the loss of communication ability leads to serious difficulties in detecting pain, particularly in more severe stages of dementia. In these individuals, pain is often also expressed in specific behaviors, such as agitation or withdrawal, that might mimic psychiatric conditions...."[29]

Saturday, last day of hospital stay: Gotta poop before going home.

Fecal impaction and dementia—Thanks to Amy M. Collins for this heads-up: "With people living longer and the likelihood of cognitive impairment or dementia increasing with age, all health care providers should be aware of the risk of fecal impaction and its potentially deleterious outcome."[30]

How quickly does Milk of Magnesia work?—Bowel movement is expected within six hours, reassures healthline.com.[31]

A Week of Haikus for Darlene

(i)

On hospital time
with Spring's Midwest prairie view,
I google "haiku."

(ii)

Japanese poem
three lines of five, seven, five
nature inspires.

(iii)

The lake with its geese
"attached by a stream to Maine"
reminds Mom of home.

(iv)

We may wonder why
we reach for the sun each day...
It's the way we love.

(v)

Goslings in the yard,
Mom would enjoy if she could—
I see for us both.

(vi)

Neighbor boy in boots
plops butt-first in the puddle,
his dad and I smile.

(vii)
The dogs tug the leash—
trees bud, flowers bloom, birds sing—
we rejoice at life.

Please Take a Look at Mom

Home from that first hospital stay, all Mom wanted was to lie in bed with Cinnamon. I was supposed to get her back to the ER to have the drain evaluated, figure out whether it was time to have it removed, and discuss what treatment was recommended next. Having spent plenty of time taking Mom to various health care professionals, I better understood their time limits, documentation requirements, and professional distance. I also better understood the importance of advocating on Mom's behalf, especially given the effect dementia had on her ability to advocate for herself. If I could ask one thing on her behalf, it would be: *Please take a look at Mom.*

I'd like to take a moment to describe the muse for this particular reflection: the rheumatologist who barely looked at Mom during our initial visit, after the clot in her eye, when he diagnosed her with temporal arteritis, staring mostly at the computer screen and interrupting our dialogue to record verbal notes on his tape recorder. When I called him after Mom's discharge from the hospital, at the hospitalist's advice, to ask him about the appropriateness of continued prednisone, given her ruptured diverticulitis and accelerated dementia, he advised me to tell her she'd go blind if she didn't take her daily dose, and it was cheaper to swallow a pill than get it in liquid form (his bedside manner would have benefited from a book I was recommended when Mom was first diagnosed with mild cognitive impairment: *The 36-Hour Day*).[32] When I told him she was resisting taking her medicines, he'd recommended I take her to a psychiatrist (I'd get right on that, once I figured out how to get her out of bed). Maybe if he'd stopped to take a look at Mom, or even ask a few questions of me in order to understand us better, we could have had a conversation that was realistic and helpful, and together we could have figured out the best way to address Mom's unique blend of needs (perhaps he was just having a bad moment; so was I—it had been a long week—so I fired his sorry ass).

Anyhoo, enough of that. Let's focus instead on those who did take a look at Mom:

~ Our awesome general practitioner, his nurses and staff, who listened, asked, and considered before laying out options and offering advice. Every time we left their office, Mom would say, "What a nice man." We actually shifted Mom's care from another well-respected and experienced gerontologist to our family doctor, not because we questioned the gerontologist's expertise, it was just that it was so difficult to reach him by phone and to schedule unplanned visits—his practice seemed too darn busy.

~ Then there was the ER doctor who paused in the midst of Mom's Stroke Alert to contact a nearby ophthalmologist and ask whether hospitalization was really the answer when Mom lost the sight in her eye without pain or other symptoms. He was there again a month later when Mom was admitted for diverticulitis and abscesses, and, lo and behold, he recognized us.

~ And the ophthalmologist that diagnosed the arterial occlusion in Mom's right eye, who made the effort to get to know her and checked in on her afterward. Having cared for his own folks as their health declined, he understood the challenges and seemed genuinely to care.

~ Also, the doctors, nurses, aides, and other staff at the hospital who, even juggling all that they did, noted Mom's resistance and adjusted accordingly, letting me help where I could. It couldn't have been easy to put a patient first when she couldn't express herself or accept help, yet they tried to find a balance that was respectful of her while recognizing my role. When they permitted me to bring in Cinnamon to keep Mom company, it was simply awesome. I am grateful that, even as Mom couldn't see them as anything other than invaders of her space, they took a look at her and gave her their best care.

~ In addition, the nice visiting nurse who sat with me at our kitchen table, explaining the significance of a hospice approach, which made intuitive sense given what I'd witnessed the previous ten days. Even with the incredible support of family and friends as we walked this walk, I sometimes felt alone. This kind soul took a look at Mom and at me, and offered her knowledgeable and reassuring guidance on where to go from there to get appropriate support.

~ Last (for now) and not least, the physical therapist who came to our house to help me get Mom out of bed and into the car so that I could get her to the hospital for her appointment, and the valet at the hospital who took the car, even with Cinnamon riding shotgun, so I could accompany Mom inside—fingers crossed that we'd get good news on her healing.

I am grateful to all who actually take a look at those who ask for their help. I see you, too.

We Shall See...One Day at a Time

"We shall see," Dad liked to reply when I'd ask him a question. I'm not sure whether he truly didn't have an answer, he wasn't ready to commit, or he was avoiding my reaction to a "No." Either way, this response reflected his focus on the present and his resistance to worrying about the unknown. I think it came back to his time in the Marines, the responsibility he'd felt for the young men in his command, and his realization that obsessing about the what-ifs could've put them in worse danger. Dad wasn't about to waste time stressing over the unknown, at least not outside his head. I'm guessing he was also trying to teach me a little patience (not exactly an inherent trait). While it wasn't easy to sit in uncertainty, this mantra was oddly reassuring. Like AA's "One Day at a Time," Dad's "We Shall See" freed me to turn my attention elsewhere.

Day seven of Mom's return home after that first hospital stay, I was hopeful. On day two of being home, when she firmly resisted the necessary medicines, nutrition, and hydration, I had lain down beside her in bed, asked her if she was ready to die, and she'd looked at me and said, "Yes." Then she'd taken my hand and we'd lain there together until she turned away—the most lucid moment we'd shared in weeks. I decided then and there that I wouldn't force; I would respect her resistance to the treatments offered, and I'd try other things to bring relief: rub her head, massage her feet, let Cinnamon sleep peacefully at her side, and nod when she asked me if that was the ocean she heard—I'd offer a "gentle presence," as my sister-in-law Heidi called it. (That clarity had brought me relief until I spoke with the rheumatologist and he'd said Mom would go blind if she didn't take the prednisone.)

The next day, when Mom resisted a bit less—taking a sip of water here, a sip of antibiotic there—I asked again whether she was ready to die; this time she shook her head no. It may sound demented to ask a person with dementia such things; however, to respect Mom in caring for her, we constantly looked for information about where she was at and how we could help, without forcing her, which had seemed to shut her down cognitively during her hospital stay. It helped when Hannah had marched in, no questions asked, and delivered Mom's medicine. After that, when Mom shook her head to my attempts, I'd say, "Mom, if you want to live, you need to take this"—dramatic, and yet it worked.

Since then, each day, our attempts to deliver food, water, and medicine had been met with increasing acceptance. Just five days into our new approach, Mom sat at the table for dinner with my brother Dave and his family, who came to visit from Maine. She even ate the bowl of pistachio ice cream he gave her afterwards. Heavens to Betsy—we did not see that coming!

I tried not to get ahead of myself, to stay firmly in this moment, assessing how best to take care of Mom. What-ifs wreaked havoc on the peace and quiet that Mom needed and deserved. So I did the research to be prepared (i.e., purchasing the mat that informed me with a loud chime at one a.m. that Mom had gotten out of bed—her first time up by herself in over two weeks) and addressed each day as it came (S.O.S.-ing the visiting nurse when Mom tore off the "sterile" bandage covering the drain in her side).

When I started to worry about Monday's return to the hospital to see whether the drain could be removed and further surgery avoided, and whether the tubing would escape Mom's curious hands till then, I caught myself: *We Shall See…One Day at a Time.* When I started to worry whether we would know the next time Mom's health turned for the worse or she was in pain, I paused: *We Shall See…One Day at a Time.* When I started to worry about whether we would be able to get Mom back to Maine for a summer visit, I stopped: *We Shall See…One Day at a Time.* When I started to worry about whether Mom would be able to live with us when we moved to Maine that fall: *We Shall See…One Day at a Time.* When I worried whether yesterday's activity was too much and she'd pay for it today: *We Shall See…One Day at a Time.*

We were doing our best to care for Mom in each moment—to offer and love, not to force or press. An approach of "gentle presence" was the best we could give. and so far, it seemed to be helping her regain her strength and her willingness to recover.

As to all the rest: *We Shall See...One Day at a Time.*

Just Listen: another parenting flashback

Listen, just listen...
Why is it so hard to do,
when I know it's what
you need from me most?
I start out trying,
and the next thing I know,
I'm speaking, advising,
wanting to take your pain away.
Listen, just listen...
why is it so hard to do?
I don't want you to feel anxious, sad, or alone,
even though I know that's part of life, too.
You'll be okay,
I'll be okay,
if I just let you be,
to find your way.
So I'll try to listen, just listen...
as long as you'll try to let me know
when it's something different
you need from me.
(Written in 2007 for fourteen-year-old Siena)

Although it's hard to watch our loved ones work through life's challenges, sometimes the very best we can do is be present, witness, reflect, listen—easy to say, hard to do. I regularly caught myself sharing my own experience, wanted or not. It's why I liked the phrase in the Twelve Step meeting welcome: "Take what you like and leave the rest." There's a lot of good advice out there—to a certain degree, though, we all gotta figure stuff out for ourselves. It's what makes us us. After her series of health concerns, caring for Mom had brought listening to a whole new level, requiring all of my senses and a setting aside, or at least a managing, of my emotions so that I could *just listen*, trusting that I'd know when I needed to take action to fix.

Guess Who's Got Her Spark Back?

"Why do I need medicine?" Mom asked, refusing her last dose of antibiotic. After a long day of explaining and re-explaining a lot of big and little things, on top of the weeks trying to nurse her back to health, I snapped. I was tired and I wanted to get her to bed so I could get to bed. All my "Gentle Presence," "We Shall See," and "One Day at a Time" flew right out the window.

"Because you've been sick, Mom, and you almost died, and the medicine's helping you get healthy again," I snapped. Nice.

Fortunately, Doug was sitting there and stepped in to explain to Mom, in a gentler tone, that it made sense she didn't remember being in the hospital, that we loved her, and that we wanted her to take her medicine so she could get all better. I quietly stepped out of the room. Guess who'd gotten her spark back? Not me!

When Siena was seven and barely in second grade, she'd come down with mononucleosis. After a couple of weeks, the school had called to ask when she'd be coming back. "When she gets her spark back," I replied. I'd heard of kids dying from mono complications, and I was not going to rush it. We'd had a great month of October while she recovered at home, playing with her little brothers and learning to read. When she'd gotten her spark back, off to school she went.

I'd learned that medical diagnosis from Mom: When I was young and felt unwell, she cared for me—taking the day off from work or, when I got older, checking in at lunch. When I had my wisdom teeth pulled, she even put a pizza in the blender; nice thought, not recommended. I'd known I was better when she said, "Looks like you got your spark back," her stamp of approval that—my eyes clear, my cheeks pink, and my energy restored—I was ready to go.

The prior seven weeks had been tough on Mom and her health. Her spark had definitely dimmed and, for a while there, I had feared it might be gone for good. The five days in the hospital that helped her survive the infection in her gut had devastated her mental well-being. By the end, frail and exhausted, she'd refused food, water, medicine, and movement. We got her home and, little by little, Mom bounced back, her mind more engaged than it had been for a while.

The weekend visit from Dave and his family was exactly what we all needed; afterwards, when I reminded Mom of the time together, she'd say, "That was fun!" Asking lots of questions and scouring her scrapbooks, Mom tried to make sense of what was going on around her. The drain in her side had been taken out and the bandage removed. She was making gains with the visiting PT and OT whom she'd initially refused. Although she still needed a lot of help, her progress was amazing. Mom had definitely gotten her spark back. Time for me to find mine.

Mom's renewed resistance to medicine wasn't because she was shut down; it was because she didn't understand why she needed it. That night, as I helped her get ready for bed, she asked all sorts of questions. Then when she lay down, she said, "I'm sorry"—I'm not quite sure what for. I said "I'm sorry" back—I'm not quite sure what for. It broke my heart even as I knew it meant that the part of her I'd feared had shut down for good was back. I lay down beside her and she put her forehead to mine. I wanted to cry. How lucky am I?

What Is Your Reason?

"What's your reason for putting on your exercise clothes?" asked another energetic trainer at Orange Theory Fitness. His question got me thinking as I did the morning workout I'd almost skipped. Over the years, I'd put on my exercise clothes for a lot of different reasons:

~ When I was little, it was all about playing and keeping up with my big brothers.

~ In grade school, I mostly wanted to beat the boys (I got that from Mom).

~ As a preteen and young teen, exercise clothes meant team uniforms: I loved to compete.

~ In my late teens, I admit it was vanity: I wanted to look my best in a bikini.

~ In my twenties, my reasons included feeling good in my wedding dress, hanging out with Doug, and running our dog, July.

~ Thirties exercise was all about balance: time with friends playing tennis, time with kids hiking in the woods, and time for me, walking July and the dogs that came next, Bubby Blue and Daisy too.

~ In my forties, I exercised to fight the ways my body was aging and to keep up with our growing kids, whom I loved to coach and help practice their sports—it also helped when anxiety peaked or depression threatened, like when Dad died.

~ When the kids started to leave for college, I launched my MOKFP—Missing Our Kids Fitness Plan—if I exercised every time I missed the kids, I'd be in great shape!—and each winter I participated in the mother-daughter basketball game of Siena's college team—a real kick for an old jock.

~ Fifties exercise was a great way to have some fun, stay healthy, and hang out with our adult kids, rebounding the basketball at the local court and tossing a Frisbee around the yard. I had long recognized that exercise provided a way to relieve stress, clear my mind, and restore my balance. And then, caring for Mom, I learned another benefit from Heidi Godman, executive editor of the Harvard Health Letter: in addition to "reducing the odds of developing heart disease, stroke, and diabetes" and helping "to lose weight, lower blood pressure, prevent depression, or just look better…exercise changes the brain in ways that protect memory and thinking skills. In a study done at the University of British Columbia, researchers found that regular aerobic exercise, the kind that gets your heart and your sweat glands pumping, appears to boost the size of the hippocampus, the brain area involved in verbal memory and learning."[33] A brisk walk counts, too![34] What better reason did I need to put on my exercise clothes than to do what I could to ward off dementia?

Huffing along on the strider, trying to get my twelve splat points, I envisioned Mom two weeks earlier, fresh out of the hospital, her blinds closed, shutting out the world. Then I pictured her after a week recuperating at home, her blinds open. An image came to mind: files spilled across the floor, Mom looking for information in the papers scattered about; for a person who'd always been so efficient, organized, and disciplined, that had to be exhausting. What a blessing that the week's rebound had restored her peace of mind. All of a sudden, I became aware of Afrojack & Matthew Koma's "Illuminate" playing on the sound system to pump us up. Hearing the encouragement to *shine on* made me smile. I don't believe in coincidence. That day, I'd put on my exercise clothes for insight and that was exactly what I got.

Guess who else was getting her spark back?

Motherhood Then, Caregiving Now: another parenting flashback

And now, for a little walk down Memory Lane. I wrote the following years before, when the kids were little and Mom was newly widowed:

It seems appropriate here to take a moment to sum up what motherhood means to me.

Its smells—dirty diapers, curdled milk, baby powder, clean hair, sweet skin, Oreos, peanut butter, laundry detergent, wet sheets, stinky feet, preadolescent armpits.

Its sounds—happy laughter, nighttime coughs, gooey sneezes, tired whining, sharp tones, deep breathing, long sighs, angry wails, sad tears, clean laundry tossing round and round in the dryer, basketball sneakers screeching on the court, the thwack of ball on bat, "what?" "why?" "why not?"

Its tastes—unbrushed teeth, coffee breath, p.b. and j., Eggo waffle crusts, McDonald's french fries, cold food.

Its touch—hugs that choke, little nails that scratch, teeth that bite, fingers that pinch, hair so soft it could make me cry, feet so smooth they take my breath away.

Its look—every color in the rainbow and more, piles of laundry, dirty dishes, constant movement by day, stillness at night, growth before my very eyes, ponytails and cowlicks, sticky faces, changing bodies, skinned knees.

Motherhood has brought me intense highs and lows: excitement, boredom, love, fear, gratitude, anger, amazement, disappointment, connection, isolation, exhilaration, helplessness, crushing responsibility, miracles, and healing faith.

In childhood I felt responsible for our parents; in parenthood I feel responsible for our children. Throughout, I've felt like I wasn't doing enough, and I've struggled to not take on my loved ones' pain, to let them feel it with faith that they'll survive.

My biggest challenge continues to be letting Mom and our kids have their own pain. I can witness it, I can acknowledge it, and in the end it is theirs. I must have faith that they will survive. To think that I somehow can shield them is not only egotistical, it's just plain wrong.

Faith is the way. To me, motherhood is living proof of a Higher Power's love.

A lot of the details had changed since I wrote these words. We'd aged. Still, the challenges I faced as mother and as daughter were strikingly similar; what had comforted me then comforted me now as we walked with Mom on her Alzheimer's path. *Faith is the way.*

To me, caregiving, like motherhood, is living proof of a Higher Power's love.

Step Five and the Transformation of Being Heard

Step Five: Admitted to a Higher Power, *to ourselves and to another human being the exact nature of our wrongs.*
                    —Al-Anon's Twelve Steps & Twelve Traditions[35]

It is this part of the Twelve Steps of AA—the sharing of our Step Four discoveries—that is so different from how I'd done things in the past, when I hid my shortcomings and denied my strengths. Born and raised a self-reliant Mainer, I'd learned to value thinking independently and feeling privately, while trying not to rock the boat (according to my friend Megan, it was the Irish in me that made that tricky). Step Five's opportunity to be honest with others who listened with patience and respect and promised to protect anonymity had freed me of the burden of hiding and the fear of being discovered. This had set me free.

Step Four's "searching and fearless moral inventory" helps us discover "the exact nature of our wrongs." Mine include perfectionism (driven by fear), which fuels obsessive-compulsive behavior, criticism of myself and others, working too hard, and difficulty letting go (no kidding). Step Five had brought me out of hiding, providing me with an opportunity to hear others' perspectives based on their experiences, which had shed new light on how I saw myself.

Step Five is a reality check. Sharing with another, still a choice, is the next step toward recovery. It's in owning "the exact nature of our wrongs" that we become ready to heal and to change, and to let them go. When I got to Step Five, I had already admitted my shortcomings to myself and to a Higher Power; it was telling another that was new. I couldn't have done that without the Twelve Steps' promise of confidentiality.

I was blown away when I realized Step Five's significance when it came to parenting. Step Five helped me to be a more patient and honest listener, willing to share my own lessons without judgment when our kids shared their concerns with me. This took availability—our kids needed to know that we were there for them when they were ready to share. It also required confidentiality—they needed to know that what they shared would remain safe; even once it was spoken, it was still theirs to do with as they chose.

I'm not saying I accomplished this all the time. After all, that would be perfectionistic! I'm saying I tried to be the kind of listener to our kids that had helped me admit the nature of my own wrongs. It wasn't always easy or convenient to listen when they were in pain or shared things that were hard to hear. However, not only does being heard set us free, being able to listen without having to jump in and rescue is transforming, too. Here's to a whole bunch of moments to connect with our loved ones with honesty, respect, and acceptance, especially when it comes to the tough stuff.

SPRINGING

After that first round of health scares that hit like afternoon thunderstorms in the Midwest, I found myself constantly scanning the horizon for subtle shifts and gathering clouds that could portend danger. I researched each new twist in an effort to prevent relapse and, where that wasn't possible, to adopt a new level of care, trying to make sense of a changing landscape, sending down deeper roots to weather new storms in the days ahead.

I realized now that, though Grandma Curtis had lived well into her nineties, that wouldn't necessarily follow for Mom. Newly aware of her fragile health, I no longer feared overstepping in Mom's decision-making and focused instead on how to offer care in a way consistent with the wishes she expressed. Conversations that I'd previously avoided I now sought out, knowing that she wouldn't remember, jotting down notes so that I would.

I attended Alzheimer's Association support group meetings in search of better strategies, like meeting Mom in the moment and not taking her anger personally,[36] as well as connection with others caring for parents in their homes, too. Finding instead spouses caring for spouses, I was awed by their tenacity as they struggled with the steep personal losses and physical demands of caring for a partner with dementia. And, instead of other kids caring for their parents in their homes, I met kids caring for their parents in memory-care facilities. I was sobered by the challenges of that job, too. I better understood that caring for a loved one with dementia is tricky business, whatever the relationship, whatever the living situation, and that we were in this for the long haul, whether Mom continued to live with us or not.

Springing from the winter of Mom's care, my hopeful optimism was layered with a better understanding of what Mom's care would require, promising new challenges in addition to new growth.

⸻

Dear Higher Power,
Please help me through this time of uncertainty and confusion.
Please help me to feel and share your love.
Please help me to accept there is anxiety for me in caring for Mom—
Please love me through it.
Please help me to give myself a break.
Please help me to do the right and loving things for Mom—
it might not always be what she says she wants—
Please give me guidance in those places.
Please help me to honor Mom while she is alive,
and also when she dies.
A DNR—natural death—is the right choice—
It's a choice Mom has made.
It's a choice I agree with.
It's a choice that hurts and relieves.
It's a choice I need to respect.
Please help me to have peace with this.
Thy will be done.
Amen.

⸻

Firstborn Fun: another parenting flashback

I wrote this the day our firstborn turned twenty-four. It was impossible to put to words all that she meant to me, so instead, I share some things about her that had held true since the start:

She's humorous, she humors us, most of the time.
She loves the color blue, and coffee talk.
She can make anything fun, even exercise, just ask the animals!

One time, as I was holding baby Siena in my arms at the airport in Prague (where we were living), I noticed another mother and child: the mom cradling her adult daughter's face in her hands, speaking to her way up close, caressing her cheek—the daughter standing there, taking it in.

It was not sad; it was beautiful. I knew immediately that I wanted that kind of open and honest expression of love with Siena when she grew up. I am eternally grateful to that mother and daughter for sharing that tender farewell; my apologies for gawking!

Seventeen years later, a friend empathized with me as Siena prepared to leave for college a thousand miles away: "I feel for you," Tina said. "You're losing a daughter, a sister, and a best friend." That freshman fall, I felt like I'd gotten the wind knocked out of me. I'd literally jumped up and down with excitement when I saw Siena's feet appear from above on the escalator at the Chicago airport when she flew home for fall break. While a tearful *goodbye* may be part of letting go, there's nothing like reuniting with a joyful *hello*.

I had never expected our firstborn to move home again after college. What a blessing this was and what a relief to know that, even when we lived apart, we stayed close (that would help when she headed off again that fall). I was grateful for the adventures Siena had ahead and, too, for the time together in the interim—it sure helped when it came to caring for Mom in our home.

～🙡🙠～

Bubby Rules
If our dog Bubby Blue made the rules, here's what she'd say:
See a treat? Go ahead and eat.
Want to swim? Jump on in.
Hungry? Help yourself.
See a stranger? Bark.
Don't hold grudges, it's a waste of time.
Tired? Take a nap.
Lonely? Get a hug.
Got an itch? Let someone scratch it.
Need to poop? Poop.
Just keep wagging your tail, and you'll be fine.
Never give up…it's the little things in life that make it worth living.
(Written in May 2015)

～🙡🙠～

Letting Go and Moving On

"Let it go," Dad used to counsel, back in the day, after a high school basketball game when I'd come home, stomach aching, fretting over a missed shot or one too many fouls. At the time, I felt like he didn't understand my frustration, like I wasn't allowed to vent. After raising three kids who played competitive sports, I got it—it wasn't that Dad meant to deny my feelings, it was that he was trying to give me relief.

When Mom had a stroke in her eye, she was put on a daily dose of eighty milligrams of prednisone to prevent another clot while she underwent diagnostic tests. Twelve days later, the soonest appointment available, I took her to a rheumatologist. After explaining her health history as she sat quietly (except to say she felt "excellent" and her pain was a "zero"), the doctor told us that the likely cause of her central retinal artery occlusion was temporal arteritis, a diagnosis that could be confirmed via biopsy. The catch? That procedure had needed to be done *before* Mom had been on the high dose of prednisone for five days, as presumably that treatment was already addressing the problem, making a biopsy inaccurate.

Bottom line? We couldn't do the test to confirm whether Mom had temporal arteritis; instead, we'd treat her "as if" she did, since the opposite could leave her at risk of a second clot. See how infuriating the *bottom line* can be?

Later, I got a call from the rheumatologist: Mom's blood test showed that her sed rate had come down forty-five percent (Yay!), indicating that the prednisone was working and that long-term prednisone treatment, with a tapered dose, was appropriate. That afternoon, as I googled while Mom napped, I learned that half the people with temporal arteritis also have polymyalgia rheumatica, a condition Mom's prior doctor had suspected a year before. When he put her on prednisone, she became subdued; in the absence of typical symptoms or expected improvement, we sought additional opinions from an orthopedist and another primary care doctor. Their conclusion? It was the bruising aftermath of a bone marrow biopsy and not polymyalgia rheumatica that was causing Mom's pain. She was weaned from the prednisone to avoid side effects like problems with mood and memory and increased risk of infection. Mom's pain had diminished and her well-being had improved, until the recent clot in her right eye. I wondered if she'd been treated for polymyalgia rheumatica all along, could we have averted the temporal arteritis and vision loss.

I realized that, in choosing to provide Mom's care at this stage of her life, given her inability to monitor changes and communicate pain herself, stuff was gonna happen that we just couldn't foresee or prevent. Still, I wondered whether there was a way I could provide her care without ultimately feeling I'd let her down. I was relieved when I remembered Dad's postgame advice—"Let it go": not an excuse, a strategy.

Then came another doozy: that first hospitalization for diverticulitis, which accelerated Mom's dementia to "severe." During our stay, I spoke up before they inadvertently doubled her dose of prednisone, and asked repeatedly whether the prednisone still made sense given the infection and change in mental status. When Mom was discharged, we were referred back to the rheumatologist regarding future treatment for temporal arteritis given the infection her body was still fighting; as mentioned previously, that phone call hadn't gone so well. The good news? Four weeks later, Mom was rebounding: She was calm, happy, eating, drinking, sleeping, interacting, and had no memory of any of this. "A miracle!" the visiting OT called her recovery.

When the rheumatologist proved unhelpful, Mom's general practitioner had recommended a different doctor in the same practice, a request refused by the rheumatologist's assistant: "You can't just change to a different doctor because you don't like the first." The prickly conversations with the doctor and his assistant bothered me. Was I being hypersensitive? I wondered, until it dawned on me that not once did either of them ask how Mom was doing. That, plus Garrett's "Mom, you're supposed to be hypersensitive in this situation; you need a doctor that understands that," prompted me to transfer Mom's care to a different practice (even though it would mean a longer wait, more paperwork, a longer drive, and a different hospital system). When I ran this by my sister-in-law, she relayed my eldest brother's advice: "Move on"—which made me smile because it was something Dad would have said, too, in addition to "Let it go."

The uncertainty of Mom's health concerns and the certainty that new twists would occur were givens. Caring for her would likely continue to feel like chasing a little red beam of light. Regret would not help; better to look to the Serenity Prayer:

Higher Power, grant me the serenity to accept the things I cannot change,
courage to change the things I can,
and wisdom to know the difference.

It was time to let go of the woulda-coulda-shouldas inherent in Mom's care and move on to what we could do for her here and now. As put by my friend Barb, who cared for her mom with advanced Alzheimer's disease, "We've got to do the best we can with the information we have in the moment. That's all we can do. Anything else would make this impossible."

We just had to keep advocating based on what we knew, learning as we went, and trying to be ready for whatever came next. Anything else would only get in the way. This was me, letting go and moving on: Note my wild eyes and clenched teeth—"the Curtis jaw," Mom used to call it, in honor of gritty Grandma Curtis from the West Coast.

⁓

"Living Is for Living"—Mom's Three Things

In the many conversations we had regarding whether Mom wanted a Do Not Resuscitate order (DNR)—as per the Alzheimer's Association, "a legal order to prevent any attempts at revival, particularly if CPR or defibrillation is needed"[37]—this was *her* bottom line:

"There's no point to living if you're not really living."

"I've lived a long, healthy life," she'd explain, "I don't want to end up sick and in the hospital." These talks hadn't been easy—particularly as she kept forgetting them so we had them repeatedly each time she rediscovered the legally required bracelet she wore to communicate her DNR decision. At the same time, these talks had been helpful when Mom was hospitalized and I'd needed to verbalize the care she wanted on her behalf. Two things I knew for sure: Mom didn't want to feel pain or prolong dying.

Dying had been exactly what we thought Mom was doing when we brought her home from the hospital that first time, liquid morphine in hand, after diverticulitis had led to sepsis. The OT told me, after the last of five visits, that on day one, she had wondered why the hospitalist had even ordered her services; she'd never expected Mom's comeback. Our goal had been to provide *a gentle presence* for Mom at home, where she'd been so peaceful and content before. It had required a whole new level of attention, which I couldn't have provided without the help of family, friends, caregivers, and visiting nurse, PT, and OT.

The time I'd spent at Mom's side in the hospital helped me take care of her after she came home. We started tracking what medicines, liquids, and nutrients she took in, as well as what her body put out. As Mom started to make baby steps toward improvement, this daily record morphed into a daily checklist (see Appendix) so we could note progress and ensure good care as her needs fluctuated.[38] As Mom reestablished her daily routine, we were more active than before, trying to prevent a fall or other setback while still promoting independence.

What a blessing that, in addition to strategizing how to provide Mom's daily care, we could consider how to help her live meaningfully, to make sure her life was more than just a list of daily to-dos. Previously, when our springer spaniel, Daisy, had gotten a devastating throat cancer that would choke her if we let it, the veterinarian had recommended we make a list of three things that Daisy loved to do, to monitor her quality of life; as long as she could do those three things—go for walks, enjoy good foods, and hang with our pack—her life had quality. Of course, caring for animals raises the question of when euthanasia is the kindest approach, while caring for Mom presented the questions of how to evaluate treatment options and alleviate pain. Nonetheless, thinking about the three things that Mom most enjoyed helped us tailor her days. We had received an unexpected gift of time, with her up and around, interactive and alert, and we wanted to continue to provide the opportunity to heal and also the opportunity to live.

Mom's three things:

1. *"…Got up at 9:30 and had a real lazy breakfast while reading the paper. That is one indulgence you'll have to tolerate. I love to have a calm and prolonged breakfast—not much food but time to read the paper and wake up."*
> —Letter to Dad, at sea with the Naval Reserve
> Officers Training Corps (NROTC), April 7, 1954

Mom wrote this when she was twenty-two. It made me smile. I never knew her to be lazy about anything. What I remembered was her getting up early, making us breakfast while Dad read the paper, and going to work. On Sundays, she made pancakes while Dad chased us around the house playing "Giants." When Mom finally retired, a year after Dad died, she admitted feeling lazy, as if she should be doing something more than taking walks with her neighbors, bringing Cinnamon to a nursing home to provide pet therapy, writing her memoirs, making scrapbooks, visiting friends, planning trips, and looking forward to the next time she'd see family. When Siena went to college far from us and near to her, Mom went to her basketball and softball games and other school events. When I'd visit, Mom and I would enjoy a leisurely cup of coffee followed by breakfast together, neither one of us rushing off to other commitments. A relaxed start to the day was one thing we could make sure to provide in her life with us, even with the additional medical appointments her new health concerns required.

2. There's nothing so pacifying or inspiring than being on the lake at sunset...
—Letter to Dad, at sea with the NROTC, June 23, 1953

Mom loved the outdoors, especially being on the water—swimming, waterskiing, canoeing, sailing, kayaking, and boating. When I was a kid, we used to go out on the boat after dinner, Mom and Dad with their coffee, while the sun set, the loons called, and the stars appeared. When Mom had her shoulder replaced in her seventies, she gave up her beautiful front crawl in favor of her solid sidestroke. I still didn't know how she floated on her back, feet crossed, the way she did. Just the summer before last, she was tossing her crutch aside to swan-dive into the lake. These days, this meant finding a way to get Mom outside or at least to look out the window, throughout the day and especially at sunset. I wasn't sure whether we'd be able to get her to the lake in Maine that summer; we were still monitoring her recovery, day by day. I was starting to understand better, though, that we could find ways to bring what she found so pacifying and inspiring about being on the lake, right there, to our life in Wisconsin.

3...I refuse to stay alone at camp tomorrow evening. I was here alone last night, and it was a long evening in a lonesome neighborhood. Then I decided one thing—I'll never by choice ever live alone. I should think Mom would go crazy.
—Letter to Dad, at sea with the NROTC, June 30, 1953

This one eased my mind considerably when I was fretting about moving Mom from Maine, where she lived on her own with Cinnamon, to Wisconsin so she could live with our family. Until I read these words, I hadn't known she felt that way. Although she'd been heartbroken when Dad died, she persevered through the first year and then sold our childhood home to move to a retirement community. In the winter months, when many headed south, she didn't complain of being lonesome. When the topic first arose, she had no interest in moving out to be closer to other people; I think Cinnamon had provided the companionship she needed. It was helpful to know that, although Mom liked her quiet time and didn't want constant attention or interaction, at her core she liked being around others, which our family life amply provided.

So as I made our daily plans, in addition to the items Mom's daily care required, I added time for three things she'd long enjoyed: a "calm and prolonged breakfast" (no appointments before ten a.m.) with cards she had received from family and friends and other fun things she could peruse; the opportunity to be pacified and inspired by nature, whether through the window, from the front porch, on a stroll around the neighborhood, or from the car as we drove by the lake; and plenty of companionship, whether it was Cinnamon snuggling at her side, a caregiver keeping her company while I was out, or family time, even when it was a bit nuts. Family was still the thing Mom thought about most, looking through scrapbooks and asking what we were all up to—though the details might not stick, the love and concern did. And, of course, there were our nightly good-nights, when I'd tuck Mom in and we'd thank each other for another nice day.

Adding *ta-da!*s to our daily to-dos—this was living.

Step Six: Readiness

Step Six: Were entirely ready to have a Higher Power *remove all these defects of character.*

—Al-Anon's Twelve Steps & Twelve Traditions[39]

According to the Jesuit priest at the silent treat I'd attended years back, "We are 'entirely ready' in direct proportion to having smashed our egos." This requires "a willingness to dispose ourselves to the grace of God, whatever that might be." Yikes—many times I thought I'd let go of some defect of character, only to have it resurface. I could see now that my job in AA's Step Six was not to let my shortcomings go, it was to become "entirely ready" for a Higher Power to remove them from me.

Having admitted my shortcomings, I'd felt urgency to get rid of them so I could find peace and acceptance. Step Six reminds us to pause in this uncomfortable spot, where we feel the pain, to do the grief and work our way through until we come out the other side "entirely ready" (once we get that the pain of the defect outweighs its benefit). Step Six is to be endured, not rushed or forced, lest we create more havoc in our lives. This is the part where we let ourselves feel a Higher Power's love, however that comes to us. For me, it could be a healing memory, a pertinent song, a sudden intuition, a dog's wag, a cleansing rain, Mom's smile, the kids' laughter, Doug's presence, even when I was at my worst.

Like Step Three, Step Six requires faith—faith that if we do the work of becoming ready, a Higher Power will remove our shortcomings. This takes patience. Despite the word *all*, the Steps have worked in my life, little by little. I still have defects of character. They are not "all" gone. Although this is a lifelong process, not a quick fix, I definitely have more peace of mind, joy, and gratitude than when I started.

For years, even as I'd felt sincere gratitude toward my parents for all the ways they'd cared for me, certain aspects of our relationships had felt unresolved. I wanted to forgive the rough spots, yet I couldn't force it. Step Six required me to pause and feel. A friend once said, "Parents have an advantage; they can always go and die on you." Some advantage. Fifteen years since Dad's passing, I'd forgiven him and I felt his forgiveness of me. I don't think I would have received this gift had I not taken the time to become "entirely ready" to let a Higher Power remove my resentments. Since then, Dad had become my ever-present ally, his wisdom helping me care for Mom each step of the way. I was so far beyond forgiveness with her that I was free to love her the best that I could, as each day brought new surprises.

What a relief that all we need to do is become ready to hand over what is holding us back and a Higher Power will do the rest. For one who is a doer, sunup till sundown, Step Six readiness offers a much-needed and eye-opening change of pace. Hallelujah!

~~~

Heads-Up: Infection and Alzheimer's Disease

Although Mom didn't remember that first hospitalization afterward, her cognition did seem clearer than it had in a while. What the hospitalist had described as "severe" dementia, online research suggested could have been due to delirium, and not necessarily permanent—phew!

Three months earlier, I'd actually told the neuropsychologist Mom was doing great—that was before the clot in her eye and ruptured diverticulitis. In caring for Mom, I sometimes felt like we were trying to solve a Rubik's Cube and someone kept adding more colors, the latest one purple. Now, as we awaited the results of another abdominal scan, online research revealed that infections impact memory and cognition in ways I hadn't previously understood. It reminded me of years before, when I'd researched childhood tics and read about a possible connection between strep infection and OCD—who knew?[40]

I did know, from firsthand experience, that a urinary tract infection (UTI) could lead to increased confusion in the elderly, which is why I'd taken Mom to the doctor six weeks earlier when she hadn't known who I was; I'd had no idea, however, that there was a potential link between various infections and the actual development of dementia. Journalist Fiona MacDonald reports on claims of an international group of Alzheimer's researchers that certain viruses or bacteria may be triggering the plaque buildup in the brain characteristic of Alzheimer's disease.[41] A study by Priya Maheshwari and Guy D. Eslick at the University of Sydney showed a strongly positive association between Alzheimer's disease and spirochetes (like Lyme disease) as well as Chlamydophila pneumoniae.[42] Note to the kids: Should I have a change in mental status, please don't forget to mention the Lyme disease that laid me low Siena's senior year of high school!

Moreover, according to researcher Frida Fak Hallenius at Sweden's Food for Health Science Centre at Lund University, another recent study indicated "a direct causal link between gut bacteria and Alzheimer's disease. It was striking that the mice which completely lacked bacteria developed much less plaque in the brain."[43] Mind-blowing to think that bacteria in Mom's abdomen might have been a factor in the development of her Alzheimer's disease. Which led to my two cents in caring for someone with dementia: Even in the absence of pain or other symptoms, *any change is reason to seek help*!

Sudden change of vision without pain? Rub eye gently with finger to dislodge a potential clot, call the ophthalmologist, and head for medical intervention (time is of the essence).

Sudden change of mental status or behavior? Get to the doctor and ask about infection as well as delirium, in addition to other potential causes, even if it requires tests of blood and cerebrospinal fluid not considered routine.

In addition, when changes in memory and cognition first appear, ask the doctor about the role infection could be playing. According to James M. Ellison, MD, MPH, "Recognition of an infection is critically important because some infections, detected early enough, can be halted or even reversed. Discovery of a treatable infectious cause of cognitive impairment is not very common, but it is an important step in the evaluation of anyone suspected of having Alzheimer's disease or another dementia."[44]

Sorry for the redundancy; it's just that some things bear repeating. We were fortunate that after all Mom had been through, her interactivity had returned, as had her sense of humor. As she slogged through another round of pre-CT scan barium, which she kept offering to share, I handed her a magazine to help pass the time. After a quick look at the holiday menus and room makeovers within, she threw the magazine down on the table.

"Housekeeping!" Mom proclaimed. "Who wants to read a magazine about that!"

⸻

Time to Be Three: another parenting flashback

Our ten-year-old, done with elementary school
and on his way to middle school,
sat at the kitchen counter one early summer morning.
"You know what I don't get?" he said to me.
"They start preparing us to be big when we're only three.
We go to preschool to get ready for kindergarten,
To kindergarten to get ready for first grade,
To first grade to get ready for second,
Second to get ready for third,

Third to get ready for fourth,
Fourth to ready for fifth,
And fifth for sixth.
Now there's
sixth for seventh,
seventh for eighth,
then eighth for ninth,
ninth for high school,
high school for college,
and college for your job."
Our ten-year-old looked at me with clarity in his big blue eyes and asked,
"When does a three-year-old get to be three?"

Today, this insightful kid continues to seek a balanced, productive, and fun life. Little had I known back then that the pandemic would bring the adult him home to work from our dining table—speaking of silver linings. My wish for Matt, as he settles back into the world out there, is that he experiences moments, surrounded by family, friends, and his big floppy dog, Tula, secure in his accomplishments, with all the ups and downs, knowing I'm at his side, in spirit, always. While this fifty-seven-year-old gets to be fifty-seven, more than anything, I wish for his twenty-six-year-old to get to be twenty-six.

My Sisters-in-Law
Sisters are different flowers from the same garden.
—Facebook post

Like Mom, I grew up without sisters. As a result, I was extremely close to her and Siena (who also had no sisters). There were times, however, in caring for Mom, when I thought it would be nice to have a sister to lean on, as I saw friends with sisters do. Though I loved my brothers dearly, they were hardly "for sharing laughter and wiping tears" (another *sister* Facebook post)—laughter, yes; tears, not so much.

Sitting in the hospital with Mom when she was unreachable, I'd had a realization. Doug and the kids were awesome, as were our friends Jen, Hannah, and Samantha, who'd all showed up so I could step away. I also appreciated my brothers' support from afar. In addition, I'd gotten some much-needed encouragement, in very distinct ways, from four special women:

My Sisters (in-law)
my brothers' wives:
Nancy, a nurse, who offered her knowledge and experience
in helpful and educational ways,
and Heidi, a caregiver, too, who checked in regularly
with empathy, insight, and concern, and
my husband's sisters:
Jennie, patient and kind, who sent me photos from her garden
—her "happy place"—
reminding me of spring's renewal outside,
and Amy, a youngest like me, who sent texts that made me laugh
and flew west to attend our youngest's high school graduation
with me and Mom
while the rest flew east for our middle's college graduation.

Even when I felt alone in my caregiving role, I wasn't. It was time to make a Facebook post of my own (thank you, Google):

Sisters-in-law, although we are from different gardens,
I love our awesome bouquet!

—⁓⁓—

Under One Roof
Under one roof—a tremendous relief—
our whole family, even when it's brief.
Truly, I'm glad they're livin' their dreams—
still, it's not always as great as it seems.
Keepin' it simple, I miss 'em when they're away—
not said to hold 'em back, just to enjoy this day.
There's nuthin' in the world like our home when it's full—
the laughter, the fun, even the bull.
A rambunctious crowd—I'd have it no other way—
this is our family, each with our say.

Monday will come, as will the fall,
we'll rearrange, still, we'll always be all.
Under one roof—a tremendous relief—
our whole family, even when it's brief.
(Trying to be present for Doug and the kids
in the midst of caring for Mom, summer 2017)

❧

Looking for Dad

The summer before, I'd been in Maine for Father's Day, which coincided with my parents' sixty-first wedding anniversary. Dad had died fourteen years earlier. Here's what I wrote later as I took the train south:

Sunday, June 19, 2016

Mom up around 9, a smile on her face. "Where's Dad? In bed downstairs? I can't find him." She looked at me expectantly. I paused, befuddled. How to break her heart. My niece Holly and her boyfriend Albert, who will spend the summer with Mom in Maine, stood near. "Mom, come with me in here." We entered her bedroom. Again, she looked at me, a glimmer in her eye, a sweet playful expression on her face, "He's not in here....where is he?" she asked. Another pause, then a step... "Mom, I think you may be confused....Dad's not here... not in the physical sense anyway...." a clearing in her eyes..."Oh..." a little laugh. We sat on the foot of her bed. "I guess I haven't woken up yet," she said. Inside my head, a crescendo of tears. Outside my head, I looked her in the eyes. "I love you Mom." She didn't even know it was Father's Day or her Anniversary...or maybe, on some level, she did. When I stepped back out into the other room while Mom got dressed, Holly and Albert stood there wide-eyed, taking it all in. "Maybe Don IS here," Holly observed. Very grateful that I was there in that moment, with Holly and Albert's encouragement, to love Mom through another challenge, and for her continued resilience and strength. Heart-breaking as it is, I feel blessed.

Since then Mom had mentioned Dad only a few times. One day I'd found her sitting on her bed at our house, holding his photo. "Isn't he handsome?" she asked and smiled. Then, more recently, as she bounced back after fighting off sepsis:

Sunday, May 28, 2017

"Didn't Don and I plant that tree for you when you first moved in?" Mom indicated the dark pink crabapple tree, as we sat on the patio out back. I nodded and, since she brought him up, asked, "Mom, do you think about Dad much?" She looked at me quizzically and said "Who's your Dad?" I paused, then asked "Who do you think of when I say 'Dad'?" When she answered "My Dad," I said, "Do you think of your Dad much?" "I can't remember my Dad," she replied, then smiled and went back to quietly enjoying the sunshine, her dog, Cinnamon, at her side.

Mom's dad had died when she was sixteen, as she, her mom, and her brother had waited for him to join them for a family vacation at Grandma Curtis's in California. I remember the first time Mom had shown me his photo on her dresser and told me about losing him unexpectedly to a heart attack—her tearful, pained expression and how much I'd wanted to help her feel better. I don't think her wound had ever healed, at least until her memory changed. "I hope I inherited Dad's patience, devotion to family, compassion, and common sense," Mom had written in her 2006 memoirs. Not only did she inherit those qualities, she passed them on to us kids.

I was constantly looking for my dad in those days. I had long kept him close in spirit, and more recently he'd felt close physically, too. I saw him in the full moon, which he once pointed out to me with the advice, "Don't ever get too busy to see the beauty around you." I saw him in Garrett, who resembled him in so many ways, including his passionate approach and rebellious flair. I saw him in Matt, whose counsel was practical, humorous, and kind. I saw him in Doug, who, like Dad, worked hard to provide for our family and didn't hesitate to share a raunchy joke. I also felt Dad's love and respect in the way my father-in-law, Cliff, counted me as one of his own. And, too, I saw Dad in my brothers, who shared his sense of adventure and commitment to what they love. It had been fifteen years since Dad had died, and I continued to look for him each and every day, grateful for all the ways he was still right here, guiding me through.

~~~

Summer Solstice 2017: The Longest Day and Grief

After a tumultuous spring, I was exhausted. Don't get me wrong, I could slap a smile on my face with the best of 'em; still, I felt tired, sad, and hesitant to admit it, given our many blessings. It finally caught up with me on Wednesday, the summer solstice, day of global celebration. That day, the longest of the year, the Alzheimer's Association encouraged doing something to honor loved ones with dementia. To me, that meant writing.

> Really enjoy reading your blog. It keeps me up to date on your Mom. Must admit, it makes me tearful, though. Reminds me of so many good times all those years ago.   —Ann

When I decided to share the experience of caring for Mom, I thought of those she'd known throughout time, like this longtime family friend. I hadn't wanted my words to bring sadness, and at the same time I'd wanted to acknowledge Mom's life—past, present, and future—the same balance I faced each day, bringing the joy while acknowledging the grief.

Even in the midst of all our blessings, and believe me, I was grateful for them, I sometimes felt loss. The family weekend that went too quickly, the kids all on the brink of moving on, Matt already off to Seattle to begin his summer job, time in the Midwest narrowing as we readied to move to Maine, and Mom at the kitchen table reading love letters from a twenty-year-old suitor she didn't recall (Dad), although she admired his handwriting. A doer even now, she regularly asked, "Am I supposed to be doing something?" When she slept more than usual (probably catching up from our busy weekend, too), I wondered if I should get her up and moving when all I wanted to do was climb into bed beside her and go to sleep, too.

According to Paula Spencer Scott, "Friends and family of someone with dementia experience two difficult psychological states at once: anticipatory grief, or coping with the very real feelings of loss for someone who is still alive" and "ambiguous loss, or interacting with someone who's not fully present socially or psychologically."[45] I would add to those two psychological states the state of constant vigilance, wondering whether Mom was okay and whether I was doing enough to care for her. Over the past year and a half, I had found a groove, thanks to all the support, which helped me to keep a healthy perspective; every once in a while, though, I lost my footing.

We all grieve a variety of losses. In my experience, grief didn't go away, it just got more familiar. Caring for someone with dementia can be confusing because, while we want to be in the moment feeling the joy, it's hard not to also feel the loss of who the person was and who they will become. Author Sid Kirchheimer writes that, according to Suzanne Mintz, president and cofounder of the National Family Caregivers Association, "As a family caregiver, you are grieving throughout the entire process, not only with the death of your loved one… You grieve with each loss—each time they go down a notch, with each reminder of what was and what it has become."[46] Even as I experienced acceptance—coming to terms with the Alzheimer's diagnosis, finding personal meaning in providing care, and enjoying being with Mom in the moment—confusion, guilt, anger, hopelessness, and sadness sometimes emerged. With respect to caregiver health, the Alzheimer's Association advises, "The stages of grief don't happen neatly in order. You may move in and out of different stages as time goes on.…Most people think grief happens when someone dies. They may not know that it's possible to grieve deeply for someone who has a progressive cognitive illness.…Accept yourself.… Take care of yourself.…Do things that bring joy and comfort, and give yourself time to rest. Ask for help when you need it, and accept the help that is offered."[47]

As these articles confirm, it's essential to take care of ourselves, accepting our feelings of loss as they surface, letting go of guilt and expectations, and leaning on others for help. As Scott puts it, "Goodbyes are always painful, and Alzheimer's is the ultimate 'long goodbye'.… Long-term studies have found that Alzheimer's caregivers who receive counseling and support, formal or informal, have better health and a lower incidence of depression. You may feel the need to put on a 'brave face' in front of the sick person all the time, when expressing your conflicting feelings is what would serve you better. A support network lets you do this. Venting on paper—writing about your feelings—can help during those moments when you can't see someone face to face."[48]

I must admit, I felt bad for feeling bad. I didn't want to diminish Mom's life in any way. I knew so many people who'd lost their moms, and I realized I was fortunate for the time I still had with ours. At the same time, I'd always hated goodbyes, feeling the loss before, during, and after. When I dropped Matt off at the airport Monday morning, I came home and I cried. Then I started to reacclimate and look forward. That night, when we spoke on the phone, I felt better. The goodbye with Mom was different—I didn't even want to think about what getting through it meant. I was not ready to say goodbye to her. I didn't want this day to end. Within its long stretch, I needed to make time to feel, to grieve, and to rejuvenate, so that the smile I wore didn't wear me down and the time that we had together could bring us both joy.

Having taken some time to catch up, to share, and to reflect, I felt better. It helped that, when Garrett played Herb Alpert and the Tijuana Brass on his cell phone, Mom proceeded to dance in her chair, head to toe—the smiles that put on our three faces were as real as could be.

～ԼԼԼ～

Pain and Delirium as They Relate to Dementia—Guess Who Has Another UTI?

No sooner did I think *Mom's having a great day* than she stood up with an "Ouch, my back hurts." I gave her Tylenol and helped her lie down, hoping rest would relieve her tired back, as it had before. When the pain persisted and I noticed Mom sleeping more, I mentioned it to her doctor. Mom's pulse, blood pressure, and temperature were all normal (probably better than mine). When the doctor asked, Mom denied any pain, in her back or elsewhere. I quietly asked him if he could test for a UTI. As we made our way to the car afterward, Mom turned to me and grimaced. "Ouch, my back hurts." Here's where I'd look directly into the camera, if there were one, and shrug.

If I had a penny for every time Mom expressed pain to me and then denied it to the rest of the world, I could give up feeling bad for splurging on iced mochas. Whether good ol' denial, the choice not to complain, high pain tolerance, wariness of medical professionals, inability to remember, or difficulty communicating—the mix evolved over time—it's challenging to help loved ones get relief when, for whatever reason, they don't communicate discomfort themselves.

In "Pain a Problem in Alzheimer's Disease," author Daniel J. DeNoon surveys the research: In a study comparing fourteen patients with mild-to-moderate Alzheimer's disease with fifteen age-matched volunteers without Alzheimer's, Leonie J. Cole and colleagues at the University of Melbourne and the National Ageing Research Institute in Australia found that pain activity lasted longer in the patients with Alzheimer's and concluded that "the experience of pain may be more distressing for these patients on account of their impaired ability to accurately appraise the unpleasant sensation and its future implications." According to Cole and her colleagues, "Pain perception and processing are not diminished by Alzheimer's disease, thereby raising concerns about the inadequate treatment of pain in this highly dependent and vulnerable group." According to pain expert Christopher L. Edwards, PhD, director of the Pain and Palliative Care Center at Duke University in Durham, North Carolina, "Caregivers have an incredible capacity—even beyond doctors—to know the behavior of the person they are caring for and to look for the times they are in discomfort or pain…using [sleeping and waking facial expressions and movements when patients are not in pain] as a baseline, [Edwards urges caregivers to] be attentive to circumstances where they seem agitated, where eye contact is altered, where there is grimacing or a facial expression indicative of discomfort…"[49]

I had noticed that, when Mom did express pain, she was unable to remember it or put it into context and usually just wanted to lie back down. As her health care agent, I was dedicated to voicing my best understanding of what she would want, if she could say. Her health care directive stated: "I direct that treatment for alleviation of pain or discomfort be provided at all times, even if it hastens my death…." Sounded straightforward; however, it could be downright confusing, particularly when delirium added another layer to Mom's communication challenges.

According to the Alzheimer's Society, "Delirium is a common, serious but often treatable condition that starts suddenly in someone who is unwell…much more common in older people, especially those with dementia….It is usually the brain's reaction to an underlying medical problem…an infection, such as a chest infection or a urinary tract infection…severe illness, surgery, pain, dehydration, constipation, poor nutrition, or a change in medication….In many older people, and especially those with dementia, delirium causes them to be abnormally withdrawn and sleepy. This is known as 'hypoactive' delirium and it can easily be missed or mistaken for depression, even by a health professional."[50] I knew from experience that delirium could cause increased confusion, disorientation, changes in behavior, and hallucinations. And I'd wondered whether Mom was sleeping so much as a result of Alzheimer's,[51] because she was enjoying relaxing with Cinnamon (after years of working full-time and suffering insomnia), because she was depressed or bored, or for some other reason. *Aha!* I thought when I read about "hypoactive delirium"—in the past, I'd known something was up when Mom said "Ouch!" Then it had been when she didn't recognize me; these days it was when she didn't want to get out of bed.

During that first hospitalization, Mom had been pale, sighing, groaning, and peering back and forth like a bird. Each time I expressed concern about pain to the nurses, who changed with each shift, I was told they'd have to hear it from Mom. Mom—big surprise—repeatedly had told all health care workers she was not in pain. I felt like one of those parents who makes up a kid's illness for attention.[52] It wasn't until a nurse and a PT heard Mom snap at me, through clenched teeth, "I hurt, I keep telling you that, and you're not helping me," that the nurse called the doctor, who ordered morphine. Mom's relief was quick and clear. The next day, Mom refused to swallow liquid Tylenol, and another nurse was again hesitant to give morphine for fear it could aggravate her dementia. Thank God Cinnamon could come to visit, providing the best relief of all.

When Mom was discharged, the hospitalist told me I was the best judge of her pain and our home the best place for her care. He prescribed liquid morphine to administer at my discretion, dabbing it on my finger and touching it to Mom's gums—yikes! I felt relief, along with sobering responsibility. At first, Mom was so weak she just lay in bed, and we thought she was dying. The one time she expressed pain to me, I'd given her the morphine as prescribed. When I checked in a little later, she'd been peaceful and relaxed. Unable to express pain, Mom sometimes got flooded and shut down; treating her pain seemed to bring her back. Fortunately, as she had recovered, Tylenol had provided the relief needed, and I hadn't given her morphine again. By then I ought to have trusted our observations, as they had helped us get Mom care for her various concerns, including another abscess, this one unreachable by drain, requiring another round of antibiotics. When Mom slowed yet again, sleeping more, feeling full, and mentioning a sore back, I hoped it was the aftermath of our full spring. Then came another early-morning epiphany: *What if it's another UTI?* Bingo.

UTIs can wreak havoc on the elderly. Jennifer Wegerer explains that "When younger people get a urinary tract infection, they will experience distinct physical symptoms….Instead of pain symptoms, seniors with a UTI may show increased signs of confusion, agitation, or withdrawal. For older adults who have dementia, these behavioral changes may come across as part of that condition or signs of advanced aging. If the underlying UTI goes unrecognized and untreated for too long, it can spread to the bloodstream and become life-threatening."[53] And according to Marlo Sollitto, "Older individuals with UTIs may not exhibit any of the hallmark signs…because their immune systems are unable to mount a significant response to the infection. On top of the lack of noticeable symptoms, many seniors do not or cannot express their discomfort to their caregivers."[54]

As it turned out, Mom's body was fighting another infection, this time a UTI, and she was dehydrated, too. So, we started another round of antibiotic and followed the advice: monitoring fluid intake, prompting her to use the bathroom, and helping her with good hygiene. Hopefully, she'd bounce back as she had again and again.

Providing Mom's care, with the challenges of pain, delirium, infection, aging, and dementia, wasn't easy. I was oddly reassured when I asked the doctor for his advice on how to make sure I wasn't over- or underreacting to the clues, and he looked at me wide-eyed with an "I wish I could…." It felt like being in the lifeguard chair on a stormy day with rough seas, circling sharks, and a nonswimmer who was trying to keep her head above water. Then I noticed those around me helping me keep watch, ready to dive in if need be, the sun peeking through the clouds, and the smile on Mom's face as she splashed around. While it complicated her care, Mom's inability to remember the pain or other details had its advantages: She loved taking guilt-free naps with Cinnamon, and when I tucked her into bed at night, she regularly gave thanks for her good health.

⌐ℓℓℓ⌐

The Happiest Days, i.e., "Going to Camp"

When Doug had gotten a job opportunity in Prague, days before our first child was due, I'd asked Mom what she thought about us moving so far away with a newborn. She, who had every reason to keep us close, living in Grammy's house, had answered instead, "Go for it." An amazing adventure ensued.

For almost eighty years, Mom had spent summers living in a cottage on Snow Pond; "going to camp," Mainers call it. After her first winter and spring with us in Wisconsin, I'd taken her back to camp for the summer, where my niece Holly and her boyfriend, Albert, with neighbors Perry and Joanne, and then our caregivers, Terry D and Samantha, had provided loving companionship and excellent care. The coming summer, with Mom's recent mix of health scares, we weren't sure how she'd weather another trip to central Maine, or how to monitor and meet her unpredictable health care needs while she was there.

As Doug and I spoke with a counselor about various challenges—kids' moves, job changes, geographical relocation, Mom's care, and our decision whether to try to get her to Maine for a summer visit, he asked in an *Are you crazy?* sort of way, "Why would you do that?" He went on to mention how vulnerable people with Alzheimer's are to changes in routine. No kidding. I couldn't come up with a quick answer to his concern, which resonated with me for weeks afterward as I continued to plan and unplan the trip, watching Mom's health like a hawk as our travel day approached. The best I could offer was Mom's own words, as written in her memoirs eleven years prior:

> …When I picture Dad, I see him…supporting the WWII War cause by creating an immense victory garden in our backyard at camp.…Mom was ill a lot my first few years, usually being cared for by a nurse at home.… Finally, her doctor prescribed a summer of complete rest away from town, which led my folks to rent and subsequently buy the gray camp at Snow Pond.…
>
> "Camp" evokes memories of brilliant sunrises, crying loons, barking dogs, family togetherness, chicken barbeques, humming boat engines, peaceful sunsets.… When my folks first rented the gray camp, we pumped water from the lake by hand and used a two-seater in the backyard! The rustic kitchen had an old woodstove, a gas stove, and a black slate sink; the shiny new refrigerator covered with an embroidered doily occupied a place of honor in the far corner of the room! During the first

years of ownership, Dad remodeled the kitchen, paneled the living room walls and ceiling, converted a bedroom to a bathroom, and glassed in the windward side porch for a bedroom for me. The family pitched in as we could—my forte was applying sealer to the living room walls…

August 15, 1945, VJ Day (victory in Japan) was joyous and exciting. I recall all of the neighbors happily joining in a huge bonfire which lasted long into the night on the front hill of the gray camp. That was the year that Dad, Tim [brother], and I built the little gray camp for bedrooms for Tim and me.…

In my earlier years, the essence of camp was relaxation, simplicity, freedom to roam, little traveling (gas rationing).…Our kids carried on the same activities, but with faster boats and more traveling. July 4th endured…before we knew it, weddings started occurring at camp.…To accommodate the growing families, we remodeled the kitchen…added a deck, making more room for all the summer birthdays. We abandoned the bony Fourth of July salmon and added the thrills of tubing and boarding. Theatrical productions on the boulder next to the gray camp continued. Still, each year, there is nothing more welcoming than the first loon call of the summer!

As we weighed the challenges of getting Mom to camp—the wear and tear of air and car travel, the uneven ground once there, the potential heat, and the distance from doctors familiar with her medical history—I remembered her advice to me, way back when: "Go for it." If Mom was resilient enough to pull through the health challenges of the past spring, who were we to keep her from camp that summer?

Our day of travel was long, almost twelve hours. The whole way Mom kept asking, "Where are we going?" When we passed the city, Mom smiled and said, "Portland." When we arrived at camp, and Matt and our neighbors, the Johnsons, welcomed us, Mom lit up. Since then she'd been soaking up her surroundings. I wasn't sure how long it made sense for Mom to stay, if at all, after I headed back to Wisconsin; however, I had no doubt that this trip, whatever its length, had been worth it.

Camp was like the back of Mom's hand—she knew every nook and cranny and got around better there than anywhere. It was her fountain of youth—she rose early to get outside and take in the day, expressing appreciation for the blue sky, the green trees, the calm lake. It was her happy place. I found myself taking in her every word, pledging it to memory, like I used to do with the kids when they were small: As Mom and I sat on our lounge chairs, drinking our hot drinks and waiting for the Fourth of July festivities to begin, Mom looked at her watch and said happily to the dog sitting in her lap, "It's only 8:10, Cinnamon—we have a long day ahead."

The next day, as I looked ahead, trying to figure out how and when to plan our departure, fretting on this side about taking Mom away from this special place, I was thankful for our time there, with all the important connections, past and present, and the kindness and concern of so many family and friends who knew Mom from before. Although this may not have been the longest day, these were the happiest days.

꧁꧂

Step Seven: Humility

Step Seven: Humbly asked a Higher Power *to remove our shortcomings.*
—Al-Anon's Twelve Steps & Twelve Traditions[55]

Back in Wisconsin, while Mom stayed on in Maine, I was grateful for Step Seven.

"Humbly…" When I first saw the emphasis on this word, I hesitated. What did it mean, to humbly ask? I didn't consider myself arrogant; if anything, I *lacked* confidence. With time, I came to see that "humbly" meant acknowledging that only a Higher Power could set us free of the stuff that weighs us down. My lack of humility showed itself in my excessive sense of responsibility: I worried that, if I even thought it, it could happen, and that, if I erred, something horrible would result. How's that for egotistical?

According to the Jesuit priest at the silent retreat I'd attended, "God is the prime mover, we just pray for willingness"; humility requires honesty and truth "to see ourselves exactly as we are, in relation to ourselves, God and to others," and it "leaves no place for judgment or comparison." It was this humility that continued to challenge and at the same time set me free. Ironically, my lack thereof was a shortcoming I "humbly asked" a Higher Power to remove.

When the kids were little and I was deep in the throes of AA's Step Seven, we were driving to pick up the babysitter when Matt asked, "Mom, why are frogs so slobbery?"

Siena the animal lover explained, "When they're born, they have slime on them; it helps them escape their predators." I nodded from the front seat. That rang true.

While my shortcomings looked and felt pretty yucky, they must have served a purpose along the way. Although they tended to keep others at a distance, they still felt familiar and comforting. It felt risky, this Step Seven, asking to have them removed. What would be left? How would I stay safe? How would I escape my predators without my slime?

As a daughter, partner, parent, and friend, I worked hard to find balance and boundaries, not easy with the responsibility I felt—which reached from raising three kids, to caring for my ailing mom, to picking up strays on the side of the road. In choosing caregiving roles, time and again, I needed to remember that I was not alone, and that when I stepped away, others would step in. Faith in a Higher Power. It's what I'd been building. It's what helped me take Step Seven. It's what strengthened me while Mom stayed on at camp, in another's care.

~ ⚘ ~

Triple Salchow—Enough Is Enough

salchow *(n): a jump in figure skating from the backward inside edge of one skate to the backward outside edge of the other, with one or more full turns in the air*

—en.oxforddictionaries.com

I'm guessing a triple salchow is three times as tough and even more rare.

As we drank our coffee, I shared with Doug Mom's repeated requests the night before, after her long day's travel home from Maine, that I take her back. It hadn't mattered what I said, Mom had circled around again at another attempt. I'd finally convinced her to rest. That morning, she'd gotten up at eleven o'clock, anxious and sad. She was already back in bed.

This was where it was tricky being daughter and caregiver. I understood, inside and out, what *going to camp* meant to Mom. Even as I admitted that the odds of getting her to Maine at all that summer had been against us, and the fact that she was safely home in Wisconsin after an awesome two-week visit was, as my brother Dave put it, "an accomplishment," I ached that she couldn't have more time there. So when she asked me again that morning when she could go back, I had to placate myself even as I tried to placate her.

Having gotten Mom home to Maine for Independence Day, and having seen how refreshed, rejuvenated, and just plain happy she was, I'd spent most of my week there brainstorming how to extend her stay. Not only had her mind been clearer than we'd seen it in a while, she'd reveled in the visits from family and neighbors. I hadn't wanted it to end, either. However, given Mom's tenuous health and my inability to coordinate full-time care with somebody familiar with its subtleties, the best I could offer was five additional days with Hannah, who'd come with us from Wisconsin.

During her time at camp, Mom had repeatedly told visitors she was spending the summer there. When I explained to her the abbreviated visit in various ways, at various times, I got various replies, ranging from "It's all okay with me as long as somebody takes care of me" to "That makes me really unhappy." One reply had set me free, the other had made me fret.

Doug counseled, "You've made the best deal you can, given the options at hand. Don't waste your time worrying about the deal that isn't achievable."

As it turns out, it all worked out for the best. Holly had picked up Hannah and Mom at camp and driven them to the airport in Boston—a huge help. Hannah had gotten Mom and Cinnamon through security and to the gate—a huge feat. Hannah had texted to tell me Mom's ID had expired a year earlier and that the grace period would expire the next week, on her birthday. In other words, had I found Mom a way to stay at camp longer, she would have ended up stuck in an airport with an invalid ID—a mess we had inadvertently avoided and a reminder that we were doing the best we could with the options at hand, and, even when I felt I was falling short, something Divine was at work.

That extra five days in Maine had given Mom time to visit the cemetery and celebrate her birthday with my brothers, to connect with summer neighbors, and to enjoy the peace and quiet of Snow Pond. That extra five days had given me time to help set up Siena's apartment for veterinary school, to spend a night with Matt in Boston learning about his job, to get home to Wisconsin to care for Doug as he underwent hernia repair, and to grab dinner out with Garrett.

Doug put it best: "Seriously," he said, "getting your Mom two weeks in Maine is like completing a triple salchow—that's something to feel good about." So, as we settled Mom back into life in the Midwest, I did my best to acknowledge her concerns, provide positive distraction, let her rest, and love her up. I'd already made her a scrapbook of her time in Maine—it was the closest I could get to getting her back there for some additional time. Enough was enough. Amen to that.

Brotherly Love on Mom's Birthday

It was Mom's eighty-fifth birthday. Of all the things I could get her as a gift, I knew without doubt that the best would be something she'd wished for in her relationship with her own brother: the promise to work things out with my brothers so that we could live our lives in peace.

As the youngest, I couldn't remember a day when my brothers weren't part of my life, even when we'd lived far apart. They were incredible guys, awesome dads, dedicated sons, and smart when it came to finding wives. When Mom had learned she had Alzheimer's and decided to move to Wisconsin to live with us, her primary concern had been being far away from them and their families. She wondered whether they'd be as surprised as she was by the diagnosis (they weren't). She often asked me not to trouble them with her health concerns—as she put it, "Why worry them when there's nothing they can do?" However, I not only appreciated their support from afar, I needed it, so I did my best to keep them in Mom's health care loop.

There was no question that, along the way, Mom's changes in memory and cognition had challenged our sibling relationships. Findings from a recent Alzheimer's Association survey showed that "in some families, Alzheimer's caregiving fosters strength and support, yet in other families, it tears relationships apart. Relationships between siblings were found to be the most strained, stemming from not having enough support in providing care (sixty-one percent) as well as the overall burden of caregiving (fifty-three percent)."[56] According to Paula Spencer Scott, while siblings have strength in numbers when a parent develops Alzheimer's, the more family members involved in providing care, the bigger the chance of miscommunication and disagreement. To keep everyone "in the loop and on speaking terms," Scott recommends agreeing to disagree, outgrowing old roles, realizing we need one another, and, to reduce caregiver burnout—"a leading reason people with Alzheimer's move from a home to a nursing facility"—dividing the labor (based on skill, strength, and life situation), sharing vital information in writing, checking in regularly, not second-guessing, and avoiding promises we cannot keep—like the promise never to institutionalize.[57]

To our knowledge, Mom's dementia was a first in our family tree. My brothers and I had been figuring things out as we went. We were blessed to have partners and children who supported us. Although our process hadn't been perfect, our intentions had been good and Mom had felt our love. Despite the daily losses to which she was asked to adapt, she was okay. I was grateful for the ways my brothers had stepped up to help, providing respite care in our home, handling legal and financial matters, sorting through her possessions, preparing to sell her house in Maine, sending flowers to brighten her days, and calling on the phone to check in. We were fortunate that Mom had financial resources to cover stand-in caregivers and other expenses, and I appreciated the trust my brothers put in me to use that responsibly.

There was no question that my brothers and I each had unique personalities, perspectives, experiences, family lives, work situations, and love for our mom. While our various styles in communication sometimes led to tension, our shared commitment to Mom helped us persist. Mom needed each one of us in different ways, and that knowledge fueled me with patience, respect, and resilience. She wouldn't have wanted to be the source of conflict and so, when conflict inevitably arose, I tried to work it through, for her and for us. Mom cherished each one of us, in different ways, and having us all in her life, in the ways that we could be, not only made my role as primary caregiver doable, it helped to make her life, at eighty-five and with dementia, complete. Happy Birthday, Mom!

Standing by Me

"Uh, Ter…this isn't moving along as quickly as I expected," said Doug, five years into our marriage, upon returning from his breakfast in the cafeteria, complete with coffee and *The Boston Globe*, to find me in the hospital bathroom in the midst of another contraction in an effort to birth our first child. Who'd have thought this would be the same guy who would surprise me twenty-three years later by setting up our son's upstairs room for us while I was in Maine with Mom, so that she could have our first-floor room when she came to stay with us.

"We're fifteen hundred miles away.…I don't want to talk about your mom," Doug, my spouse of almost three decades, replied when I began to fret, on day four of Garrett's senior spring break, before he headed to the casino to blow off steam. Yep, this was the same guy who took care of Mom on our twenty-ninth anniversary so that I could accompany Garrett to Turks and Caicos for the opening ceremony of a basketball court he'd helped renovate.

No question, caring for others, even in the best-case scenario, can challenge relationships, so it's no surprise that this applies when it comes to looking after a loved one with Alzheimer's disease. According to Connie Matthiessen, a Caring.com marriage survey that looked at how caregiving affects a caregiver's relationship with a partner found strong feelings, both positive and negative, about the impact on everything from "family finances to sexual relations to leisure time." In fact, "Eighty percent of respondents said that caregiving put a strain on their relationship or marriage."[58] Another survey by the Alzheimer's Association found that, of the thirty-five percent of respondents who said caregiving actually strengthened their relationships with family members, "relationships between spouses/partners were strengthened the most from the experience, with 81 percent believing that 'being emotionally there for each other' was a source of strength they drew upon for caregiving."[59]

"I think I cured Alzheimer's," Doug had declared on day three of Mom's first hospitalization, after bringing me dinner and sending me outdoors for a walk. When I returned, Mom was smiling and laughing as he told her stories about her homeland, Maine. When he returned the next night and tried again to engage her, she lay there blankly, even when he'd shared his best jokes. The next night, when he recounted seeing a wild turkey that day, and then, to her unresponsive stare, asked if she'd ever seen one, she nodded slowly, pointing her index finger directly at him.

I'd be lying if I said I hadn't shed more than a few tears during our married life, which bugged Doug, as he preferred to fix things, not cry about them. This one wasn't fixable, though, so he was learning to let me flow. I was glad he was at my side, supporting me the best he could, and I tried to do the same in return. I appreciated the ways that prior challenges to our relationship, like job stress and parenting concerns, had prepared us for this phase, and that together we were still having fun. It was key that both of us had a safe place to vent and that we found a regular time (our morning coffee) to do so with each other.[60]

Let's be honest: Doug and I had our crunchy moments. Our kids could tell a great story about the year our Christmas tree had tipped over and how beautifully we'd communicated—har-har—as we tried to save it. Plus, there'd been numerous rambunctious road trips between Wisconsin and Maine. Fortunately, like the two of us, our marriage was stubborn, too.

As we prepared for Garrett and Siena to leave in two and a half weeks for their next adventures, people kept alluding to our upcoming "empty nest." While our nest was going to change dramatically, it wasn't going to be empty, nor did I want it to be. I'm grateful that Doug not only had my back, he helped me in big and little ways every day, and, through it all, he played with Mom, like he did with the kids, and it made her, and me, laugh.

Way back when, when we danced that first dance as husband and wife, I hadn't known exactly how the words to the song's refrain would apply, only that we'd have ups and downs and I hoped he'd be at my side through both. Those words continued to apply, and I was grateful for all the ways Doug continued to, like Ben King croons, "Stand by Me."

⌁

Step Eight: Discernment

Step Eight: Made a list of all persons we had harmed, and became willing to make amends to them all.

—Al-Anon's Twelve Steps & Twelve Traditions[61]

When I first turned my attention to AA's Step Eight, I felt gripped by anxiety. Making a list was easy; I'm good at lists. The "of all persons we had harmed" was trickier. I wasn't so good at discerning whom I'd harmed.

According to *Al-Anon's Twelve Steps and Twelve Traditions*, the feeling of gnawing guilt signals whom we have hurt and who belongs on our Step Eight list.[62] My gnawing guilt, however, wasn't always earned: I used to think I could hurt others with my thoughts and feelings. I'd come to understand this wasn't so and that flogging myself for uncomfortable thoughts and feelings only exacerbated them, making me unwell and fueling obsessive-compulsive go-rounds. It's what we *do* with our thoughts and feelings—our actions or lack thereof—that matters.

Over time, I'd developed a better sense of whom I'd harmed, including myself, through obsessive-compulsive behavior, perfectionism, poor boundary-setting, holding on to hurt feelings, and failing to slow down and just be. The beauty of the Twelve Steps is that there's no call to beat ourselves up for harms we've caused; instead, it's the pain that led to that exercise that gives way in Step Eight to the willingness needed to move forward.

In the past, I'd let the fear of making amends in Step Nine get ahead of the "becoming willing" required of Step Eight. In the midst of caring for Mom, I didn't know what amends I'd be called upon to make when I got to Step Nine; however, I did know that carrying unnecessary guilt only fueled dysfunction. According to the fortune cookie I'd recently opened, my life was about to get more interesting. It was time to move on with faith and open up to the healing ahead.

~~~

Beast Mode

go beast mode *(v): …to become tougher and persistent in order to accomplish a goal*

—www.onlineslangdictionary.com

Two years earlier, when Siena left to work on a wildlife sanctuary in Malawi, Africa, I'd committed to something bold. I'd joined Garrett's CrossFit gym and started working out regularly with Nicole, trainer extraordinaire. She was so funny, kind, and low-key, I hardly noticed she was kicking my ass. We shared all kinds of things, including our common experience with a loved one's dementia.

When Nicole decided to move on to a new career, she gave me a neon pink bracelet, the words BEAST MODE attached. A year ago, as I readied to leave Wisconsin to take eighty-three-year-old Mom back to Maine for the summer with Holly and Albert, I put on that bracelet as a reminder that I was up to that task. In the year since, I had been in beast mode a fair bit, caring for Mom as her health ebbed and flowed and Alzheimer's progressed. I'd also had moments of letdown, just plain overwhelmed with concern for Mom's health challenges and our kids' upcoming departures.

As I started to think about the coming week, when I'd again leave Mom in another's care so that we could take Garrett and Siena east to school, I made a mental note to dig out Nicole's BEAST MODE bracelet as a reminder that I could do whatever was required to care for loved ones, even as their needs pulled me in different directions. When our go-with-the-flow niece Ali came to visit, the fun was cut short when we found ourselves back at the hospital again, the third time in six months, Mom being evaluated for another intestinal ailment—her blood loss severe enough to warrant a transfusion. I realized I couldn't wait another week to gear up. Ready or not, it was time, once again, to go BEAST MODE.

❧

Curveball Complete: What I Learned During Mom's Second Hospital Stay

At the start of the week, my to-do list had focused on organizing caregiving for Mom and the animals and getting ready to take the kids to school. I had started to feel emotional about the changes ahead and grateful for the prospect of time together beforehand when I noticed blood in Mom's toilet—a "complete curveball," Doug called it—a classic example of the importance of "Letting Go of Expectations," as they say in AA.

While I did my best to take care of, advocate for, and comfort Mom as she underwent blood transfusions, colonoscopy preparation, failed IVs, and capsule endoscopy, I had moments sitting beside her in the hospital when my mind started to wander and my thoughts to spin. After twenty-four years of having kids at home to parent, time with them felt fleeting. Mom, of course, had no notion of this—her concerns were immediate. Unlike her first hospital stay that spring, this time around she unintentionally charmed all with her wit; still, given her inability to remember the details of her medical needs, I stayed at her side, night and day, with wonderful breaks, thanks again to family and friends.

In a nutshell, after Mom's second five-day hospital stay, we learned there was no evidence of cancer or other tumors in her digestive tract—Hallelujah! However, she did have a small hiatal hernia, diverticular disease throughout her large colon, and a bleed in her small bowel, which appeared to have stopped. Phew! If Mom got another bleed, we'd have to consider surgical intervention, which I was told could be brutal at this stage. After four days of trying to keep her from removing various medical apparatuses, including the IVs so difficult to attach to her veins, I shuddered at the thought of helping her heal through surgery, and I worried about further damage to her memory and cognition from the anesthesia that would be required—a classic example of the importance of "One Day at a Time," as they say in AA.

So, instead of worrying about what might happen next, I focused on what we could do to prevent another intestinal bleed, which meant a new to-do list, per Mom's discharge instructions: cut out baby aspirin and other blood thinners; keep Mom hydrated; prop up her head when she lies down, and provide a low-fiber, anti-reflux diet; contact her rheumatologist to see if we could further reduce her daily dose of prednisone from twenty to ten milligrams given that it can mask infection and she had mild erosion in her stomach and a bleed in her small intestine; follow up in a week with her regular doctor and in three weeks with the specialist; as always, pay special attention to any changes in sleep, energy, appetite, bowel habits, cognition, and pain; and, any concerns, back to the ER we'd go.

Curveball complete, I was excited to get Mom home, safe and sound, the feedback on her health as good as it could be, given the amount of blood she'd lost, with six days left till Doug and I would take the kids east, with the help of my sister-in-law Nancy, who would hold down the fort in our absence.

P.S.: Here's what I found googling gastrointestinal (GI) bleeds our second hospital stay:

~ According to John B. Adams, MD, and David A. Margolin, MD: "Diverticular hemorrhage is the most common cause of lower gastro-intestinal bleeding in Westernized cultures. Fortunately, the majority of diverticular bleeds will spontaneously resolve; however, 20% of patients will require therapeutic interventions to obtain hemostasis."[63]

~ John P. Cunha, DO, FACOEP, and Bhupinder Anand, MD, advise that "Treatment for GI bleeding usually includes hospitalization because blood pressure may drop and heart rate may increase and this needs to be stabilized. In some cases, IV fluids or blood transfusions are needed, and surgery may be required."[64]

~ T.O. Kovacs observes: "The management of patients with small bowel bleeding remains a diagnostic and therapeutic challenge."[65]

~ "After initial evaluation, colonoscopy provides not only the best method of evaluation, but also the best method for treating patients with lower GI bleeding," says Maxwell Chait, MD.[66]

~ However, Otto S. Lin cautions: "Colonoscopy in very elderly patients carries a greater risk of complications and morbidity than in younger patients. Thus, colonoscopy in elderly patients should be performed only after careful consideration of potential benefits, risks, and patient preferences."[67]

~ As per Deepak Gunjan, et al., "The pharmacological treatment can be helpful in recurrent, refractory, inaccessible angiodysplasias lesions and in patients at high risk for other interventions. The role of surgery is declining, however it is last resort in failed endoscopic treatments and recurrent bleeding."[68]

~ "Capsule endoscopy is a procedure that uses a tiny wireless camera to take pictures of your digestive tract. A capsule endoscopy camera sits inside a vitamin-size capsule you swallow. As the capsule travels through your digestive tract, the camera takes thousands of pictures that are transmitted to a recorder you wear on a belt around your waist."[69] Thanks, Mayo Clinic Staff.

~ And The American College of Gastroenterology notes: "Patients taking NSAIDs who also are taking a prescription corticosteroid, medications like prednisone (in doses over 10 mg), have been found to have a seven-fold increased risk of having GI bleeding."[70]

The Middle of Us: another parenting flashback

As I drove Mom to see the GI specialist, I recalled a reverse trip twenty-two years earlier, when she'd brought me home from the same hospital, in the way back of our van, after I'd been hospitalized for a back injury suffered when I was seven months pregnant with Matt. Mom had made sure I'd gotten home to a hospital bed on our first floor where I could recuperate, enjoying Siena's two-year-old antics while our second grew inside me. It was hard to believe that, already, that very day, he was turning twenty-two!

On his third birthday I'd written:

> …This blond-haired and dimpled three-year-old is so sensitive it scares me sometimes; when reprimanded, however gently, he either goes into hiding or comes out fighting, pain written all over his face. He's a warrior; just the other day, after days of nonstop rain, he came to the kitchen, proud to show me the gun he had made of blocks to shoot the thunder and lightning. And he is also so gentle, when others are sad he tries to make them feel better. I worry that he didn't have the same easy transition to our world that our daughter had, that I was not able to give him all that he needed when he was an infant because I was balancing two. What a relief that there is something much more than just my mothering going on here, that he is sharing the gift of siblinghood with her.

Soon afterward, when Garrett came along, I was mindful of the potential sandwiching effect on our Middle, though it was abundantly clear that he didn't see his little brother as rain on his parade. There's no denying the special bonds Matt shares with his older sister, his younger brother, his dad, and me. Not that he has to, still, it's a fact: He brings balance to our family. Thinking of him reminds baby-of-the-family me to step back, take a deep breath, and calm myself—to try to be less tornado and more glue.

According to Catherine Salmon, PhD, and Katrin Schumann, authors of *The Secret Power of Middle Children: How Middleborns Can Harness Their Unexpected and Remarkable Abilities*, "We have a lot to learn from middle children. As negotiators they take the time to see things from other points of view. This give-and-take serves the best interests of both parties. As trailblazers, middles take considered risks and discover that the less trod path is often the best one. And our society will certainly continue to need justice seekers who understand that there is more to life than financial rewards....If we could all be a little more like middleborns, that would be a good thing."[71]

So here's a shout-out to Matt: You have no idea the impact you have on those around you and how sorely you are missed when you are out there in the world doing your thing—even as we enjoy watching you adventure from afar. Thank you for being the Middle of Us.

Putting Out Fires

Happily home from her second hospital stay, eighty-five-year-old Mom, her Alzheimer's back to "moderate," received a visit from the fit physical therapist assigned to determine her need for in-home care, thanks to Medicare. He was impressed with her spryness as she showed him around. A lengthy interview ensued at the kitchen table, during which he explained various papers we needed to sign and asked a series of questions to determine Mom's safety in our home.

"Do you have a plan in case of fire?" he asked.

She looked him in the eye and answered definitively, "I'd put it out."

He glanced my way, eyes wide, then back at her. "I mean, do you have a plan of escape in case of fire?"

Mom nodded in my direction. "That's up to her."

Fountain of Youth: Hanging Out with Our Millennial Kids and Their Millennial Friends

Every time I heard a rant on millennials, like one I'd recently caught on Sunday morning TV, I wondered who the ranter was talking about. The millennials I knew actually gave me hope for the future. They were the kids I tutored who were trying to figure things out, the health professionals at the hospital who took great care of Mom, the caregivers who patiently looked after her when I needed to step away, the trainers who helped me get stronger, my nieces and nephews and our kids and their friends who raised me up, made me laugh, and reminded me what it was like to find my way in a world with unique challenges.

Some people warn against being our kids' friends. I don't get that, either. Being friends doesn't have to come at the cost of parenting. Any good friendship requires mutual respect, honest communication, healthy boundaries, acknowledgment of pain, willingness to brainstorm solutions, and helping one another stretch and grow. I actually appreciate dialogue that goes both ways, as it's necessary for working through the big, and little, issues of the day.

One of the unexpected gifts I received as a friend of our kids was getting to be a friend of their friends, who honored me with nicknames like Mitmama and Tarbus (we somehow got there from Ter Bear). These days, they were adults, set out on their educational, career, and even marriage paths. It had been fun watching them grow. I was grateful for the love they'd given our kids and, furthermore, the love they'd given me and Doug. In the loaded life we led, their dropping in unexpectedly—with a "Hey, Mitmama!" or a "Waddup, Tarbus?"—lifted my spirits. Although I knew we'd stay in touch (thanks in part to the social media that others lament), I'd miss the regular drop-ins, the errant FaceTimes (not intended for me), the weekly Game of Thrones, and all the other overlaps.

I find millennials to be open-minded, adventurous, resourceful, questioning, and humorous. I couldn't imagine caring for Mom, our not-so-silent silent generation elder, without them. I'd even go so far as to say being friends with my kids and their friends was like finding my own fountain of youth. When I wrote this reflection, little did I know a pandemic was headed our way, and how it would ask millennials to adapt and persevere; again, speaking of resilience, I'm hit with profound respect for the ways they're trying to carry on in such uncertain times.

Boomerang, and the Almost Empty Nest

boomerang *(v): …return to the originator, often with negative consequences*
—www.google.com

According to the folks at the Mayo Clinic, "Empty nest syndrome is a feeling of grief and loneliness parents may feel when their children leave home for the first time, such as to live on their own or to attend a college or university. It is not a clinical condition."[72]

I confess, Wikipedia may not be the ideal place to seek spiritual guidance. However, late at night, far from home, when a tired spouse has rolled over to go to sleep, a bereft mom—in the midst of sending off two kids in the same week—has gotta find emotional reassurance where she can. Seeing the pain I felt in someone else's words comforted me. Plus, thanks to F.T. Cohen, et al., I learned the term *boomerang generation*:

"...the so-called 'Boomerang Generation'—young adults who return to live with their parents—have changed the traditional empty nest... Census data from 2008 showed as many as 20 million 18–34-year-olds (34% of that age group) were living at home with their parents. A decade earlier, only fifteen percent of men and eight percent of women in that age range did so."[73]

Even outdated, this Wikipedia entry redirected me to gratitude. I'd never expected Siena to come home to live between college and graduate school. There was no question that our boomerang changed our dynamic. She provided Garrett a confidante as he made his way through high school, Doug a companion as he stayed up late watching TV, and Mom a friend as she sat at the kitchen table enjoying the birds outside. She also showered our pets with love and attention, and added to our family zoo; thanks to her, we adopted Berry the beagle, picked from her litter in front of a bar at Strawberry Fest, and Peach the kitten, a rescue from the humane society on Siena's last day. And, too, our boomerang had given me a partner for exercise, iced mochas, walks, and so much more (not to mention the awesome friends she'd brought through our door).

When Siena was just eighteen months old and we were new to Wisconsin after living overseas, I left her in the Sunshine Room at the YMCA while I attempted yoga; fifteen minutes later, the attendant came looking for me because our sunshine was inconsolable. That was the last time I tried that. As she grew, becoming big sister to one and then two, her independence had expanded, as had her confidence. Over the past six years, she'd attended college in Maine and traveled and worked abroad, so I was used to having her far away. I loved the adventures she pursued; it's just that I was thankful she'd boomeranged home for a prolonged stay, too. Although *boomerang* can connote an undesirable return, we'd had a blast, and the only negative I could see was that now we had to readjust to being far apart again.

As she settled into her next stage at veterinary school, I was grateful for Siena's opportunities and excited for what lay ahead for her; still, there was no denying I missed her (and Edith, her three-legged cat), and I looked forward to the next time they would land back home, whatever the duration. As it turned out, the pandemic would bring these two and the siblings back home for another year, this time to Maine. Who knew?

What Next: Dropping Our Youngest Off at College

Earnest eighteen-year-old you with me in your heart,
asks me straight up, "What next?"
You don't want me to miss out on my life
making sure that she doesn't miss out on hers.
"I'm not sure," I admit—I tell you the truth,
cuz I value your two cents, and you'd see through anything else.
"I'm taking it a day at a time, trying to draw out this phase,
trusting I'll know when it's time for a change."

I wrote this after a conversation with Garrett, so supportive in my effort to care for Mom, while also trying to care for his mom—me! I'd been sitting on the couch, midafternoon, catching my breath while Mom napped, when Garrett came home from working out, energetic and enthusiastic. Seeing me there, he paused and asked, "You okay?" to which I nodded and explained, "I'm just tired, taking a moment to regroup." With that, he put down his backpack and gave me a big hug and an "I love you, Tarb."

Seriously, how lucky am I, that in the midst of your world,
you see me sitting here, and give me just what I need.
Although I'm still not sure what is next,
I promise to take care of me the best I can, in the mix.
All I ask is you do the same… What's next for you?
Great things, I have no doubt—and I will cheer your every step.

As we settled into the next phase, after dropping Garrett off for freshman year of college far away, in addition to the intense mix of emotions I felt, I was excited to see "What next?"

Still Smiling

"You can still smile, so that's okay," said Mom, sitting at the kitchen table folding laundry as we talked about the kids, newly away at school.

Growing up, every time I'd face a challenge, Mom would advise: "Put a smile on your face and you can do anything." Whenever she left me a note on the kitchen counter, which she often did while managing our home with a full-time job, she'd sign off with a quirky little smiley face. This approach had helped me through all kinds of challenges, and it was helping me now, as I settled into our emptier nest.

Recently, I'd come across a letter from Mom to Dad back when they were courting and he was away doing his summer service with the Navy. Mom wrote:

> *This Dale Carnegie book is really doing me good. One of his cardinal principles is—SMILE. This I've tried consciously the last couple of days, and I've found the world smiling with me to a greater degree. After all, my troubles are minute as compared with those of the armless fellow or the crippled teenager or the bankrupt contractor or the landless farmers I've seen recently.*
> —Letter to Dad, at sea with the NROTC, 7/11/1953

Mom was referring to Carnegie's "Principle 2—Smile":

> …It costs nothing, but creates much. It enriches those who receive, without impoverishing those who give. It happens in a flash and the memory of it sometimes lasts forever. None are so rich they can get along without it, and none so poor but are richer for its benefits. It creates happiness in the home, fosters good will in a business, and is the countersign of friends. It is rest to the weary, daylight to the discouraged, sunshine to the sad, and Nature's best antidote for trouble. Yet it cannot be bought, begged, borrowed, or stolen, for it is something that is no earthly good to anybody till it is given away…nobody needs a smile so much as those who have none left to give![74]

The day before, I'd taken Mom to the GI specialist for her two-and-a-half-week post-second-hospitalization checkup. When her vitals were normal, Mom had exclaimed, "Yay for me!" which, of course, made the nurse and me smile. That morning, I'd woken up humming Old Dominion's "No Such Thing as a Broken Heart." Sorting through various piles that had accumulated as I'd cared for Mom during her GI bleed while helping our kids pack for school, I came across a cookie fortune I'd saved in that haze: *Before you can see the light, you have to deal with the darkness.* I realized, like Mom had in 1953, "my troubles are minute as compared with" the unexpected and devastating losses faced by so many others. Still, keepin' it real, I felt pretty wiped out. It reminded me of when I was pregnant with Garrett and went to the midwife for our six-week checkup. She'd asked how I felt and I told her I was exhausted. With that, she'd replied, "That makes sense—your body just finished building a human heart!"

That memory comforted me now. The exhaustion I felt made sense—I'd just finished twenty-four years raising kids, the last couple caring for Mom, too. Finding renewed energy would take time, patience, settling in, and a new groove. I was grateful I had gotten to parent with abandon—like there's "No Such Thing as a Broken Heart"—and I would allow myself space to deal with the current growing pains. I'd find my way back to joy. Doug, who'd been waiting for me patiently and still made me laugh, deserved that. Thanks to Mom, I'd learned to smile, even when it wasn't easy. Thanks to Mom, I was still smiling—even in our almost empty nest.

⌒↬⌒

Step Nine: "Let Me Be Free!" and the Relief of Making Amends

Step Nine: Made direct amends to such people wherever possible, except when to do so would injure them or others.
—Al-Anon's Twelve Steps & Twelve Traditions[75]

I hope I never forget the vision of five-year-old Siena, in her blue floral snow suit, zooming down the snowy hill on her sled shouting at the top of her lungs, *"Let me be free! Let me be free!"* It made me laugh out loud then, and it makes me laugh out loud now.

By the time I started down AA's Twelve Step path, I'd done lots of apologizing, not only when I'd caused harm, but also to put an end to conflict. Any lingering resentment I felt afterward was better than feeling unloved in the midst of an upheaval, or so I thought. Those resentments, however, didn't always go away; sometimes they accumulated, weighing me down. I needed to find a more balanced and honest approach to taking responsibility for my actions than saying "Sorry" just to make peace.

Today I understand that making the direct amends called for in Step Nine isn't about saying "Sorry," it's about owning and changing our problematic behaviors. I'm not saying that finding the words isn't important; in fact, journaling letters to the people on my list helped me to better understand the nature of my harms, real and, in some cases, imagined. In sharing my list of amends with a sponsor, however, I realized that meaningful amends would require me to choose new actions and reactions. While finding the words might be relatively easy, changing behaviors and sticking to those changes was much more difficult. Faith, humility, discipline, and remembering the pain of before kept me on course. Although I sometimes slipped back into old patterns, I knew the relief of a different way.

There are times when making amends can produce its own harms: to ourselves, to others. If this is so or if we're unsure, we can start by changing our behavior in the present so as not to repeat the injury, and then pray for guidance whether there's more we need to do. In those cases, it helped me to focus forgiveness and acceptance on myself, Doug, and our children, knowing I could share what I've learned with them, when and if it fit. And when we are unsure what amends to make, it helps to ask our trusted others for insight. Still, only we, with a Higher Power's guidance, can know what's appropriate. According to *Al-Anon's Twelve Steps and Twelve Traditions*, "In this Step I am very much on my own; it is up to me to decide how its key words and phrases apply to my life."[76] This is where the discernment developed via the preceding eight steps comes in handy.

As I cared for Mom, it helped to take responsibility for that which weighed me down, to set it right the best I could, and to start fresh each morning, the best I could—which reminded me of the adventurous yet sensitive little girl inside of me, zipping down another hill, shouting at the top of my lungs, "*Let me be free! Let me be free!*"

No Need to Yell

Speak quietly with confidence, no need to yell.
Speak quietly with confidence, till then listen well.
Don't speak out of turn, when it's not mine to learn.
Let them hold their own, now that they're grown.
Forgive myself, I meant no harm.
Living, learning, here on the farm.
(February 13, 2015)

Often the first to dive into the fray, I wrote this to myself when the kids were twenty-one, nineteen, and sixteen—a rambunctious time in family life. In political times, when family doesn't always agree, it's more important than ever to listen, respect, and love—to acknowledge difference and celebrate common ground, and to trust we can work it out, one way or another, without me jumping in. Because I was raised to keep the peace, married to a partner who speaks his mind, and having raised our kids to express theirs, there were bound to be tense moments. When I found myself perched on the edge of losing my cool, I could choose instead to step back, observe, and figure out what it was, if anything, I could add. A wee bit emotional, I was still learning: there's no need to yell.

It had been two weeks since we dropped Siena and Garrett off at school and, wow, it was quiet 'round here. I had to admit, I actually missed the noise! I was grateful for the reminder this poem provided that, when life is wild and a bit chaotic, it will not always be so, as well as the reverse: Our emptier nest would not always be this quiet. As I typed this reflection, I could hear a persistent growling at the front door—the kind that sounds like it could shortly morph into a full-out howl—and I realized we still had a rather loud beagle our boomerang eldest had brought home, who loved to stand at the window or in the yard yowling at the moon and every other little thing. (Sorry, neighbors!) If I could just find a way to convey to her: *No need to yell.*

Empty Nest Plus One

Along the way, I'd wondered whether we were doing the right thing, caring for Mom in our home. Back when she could, she had often said she never wanted to be a burden. One of the best and worst things about Alzheimer's had been that, until recently, she simply hadn't registered the degree of unraveling in her thinking and health. She didn't remember what she didn't remember.

I was grateful for how my family had welcomed Mom in to live with us two years before, even though it inevitably altered our family life, starting with my availability. Now that the kids had flown the coop, I realized even more how their presence had brought balance, providing regular respite in Mom's care. What I appreciated most was the way they loved Mom, seeing her as a natural extension of our family, while also encouraging me. Garrett had commented, "Mom, I see the way you care for Lala, and I will do the same for you." I teared up just thinking about it.

These days, I appreciated more than ever Doug's continued support. When we couldn't find a caregiver for the local Color Run, he suggested we bring Mom along: "She might just have a blast!!!" he texted. It helped that Mom was so darned good-natured, though I had to admit, if she was snarky with anyone, it was him. Which I also must admit, he kinda deserved, as he was always the first to give her a razzing. Even as Mom sometimes forgot who I was, she continuously asked about him when he was away and enjoyed interacting with him when he was home. Although our empty nest may not have looked the way he'd expected it would, he rarely complained and, better yet, together we made the best of it.

Before her August hospitalization, I'd taken Mom to the doctor covering for her doctor, who was on vacation. Despite my concern regarding blood in Mom's stool, when Mom rated her pain at one and said she felt fine, the doctor had referred us to a GI specialist the following week and sent us home to "monitor" her blood loss. It turned out that peering into the toilet is not the best way to determine significant blood loss—that requires a blood test. Fun stuff. On the way home from that appointment, I explained to Mom that Siena and I had planned to take Doug out that night to celebrate his birthday while one of our helpers kept her company. When I mentioned it might be better for me to stay home to care for her, she replied, "Why would you do that? It's not like I'm going to die." Then she looked at me and smiled. "And if I do, we'll blame Doug."

We'd both laughed out loud at that.

It turned out the Color Run wasn't in the cards. When Mom's back pain became unbearable, the doctor prescribed tramadol, which had helped her through an injured rotator cuff the year before. This time, after just a couple of doses, it led to heightened agitation, intense confusion, and sleepless nights. Little did we know that tramadol, while it mitigated pain, could also lead to hallucinations and other adverse side effects, especially in older adults.[77] Sunday morning, two days after we stopped the tramadol, as Mom tried to make sense of the prior couple of days, she asked, "Who's going to keep me from going crazy?" I was glad I could answer, "I will do my best, Mom, and Doug will help, too." She smiled thankfully, as did I. What a relief when, four days off the tramadol, Mom's pain ebbed and she was at peace.

No, our postgraduate nest didn't look the way any of us had expected. Not exactly empty, it was more an *empty nest plus one*. I was grateful, even when I wasn't sure what was next.

~ ♪♪ ~

"Lady Girl"—When Mom Forgets Who I Am

The first time it happened, to my knowledge, was after I'd been away for a couple of weeks on spring vacation and returned to an infection raging in Mom's gut, causing delirium. The most recent time it had happened was the prior weekend, when she was suffering intense back, hip, and shoulder pain, likely (we hoped) the result of overdoing it with the visiting OT and PT (far be it from Mom to say "uncle"). Megan, a long-time friend, texted me that she couldn't imagine the ache I felt when Mom forgot who I was. It gave me pause. These days, I used the degree to which Mom knew me at any given time as information about her health and what might be lurking behind a wince, a sigh, a nap. However, I had to admit, when I stopped to think about it, I did feel an ache, as well as a fear—what if I lost my ability to ease Mom's way as she lost her ability to know I was her ally?

The first time Mom had been hospitalized that spring, her Alzheimer's had become so severe she hadn't even known me, so that even I struggled to get her medicine in. The second time we were in the hospital, that summer, when the OT had asked Mom if I was her daughter, Mom had laughed and responded with a shake of the head, "No, I'm *her* daughter," after which the OT had turned her questions toward me. In the past week, Mom had referred to me as her sister and her friend. As tramadol messed with her mind, she'd asked me if I'd be her secretary and, later, my personal favorite, her "Lady Girl."

Back when she knew me, Mom had been so independent, proud, and private that these days I sometimes wondered if I was violating her trust by sharing our Alzheimer's journey. At the same time, sharing my reflections helped me cope. Not only did it give me something to do during the hours I sat quietly at her side, it gave me an outlet, a way to make some sense of this brutal disease and, I hoped, to help others. Doug, who knew me best, eased my mind: "Your mom would want you to be okay, and writing helps you be okay." So I wrote, and sharing made the ache bearable. The messages I received back—a hug in a parking lot, a text on my phone, a post on Facebook, a comment on the blog—came when I needed them most, often when I was questioning myself, helping me to keep the faith and stay the course.

Whoever Mom thought I was at any given moment was okay; it had to be. I was just grateful that she still trusted me in the most fundamental ways, allowing me to give her care. There is no taking for granted anything when it comes to Alzheimer's disease, so we count our daily blessings. I was just glad to be Mom's Lady Girl or whoever else she thought I was, as long as she still knew I was on her side.

❦

"First Things First"

When a sleepless weekend led to another round of pain, blood, and breathlessness, off we went to figure it out. As I drove Mom through the morning fog, I started to feel breathless myself, with all the what-ifs. Then I remembered AA's slogan "First Things First."

The prior week's multiple unsuccessful blood-drawing attempts had left us without information, so this time it was to the hospital we went, me wondering whether to veer left to the ER or stay straight for outpatient testing and treatment. I'd been told that our next ER trip would likely take us to surgery for intestine removal, an alarming thought having seen Mom rip out IVs and generally unravel during hospital stays. *First Things First*, I reminded myself.

The nurse drew blood and collected urine in record time; free to go, we stepped out into the fresh air and I asked Mom what she wanted for lunch. "Something meaty," she replied. So off we went for Wisconsin's finest: Culver's ButterBurgers, eaten in the car while we enjoyed a fog-laden view of Lake Michigan. *First Things First.*

When he called with results, Mom's doc said her labs showed a falling red-blood-cell count indicating blood loss and a climbing white-blood-cell count indicating infection. I expected him to send us back to the hospital. Instead, he recommended antibiotics for a suspected flare-up at the site of prior internal bleeding, followed by a blood recheck in a week to ensure she was healing. So relieved to have a treatment plan allowing Mom to stay put, I told him I loved him. I do realize I gotta work on better boundaries; for now, though, I exhale. *First Things First.*

❧

Moving Mom, Again

Of the biggies we had made in caring for Mom, one of the most challenging decisions had been moving her away from her home in Maine. It was, after all, the place she'd built after Dad died. Always disciplined, she'd taken her first year of widowhood and stayed put in our family home. A month after the first anniversary of Dad's death, she called me on the phone:

"You'll never guess what I did today," she announced.

"Give me a hint," I replied.

"It's the last thing you'd ever expect me to do," she answered.

"Got married?"

"No!" Mom had laughed. "I bought land to build a house in a retirement community..."

"What?" My disbelief had mixed with hope.

And so Mom had set about planning her new home—designing every nook and cranny to contain her favorite things and painting the shingles red (it turns out she'd always wanted a house that color). When it was done, she packed up our home of forty years and moved north, closer to where she'd grown up. Mom had spent fifteen great years there, her neighbors becoming dear friends. She had adopted Cinnamon and the two had become inseparable. When Siena had gone to college ten minutes away, Mom's new home had provided her a second home, too. Dad used to joke that he would die first and Mom would marry a younger man. That's sort of what happened: After a year grieving, Mom had grabbed what life had to offer and carried on, Cinnamon at her side, making Dad proud.

As Mom's needs evolved, I'd arranged regular caregiving visits from a nearby agency to help with medicines, household chores, errands, and appointments (although Mom managed to evade them a fair amount of the time). I called twice a day from Wisconsin to check in. My brothers and I had a series of conversations with Mom as our concerns mounted; she'd listen patiently, sort of, and then tell us she didn't see what we saw and she didn't want to give up the life she was living. One time, my sis-ter-in-law Nancy called me from Maine asking after Mom's whereabouts. Last I'd heard, Mom was planning to take the ladder up to camp to climb in the window because she couldn't find the key. Ayuh.

Doug and I visited frequently during the long winter months when Mom was the only non-snowbird on her isolated street. Finally, requir-ing medical care during one of her winter visits to Wisconsin, she sim-ply stayed on. That winter, when the neuropsychologist diagnosed Mom with Alzheimer's disease and expressed concern about her living alone, I asked him to lay out the alternatives: assisted living, in-home caregiving, or moving in with family.

"Given the choice," Mom said, "I want to stay here with Terry and her family."

In the car afterward, she fretted about moving away from the boys and their families, before declaring, "Looks like you're stuck with me." When we got home, she asked me not to tell the kids—"They don't need to worry about that"—and then promptly forgot the whole thing. That spring, Mom had frequently asked when she was going home to Maine. She felt unsettled; I felt responsible. It helped when Matt wisely offered to do the same for me someday, if it was what I would need to stay safe.

This April, returning from spring break with Doug and Garrett, I'd asked at bedtime, "Are you happy here, Mom?"

"Yes, I'm happy here," she said. "I'm happy wherever I am." Music to my ears.

It had been a year and a half of highs and lows since Mom moved in with us, and with our kids now in school out east, we'd decided it was time to move Mom again, with us, back to Maine. Sorting through twen-ty-four years of nostalgia as I readied to pack had given me something to do in the kids' absence. Recently, though, the significance of leaving the home where we'd raised our kids and taken in Mom was starting to sink in. Although I was excited for what lay ahead and it was a great distraction from our *empty nest plus one*, I worried about the effect of moving east on the kids and our family life and the impact on Mom of moving to a new, unfamiliar house, now that she was settled. I'd also miss the life and the friends we'd made over our twenty-two years in the Midwest, although, thanks to modern technology, I trusted we would keep in touch and visit back and forth.

When I awoke to hear Mom up and about downstairs, I turned on the family room light to find her perched on the arm of the couch, holding the lamp in her hands, her crutch on the floor across the room, her knee and elbow bleeding. She peered at me and asked, "Are you my daughter?" After I reassured her regarding the sounds she thought she was hearing outside, she looked at me and said, "I was trying to find my way home....I guess I'm here."

Home means different things to different people, and the notion can change over time, sometimes by choice, sometimes by necessity. The time had come to get Mom back to my brothers and their families, extended family and friends, our kids, and familiar territory. "Home is where my mom is" read the plaque Siena had left on my dresser before we took her to veterinary school. She'd known it would bring me comfort when I returned to Wisconsin to start packing—that wherever I was, she would find me. It had comforted me as we prepared to move Mom again, this time back to Maine. Fingers crossed, her health would remain stable until we got her there.

⌐⌐⌐

Nine Squares

When Siena was eight weeks old, I was getting ready to move to the Czech Republic for Doug's new job. The only thing I'd insisted on was that we bring along our dog, July—turns out sometimes yelling *is* necessary.

As our departure approached, my cousin Margie came to visit in Milwaukee, where we were living short-term. When I told her about my new-mom-moving-overseas concerns, she recommended a book, which I tucked into my suitcase and found extremely helpful over the next year and a half. It helped me again, eighteen years later, when Siena left for college and I felt like I'd had the wind knocked out of me. I had a feeling it could help me now, as I adapted to our empty nest plus one and prepared to move Mom back to Maine.

In *Feel the Fear and Do It Anyway*, Susan Jeffers, PhD, emphasizes the importance of developing a healthy balance in order to break what can be a vicious cycle of fear and anxiety.[78] One of the strategies she recommends is creating a Whole Life Grid, which looks like a tic-tac-toe field, the nine boxes reflecting various aspects of our lives. The point is, if we pour all of ourselves into only one or two of the boxes, we're bound to feel panicked if things don't go well there. By committing ourselves to our other boxes, too, we create balance to help us through the inevitable ups and downs. As part of the exercise, we visualize what we'd like each box to look like, writing it down in detail and then listing what we need to do to make that box reality. We use this list to set daily goals, committing time and energy to all the boxes in our grids.

As a new mom living in Prague with an infant, a dog, and a traveling spouse, I used this strategy to format a meaningful life, far away from the people and places I had relied on for support—it helped me to step out when I could have easily hunkered down. Again, when Siena went to college eighteen years later, this practice helped me reevaluate and recommit to the things that make me me. Within a year, I had so much going on that I could be selective, which led me to five full and productive years, even with plenty of stress. When Matt went to college and I felt the familiar ache, I had confidence I could get through, and was able to help Doug and Garrett adapt, too. At times of high stress, when my focus starts to narrow and my obsessive-compulsive tendencies gather steam, recommitting to my nine squares helps me stay on track. It was time for another go-round.

This time, my nine squares included: Me, Marriage, Mom, Kids and Pets, Spirituality and Faith, Extended Family and Friends, Home, Recreation and Fun, and World. What struck me was that, when I looked at my prior grids, they were pretty much the same as my current one. Although they differed in detail, the categories were consistent. What mattered most was committing time to each endeavor—that is what had fluctuated with the various stages of my life. Notably, the Ninth Step amends currently on my plate reflected my nine squares status: The squares I'd cheated in time and energy were the places where I needed to recommit.

Bottom line: While tweaking where I put my time and energy would lead to more balance for me, I owed it to others as well. As I drove by a local church, I saw a sign out front that read: THERE IS A TIME FOR EVERYTHING. BE SURE TO MAKE TIME FOR GOD. It looked like my middle square—Spirituality and Faith was a great place to start. (P.S.: Yes, I did put our kids and pets in the same square!)

Celebrating Our Youngest: another parenting flashback

Garrett away at college and turning nineteen—our family in the midst of change—it was fun to look back at my journals and celebrate some of the things parenting him had taught me:

September 26, 1998:

After weeks of wondering…I awoke at 12:30 a.m. and I was sure of one thing: My water had broken. When I woke my mom, her first words were, "You're on your way?" So simple, so sweet, and so ready…

By the time we reached the hospital, the contractions were three minutes apart….This time through, I felt the pain. I did not use mantras to cope as I had with our eldest or drugs to survive as I had with our second. This time I was present. At moments I doubted I'd make it through. Then, there he was. Out of my body onto my chest and into my arms. Eight pounds, nine ounces. 5:28 a.m.….What relief. What joy. What a gift…

My friend Tina nailed it when, in describing the wonder of a newborn, she talked about having the opportunity to fall in love, all over again. I know of no greater gift than this: falling in love, all over again, this time with baby number three.

September 26, 1999:

…How could we be so blessed a third time around? He's so many things…among them a constant reminder that this is not a limited supply of love and beauty we are dealing with, it's an endless one. Crawling with such determination, into absolutely everything, drawn like a magnet to outlets, toilets, and sharp objects. So easygoing, so happy, so funny, and so interested in everything around him.

Growing bonds with his big brother and sister: their very own relationships... When I went from one child to two, I feared it might mean less love for each; now I know in going from two kids to three, the love only increases. The key is that I am not the source of the love, just one of its many expressions. It's the power higher than us that supplies it.

When I feel exhausted I tend to close my connection to that source and I feel all dried up, like a sponge wrung out. If I could only remember at these moments to throw the faucet wide open, to let the love run right into me, fill me up, and flow over. Ahhh, these kids are a reminder: it's not just about me....

September 26, 2000:
...Already two! Talking up a storm, on the move almost constantly, a person in his own right. Powerful in his sense of humor...in his first friendship...and in his love....

One morning, as a babysitter arrived so I could go to the library to write, our littlest decided it was time to take Bitty Bunny for a walk in the rain. I could have passed him over to the babysitter—thank God I didn't and instead I walked along barefoot beside him as he, still clad in his blue footsy pajamas adorned with yellow stars, pushed Bitty in the stroller around the block, unfazed by his runny nose or the rain coming down.

On his own little adventure, in his own little time zone. I was lucky enough to tag along.

September 26, 2017:
We can't always predict how change will change us. We can hope, and still we need to keep our eyes up, our hearts open, and our minds willing to learn. I'm grateful for the faith that parenting has brought me. Even as I missed this kid and the time we'd shared, I was excited for what lay ahead. I was—and still am—tagging along, even from afar.

SUMMERING

Living away all those years, summers meant returning to Maine, for as long as we could, an expanse that shrank as the kids grew. Whether a month, a week, or just a few days, as soon as we crossed the bridge from New Hampshire to Maine I'd breathe easier. The smell of the trees, the call of the loons, the taste of Mom's cooking—all reassured me, as if everything had changed and nothing at all. Without fail, no matter what time we arrived, Mom was waiting to greet us.

Got to camp after midnight, worried Mom would be worried.
Through the window I spotted her:
sitting on couch, reading book, blond hair gleaming in lamp light.
When Cinnamon started to bark, she threw down her book,
grabbed her cane, and came to let me and Garrett in.
She was happy and well, and she remembered me!

It follows that this next set of reflections, Summering, begins with moving Mom back to Maine for good. After all we'd been through in Wisconsin, this next phase promised time with family and friends while walking the familiar paths of Mom's and my youths, which we hoped would restore her health and well-being. At the very least, getting her back to her geographical home allowed our worries to ease and our pace to slow, so that we could live more fully into each day, even if that meant watching *The Sound of Music* again and again, Maria (i.e., Julie Andrews) twirling in the meadow singing the title song, Mom swaying in her favorite chair smiling, and asking, "Have you seen this before?"

Just as summer is all the sweeter for the knowledge that fall is ahead, so this phase of Mom's care was touched by a better sense of the shadows that Alzheimer's casts and the importance of capturing the moments, finite and infinite, in the warm sun. I'm so thankful that we got Mom back to Maine in time, not to die, but to bounce back, to live—to reconnect with old friends, to make new friends, and to have some good old-fashioned summertime fun.

Dear Higher Power,
Please grant me the Serenity
to accept Mom's Memory Loss.
Please help me to better understand, to adapt,
to re-find my balance, my joy, my self.
Please help me to care for her in the best way possible,
while staying healthy, too.
Please help me to rediscover my connection with Doug,
and to forgive things said in anger and in grief.
Thank you, Higher Power, that I am not alone—
I feel your love.
Thy will be done.
Amen.

"Retiring" the Car Keys: in retrospect

"It's going to be hard to see my friends without my car," Mom said, after not driving for close to two years, as we sat at the kitchen table discussing our upcoming move back to Maine.

When I reminded her that her license had expired and reassured her that I'd be happy to drive her anywhere she wanted to go, she nodded and smiled. We'd come a long way. What a relief that the driving question was behind us. That one had made me sweat for years before we'd gotten it resolved, and then only by virtue of moving her to Wisconsin, "to winter" with us.

Someone had once suggested we talk about the whole thing as "retiring" the car keys—Mom hadn't bought that for one second. "That would mean giving up my independence, and I'm not ready for that," she said adamantly and repeatedly, voice stern, Curtis jaw set.

Mom had loved to drive and frequently did, for work and recreation; adventurous to her core, she'd made good use of a full tank of gas, something she didn't take for granted, having grown up with rationing. As a kid, I much preferred driving with her over driving with Dad, who favored the passing lane and putting the pedal to the metal. In Mom's retirement community, she had chauffeured her neighbors around, sharing her knowledge of Maine as she'd shown them her favorite places.

During a summer visit, I'd gotten a wake-up call when Mom had turned left, me riding shotgun, right into the path of an oncoming truck. To my surprise, Mom hadn't even seen it. After that, when we were together I would drive—a change she never questioned. Otherwise, she continued to drive to and fro.

When my brothers and I shared our concerns about her safety on the road, Mom had resolutely marched herself down to a nearby driving school she'd found in the yellow pages, calling afterward to proudly report: "I passed my refresher course in flying colors!" Which had done little to ease my fears: I wasn't so worried about her on familiar ground, I was concerned about her behind the wheel if something unexpected were to occur: bad weather, car trouble, a detour, an animal in the road, another unpredictable driver. Mom had gotten confused behind the wheel before: One time, she'd taken our kids out for ice cream and ended up forty-five minutes north; another time, she'd lost her way going to visit a friend; and on another occasion, she'd gotten turned around driving an hour south to replace her American flag.

Concerns mounting, I'd hired a couple of caregivers to take Mom to appointments and help with errands; it wasn't unusual for them to arrive at her little red house, she, Cinnamon, and the van long gone. What made the whole driving question so challenging was that, even with our repeated conversations in which Mom would acquiesce, she kept forgetting and was surprised anew by the whole notion—just the past winter, more than a year since she'd driven, when Uncle Bill died, Mom had wished she had her car so she "could help the girls run errands."

My brothers and I had wrestled with this one for quite some time until Garrett said, "Mom...she's gonna hurt somebody!" (this after she'd driven him to school, down the wrong lane, twice). Needless to say, I was deeply relieved when Mom moved in with us in Wisconsin, making the driving dilemma moot, at least until she went back to Maine for the summer.

Recently, I'd been sitting in a coffee shop writing when I overheard an elderly woman talking with her friend about her kids' efforts to take her keys:

"They're only thinking of themselves," she said. "They don't want to feel guilty if something happens."

I'm sorry; I wasn't eavesdropping. I was just sittin' there doin' my thing and they were talking loudly. While I admired the friendship and support they shared, wishing the same for Mom, I gotta say, when it came to "retiring" Mom's keys, I wasn't worried about myself, I was worried about the world. I'd seen enough tragic stories on the local news to know better, plus how could I continue to duck the issue with Garrett calling me out?

In the midst of all this, I said to Siena urgently, "Someday, when you think I'm not safe on the road anymore, please take my keys. Don't worry about my independence or my resistance; just do it. I trust you."

She answered calmly, "Don't worry, Mom, I will—I don't think you're there yet."

Some might disagree, like the police officer who stopped me as I slipped through a yellow light, trying to keep the turtle sundae I was bringing home to Mom from flying into the dashboard. Long story short, a mistake at the DMV and I got an ominous letter. I'd had to laugh—all my worries about Mom, and I'd been the one with the suspended license. Whoops.

So, as we prepared to move back to Maine, I was glad Mom looked forward to reconnecting with friends and relieved we didn't have to worry about her behind the wheel. I would happily drive her wherever she wanted to go! And don't think for one moment I was going to leave my car keys lying around. The morning I left Mom in Maine two summers earlier, as Holly had driven me to the train, Albert had found Mom in the garage with a handful of keys, trying to start her van. She wasn't pleased when he bravely disarmed her. "Disconnect the battery!" I urged him afterward. At summer's end, when Mom told me she couldn't understand why her van had been hanging from the rafters in her garage all summer, I was grateful we'd taken action, even though it had felt sneaky.

∾

Glad to Be Acadia Manset's Granddaughter

It was Grammy's birthday—she'd be 116! It was also Dad's birthday—he'd be eighty-four! I'd been living in Grammy's house in Massachusetts when she passed away twenty-four years earlier. My parents had moved her to Maine "for the winter," and she had asked Doug and me to take care of her home until she could return in the spring. After she died that February, in a nursing home, it was for me to pack up her home of sixty years, preparing it to sell.

Pregnant with Siena, I spent endless hours, when I wasn't practicing law, sorting through all the things Grammy had so carefully kept and trying to figure out what to do with them next. Of the many things I rehomed, the records which Grammy had shared with me, I kept. It was in reading them years later that I discovered Grammy had written for the local newspaper under the pen name Acadia Manset—a shout-out to her favorite summer haunts in Maine.

What a surprise to discover that this gray-haired ninety-three-year-old woman—her mind open and sharp—had written in such beautiful detail about the trips she and Grampy had taken around the world as passengers on tanker ships. What a blessing to learn about her daily life, starting from childhood, to losing her father, to meeting Grampy, to adopting and raising Dad, to caring for her aging mother, Dora.

While eagerly awaiting news of Dad's (Don's) whereabouts while he served his summer duty in the NROTC, Grammy and Grampy (Eustace) had welcomed Dora into their home:

> *Monday, July 13, 1953...MOVING DAY....[Eustace] off &*
> *I to [Mother]....Movers there by 12. Packed Lucy [the car] &*
> *unloaded before they arrived here. All done by 1:50 & gone. I back*
> *for [Mother] & last odds & ends. [Eustace] stayed in to work in*
> *office. Settled worst bulk & it's not too bad really! Bed 11:30.*
> *Saturday, July 18, 1953...Don flew to Corpus Christi...41*
> *NROTC killed in [Florida] on way up to Norfolk from [Corpus*
> *Christi]. Hard day of anxiety. [Mother] settled her room—I put*
> *light on porch, fixed lamp, etc.—knees weak...[Eustace] home*
> *5:15. TV 7:30–9 then call from Don—SAFE!...*

It had been reading Grammy's diaries and recognizing parallels in my growing concern for Mom that had helped me realize that having her live with us, like Dora had with Grammy and Grampy, was an option. When I read that Dora had died in Grammy's living room, Grammy at her side, I was inspired to give Mom the same care and companionship Grammy had given Dora:

> *Friday, September 20, 1957... A lovely day fair, breezy & warmer. [Eustace] off 9—[Mother] sleeping but no food—only juice. Had washing to do for her & gave her water by spoon. Mended [Eustace's] suit & pressed & ironed in A.M. Sat at foot of bed all P.M. & mended. Water frequently—speech very difficult. Knew [Eustace] when he came just before 6—but failed to swallow by 6:45. An extra deep sigh at 7:35 & Mother went to sleep. [Eustace] in from uptown in few [minutes]. Mr. McGown here 9 or so—[Eustace] & I dismantled bed after they left. Talked till almost 4.*

When I was a child, I often said to Grammy, "I can't wait to see you," to which she'd reply, "Well, you're going to have to," humor in her voice. I was so grateful for the records she kept, and the ways they allowed me to feel her presence in my own empty nest plus one. In honoring Grammy's birthday, I celebrated the ways she had inspired me to care for Mom, in the sanctity of our home, writing as we went to keep track of our journey, just one of the many reasons I was, and am, glad to be Acadia Manset's granddaughter.

Step Ten: "Progress Not Perfection"

Step Ten: Continued to take personal inventory and when we were wrong promptly admitted it.
                              —Al-Anon's Twelve Steps & Twelve Traditions[79]

I needed to make clear, as I continued to peck away on my laptop, that I'd made plenty of mistakes—as daughter, sister, spouse, mom, friend, and caregiver. Although I tried to share the lessons I'd learned, I wanted to acknowledge that caring for others is such a personal and specific endeavor, there are no blanket solutions.

When the kids were little, I'd sometimes try a new approach, only to be so inconsistent because it didn't fit my personality that it wouldn't work, or, just when I thought I'd found a groove in my parenting approach, things would shift and what had been working stopped working, or what was effective with one kid was not for the next. PROGRESS NOT PERFECTION read the slogan on the wall of the room where I'd attended Al-Anon meetings for close to a decade—what a novel thought, one that helped me then as our kids' parent and helped me now as Mom's caregiver.

According to *Al-Anon's Twelve Steps and Twelve Traditions*, Step Ten tells us, "We need to keep observing what we did and why we did it. Examining our motives provides us with the tools we need to free ourselves of many problems that had beset us in the past."[80] As the Seventh Step reads, the word *continued* suggests that AA's Twelve Steps are not merely a list to get through and be done with, they help us create a way of life long after the crises that brought us subside.

Furthermore, continuing "to take personal inventory" is not limited to noting our negatives; it also includes acknowledging our positives—our progress and growth. The point is to build ourselves up, not tear ourselves down, so that we can be aware without being sick and make better, more responsible decisions about our lives, in the present.

At the silent retreat I'd attended years back, the Jesuit priest had noted that Step Ten requires perseverance. Having established a connection with a Higher Power in Steps One to Three and having addressed old pain in Steps Four to Nine, Step Ten gives us a process for dealing with stuff as it happens, or soon after, so that we can avoid the buildup of unresolved pain. This can be accomplished via spot checks, daily checks, and retreats.

Even though I no longer attended regular meetings, Step Ten helped me stay on track. I was thankful for how it helped me to pause, assess, and address things, head-on. Caring for Mom, with the way her Alzheimer's disease anchored her right here in this moment, I appreciated how Step Ten helped me stay right here with her, if not all of the time, at least some of the time: Progress Not Perfection.

Fingers Crossed: All Packed Up and Ready to Go

It was so close I could see it in minute detail. It was so far it seemed improbable. I got up that morning sleepy, again, after another wakeful night, wondering whether we'd pull this off.

The joke had been on me a couple of days earlier, having recently written about driving and Alzheimer's disease. Yes, it had been a relief when Mom's driver's license expired, putting the matter to rest, until I realized that that would make it difficult for Hannah to get her through airport security. I'd spent the afternoon searching for Mom's passport, fearing it was in the PODS container headed east, when a photo I'd saved on my computer revealed it had expired, too. Online research told me I couldn't get Mom a new ID without taking her to the DMV.

As I pondered the feasibility of packing Mom up for our cross-country drive, with four dogs, a cat, a rabbit, a chinchilla, and a U-Haul, it had seemed far-fetched. Then a call back from the airline assured me Mom could get through security with an expired ID, as long as she had a birth certificate to back it up, which had led to another online search, the purchase of a new birth certificate, and relief when it had arrived in the mail two days later. Fingers crossed.

And, too, there was the matter of Mom's fitness to travel. My biggest fear as the days counted down to our departure, in addition to Hannah getting her and Cinnamon through TSA, was that Mom's health would slip once Doug and I were already on the road. She'd been through so much in the preceding six months, including a series of recent medical appointments to prepare for the move. Cancerous cartilage on the tip of her nose had been removed (the scab still healing), prednisone was being tapered, and white- and red-blood-cell counts were stable.

Mom was excited to get to Maine, even as the details escaped her. I had made appointments with new doctors there, as it was unlikely her doctors in Wisconsin would accept her invitations to come with. As I lay in bed at night listening on the monitor to Mom's gnarly cough, I prayed it would ebb. In the morning, as I noted her soggy briefs, I hoped it was the cough combined with the fluid we'd been pushing, not another UTI. Fingers crossed.

Then, of course, there was the matter of readying our home in Maine, between our unloading and Mom's arrival. There was no way the slew of renovations we'd undertaken would be done, so we would do our best to set up shop in a way that would work. This was the least of our concerns—as Mom's doc had advised, given her fragile health, we needed to grab this window of stability and "go for it." Once we got to Maine, we'd figure out the rest. Fingers crossed.

It went without saying, I was a horrible partner right now. I hoped Doug didn't leave me before we hit Thiensville, just down the hill! Fingers crossed.

At least he had a cross-country bike trip to look forward to, which I wholeheartedly supported. Getting Mom back to Maine among family and friends, the ocean near, was my own bucket-list odyssey. "Some dreams do come true," said Bernie, the counselor I'd seen since experiencing the postpartum blues two decades earlier. I hoped she was right. Fingers crossed.

As Doug and I left Mom to drive east, I blogged to my friends in the Midwest, and everywhere else, that if they heard a wind blowing their way Sunday evening, it might just be my huge sigh of relief making its way from Maine, letting them know that Mom, Cinnamon, and Hannah had arrived, safe and sound. Fingers crossed.

Healing as We Go—UTIs and Mohs Nose, Mom and Me

As Doug and I headed east, I hoped things wouldn't unravel. A recent visit to Mom's doctor had confirmed what I'd feared: another UTI. With his advice, we were sticking to our travel plan, hoping the antibiotics would kick in and bring relief like before. It struck me as ironic that it had been a UTI that had piqued my concern during Mom's visit from Maine to Wisconsin two years earlier, just before she'd moved in with us "to winter."

It was also ironic that Mom's first and last medical procedure in Wisconsin was Mohs surgery to remove skin cancer from her face.[81] I had wondered whether it was the right call, with our upcoming move and Mom's other health concerns, until the skin doctor told me the tumor was precariously close to a nerve to her brain—this within a week of her dog having a lump removed from the top of her furry little head. I knew by the way Mom had picked at Cinnamon's stitches with her curious hands that stitches on the end of her own nose wouldn't stand a chance. When I warned the nurse, she looked Mom sweetly in the eyes with a "Leave the bandages in place, okay? It's really important to let your nose heal." Mom had smiled back at her equally sweetly. The bandages were off by the time we hit Main Street, the stitches bleeding by supper.

At my farewell appointment with Bernie, she remarked, "Look at how your relationships have transformed since we began, especially with your Mom," which had set me to thinking as I drove home, tearing off my own metaphorical bandages by the time I reached Main Street. So used to trying to stay in the moment with Mom so that I could provide good care and good company, I was touched by the stream of memories that ensued.

"Your mom never put you down when you were little, either," noted Aintie Jono (aka Aunt Joan) when she saw me parent. Although that came as a bit of a surprise because I remembered Mom being more practical than coddling, busy juggling work inside and outside our home, I liked hearing that we shared that in common. It made sense.

In middle school, during rocky social times, Mom would lie down with me at night, sharing her go-to strategy when worries kept her awake; I loved the way she talked me through tensing my body and then relaxing, bit by bit, from the tips of my toes to the tip of my nose.

I also remembered, somewhere in there, Mom showing me the photo of her dad and describing tearfully his unexpected death when she was a teen. I just wanted to ease her pain.

I recalled, too, when Mom went through midlife health and work changes and the relief I'd felt when her grumpy funks would dissolve into cleansing tears—it was like the sky cleared so the sun could shine.

In high school, when Mom's "some men still want to marry virgins" pep talk didn't inspire me the way she had hoped (and kinda put a damper on the Deering's Big Beef sandwich and chocolate frappe we were enjoying), I stopped confiding in her, as I simply hadn't wanted to let her down.

When I was in college and Mom's mom, Gum, was diagnosed with lung cancer, it was not unusual for Mom to forget our evening conversations, so I stopped calling her after seven p.m. When Gum died in my senior year and Dad asked for my help, I realized how much Mom hurt from the loss.

I also remembered Mom shedding tears of concern for Dad when I was young and he left for another business trip, and tears of anger years later as she vehemently defended my brothers' and my concerns: "We use alcohol to deal with stress," she'd said, something I understood better these days.

Months after I wed, Mom warned me that the competitive spirit Doug and I shared could be hard on a marriage—sometimes one has to give. She was right about that!

When I started having my own kids, Mom was there for every birth. I remembered thinking that, if I could take one person into battle, it would be her. She was the one to bust me out of the hospital during pregnancy number two so that I could recuperate at home near Siena, just two.

Then there was the time we stood in the kitchen of my childhood home, the kids one and three, and Mom looked at me crossly and proclaimed, "I don't understand you. You're so emotional. You don't make any sense."

A couple of years later, trying to respond to my request that we communicate more openly, Mom called me after a visit and said carefully, "I don't think you need to talk to your kids as much as you do." That one still cracks me up.

Then there was the April afternoon when we stood in a hospital room, moments after unplugging Dad per his wishes, when Mom hugged me close, consoling me, "I know how hard it is for a daughter to lose her father." Together, we walked out of the hospital, blinking into the late-afternoon sun; the next day we picked out Dad's funeral clothes, including his Birkenstocks, and, on the morning of his funeral, took a walk down memory lane at nearby Fort Williams. It was brutal to leave Mom in Maine to return to life in the Midwest.

A year later, when Mom surprised me at my fortieth birthday party, our emotional hello, amidst my Wisconsin friends, was raw and real, as was her sharing later the comforting feeling that Dad had been near when she cleaned out his closet and her tearful admission the day she left: "I don't know why I can't stop crying."

In addition, there were all the times we'd spent together since, during summer visits to Maine when she'd wait up late for our arrival, welcoming our animals and all our craziness into her home, and her regular visits to Wisconsin when she'd eagerly help however she could, and Siena's four years attending college in Maine, when Mom cheered her on in my absence. And, of course, the time I held her in my arms when she was in anaphylactic shock from fire ant venom, the island nurse reassuring me, "Don't worry, child—the Lord ain't ready for your mama yet."

And now, Mom's incredible resilience, her indomitable spirit, and the joy she still found in the little things, making it possible for us to care for her in our home as Alzheimer's and other health concerns took their tolls. Even when she didn't know us, she trusted us.

Recently, when I'd asked her if she knew who I was, she answered, "You're Nobody." Together, we and Hannah had laughed.

Then, the day before Doug and I hit the road east, when I asked Mom if she knew who I was (one of the ways I monitored her fluctuating confusion), she answered, "You're my best friend."

It's true, I was incredibly fortunate to have the relationship I shared with Mom. That didn't mean it had been without pain or that I'd always felt the love. Sometimes I missed who Mom *had* been so intensely it took my breath away, sometimes I felt deep sadness that she could no longer join in the way she once could, sometimes I felt tremendous responsibility for making medical decisions she could not comprehend, and sometimes I feared what was coming next.

Then I'd look over at Mom sitting beside me in the kitchen, asleep in the rocking chair, her scabby nose and layered shirts, and I felt such an intense love. I was so grateful for the time we'd had together to forgive, to forget, and to mend.

While waiting at the hospital for another blood draw, the second time in three days because the nurse had entered the wrong orders, Mom sat in a wheelchair in front of me. While I rubbed her shoulders, she looked up at me and asked, uncharacteristically, "Do you love me?" to which I responded, "Yes, Mom, I love you more than I can begin to capture with my words." To which she replied, characteristically, "Good, then we don't have to talk about it." The lady was consistent even when she wasn't.

As Doug and I drove twelve hundred miles east, I tried to be brave, to count my lucky stars, and to practice my faith; my fingers were still crossed, this time in prayer:

Dear Higher Power,
Thank you so much for the relationship Mom and I share.
Please help her, Cinnamon, and Hannah make it to Maine, safe and sound,
so that we can start the next chapter together.
Thank you, too, for sharing with us our wonderful friends—
Jen, Samantha, and Hannah—who care for Mom in my absence,
providing selfless attention and encouragement.
Please encircle us all in your love. Thy will be done. Amen.

Green Monster of the Midwest, aka "How Time Flies..."

"How time flies…" texted Jen's spouse, Mike. Over the prior seventeen years, the pair had become our dear friends—neighbors first, family now. Our kids were their kids and vice versa. A favorite memory was when our blended crew of Brewers and Red Sox fans set up Fenway's Green Monster in our backyard in Wisconsin.

Mike's text sent me to googling one of my all-time faves, James Taylor's "Secret o' Life." The lyrics celebrating *the passage of time* resonated with me when I was eighteen and leaving Maine to pursue my dreams, and fit more than ever as, at fifty-three, with our empty nest plus one, we were returning to Maine to begin our next chapter. I realized that all that was left to say was a deep-felt thanks to our many Midwest friends for sharing their time and love with us over the prior twenty-two years and for sending us good wishes and encouragement as we headed east. Recalling another James Taylor great, "You've Got a Friend," I hoped that technology would help these friendships endure.

Finding a Samantha in Maine During Hospitalization Number Three, This One for a DVT

Day two after Mom's return to Maine and feeling very much alone, I lay in the dark on the cot beside the bed where she slept, her left leg swollen, purple, and painful thanks to a blood clot. After weeks of watching for signs of another intestinal bleed, it had been the very opposite that had landed Mom in the hospital, again, this time in Maine.

The day before, during our eight-hour stint in the ER, Mom had told me repeatedly she'd seen Samantha as she was being wheeled off for a

CT scan to inspect her veins. When I asked if it could be someone who *looked* like Samantha, Mom had insisted, "It's Samantha. I could tell by the way she greeted me." Samantha had helped, in every single way, over the prior couple of years—caring for the animals, cleaning the house, hanging out with Mom. You name it, Samantha had brought her laid-back, upbeat, hardworking, can-do approach. She had been hard to leave behind. I understood why Mom's face lit up when she thought she'd seen Samantha in the midst of another long day in the ER.

That night, when the evening nurse came into the room where Mom was settled for the duration, I did a double take of my own. As she came and went all evening, Mom kept asking if she was Samantha. We agreed the resemblance was striking. The friendly nurse, whose name tag read MELODIE, told us with a smile, "You can call me Samantha if you want." She knew from listening to us converse that our doing so would be the highest compliment.

Day two, about four a.m., just after a doctor woke me to tell me the heparin they were giving Mom by IV to thin her blood, in order to prevent the formation of additional clots and to keep the existing one from getting bigger, in the hope her body would break it down and reabsorb it, appeared to be causing a bleed elsewhere—a risk they'd been monitoring throughout the night with regular blood draws. As we awaited the blood transfusion intended to replenish the hemoglobin Mom had lost, I started to fret. What if, in my determination to get Mom back to Maine, I'd inadvertently brought her harm? What if, in all the distraction, I'd missed a sign that could have protected her from all this? What if all my finger-crossing had been in vain?

Enter the one and only Melodie, aka Samantha. Noting the tears streaming quietly down my face, she asked if I needed anything. When I shared my worries, she said, "Your mom is eighty-five. She has a complicated health history, with Alzheimer's, diverticulitis, kidney disease, infection, limited activity level, and dehydration. This clot is so big it didn't just happen in travel; this condition's been developing for a while. This is not on you." Her words took me from feeling all alone to feeling the love, so that I could catch a few Z's which I'd need to get through the decisions ahead.

"What does *Samantha* mean?" I googled on day three of our third hospital stay, a filter inserted in the vena cava in Mom's abdomen to protect her lungs from a breakaway clot, her tender leg on the mend, a compression stocking in the works, the heparin being transitioned to Coumadin in hopeful preparation for a hospital discharge.[82] According to the advice of experts at babycenter.com on how to pick a name, *Samantha* means *listener*. Sounded just about right!

Finding Our Balance in Maine—Look Who's Boomeranging Now

"Thank you for the nice day," Mom said at bedtime, on day four of our hospital stay, a day that had started with four a.m. blood draws, another transfusion, and "good news"—she was done with the heparin IV, her body unable to metabolize it, so she'd be solely on warfarin, aka Coumadin, delivered by tablet—a step closer to going home. A day in which things seemed to settle—by evening, the levels of hemoglobin and warfarin in her blood were promising.

A week earlier, when I reminded Mom on the phone that she and Hannah would be flying to Maine to join us in two days, Mom had said, "I think I can last that long," to which I'd answered, "You better!" Together, we'd laughed.

Mom had gotten up that Sunday morning, travel day, left ankle swollen; she'd still been game to go, so we'd stuck with the plan. I was glad it was just a two-hour nonstop flight. When Mom, Hannah, and Cinnamon arrived in Maine, Mom had been exhausted and confused, her leg all puffed up. When I asked if she needed to see a doctor, she was adamant: "No, not at all." At bedtime, when I'd lain down beside her, she turned toward me and said, "I'm glad I'm here."

Doug and I had slept near, hoping a good night's sleep would bring relief and help Mom get through whatever came next. In the early morning, when I'd heard her talking to Cinnamon, she had sounded content. When she roused again later, she seemed happy and energized, albeit confused. Hannah noticed her leg was discolored; when we were unable to get her up to the bathroom, we called 911. That morning, Mom's first back in Maine, I rode with her in the back of the ambulance to the hospital where Dad had died.

Six days later, her DVT scare already forgotten, Mom sat at my side, in our new family room, peacefully asleep. As I processed the past week—the highs and the lows—I felt more out of balance than in quite some time. "Balance" isn't always the point in the middle or the line through the center. Sometimes it's one thing way out there and then another thing way back here, more like a bunch of extremes than something steady, stable, or poised, as googling it would suggest.

Safe and sound in a familiar routine—
A daring cross-country move
Leaving a community of awesome people—
Moving to another community of awesome people
The Midwest Prairie—The Atlantic Ocean
Encouragement—Discouragement
Remembering Mom's "Go for it"
and Dad's "Don't let the weather get in the way"—
The reality of Mom's third five-day hospital stay
Mom saying she's so glad she's here—Then forgetting where here is
Mom insisting she does not need a doctor—
A doctor is exactly what she needs
An intestinal bleed due to too little clotting—
Deep vein thrombosis due to too much clotting
Warm welcomes—Cold shoulders
A medicine that stops a clot in its path—
The same medicine threatens another bleed
Worrying whether I pushed too hard to get Mom back—
Witnessing her joyful reunions with my brothers and their families
Feeling alone at four a.m. at the foot of Mom's hospital bed—
Feeling support at nine a.m. when brother Dave surprises me with coffee
Questioning whether I'm fit for this job, after another sleepless night—
Refinding my way, thanks to a prayer written by Megan,
a dear friend in the Midwest
An unfinished house—
Everyone involved going above and beyond to get it ready
Mom speculating about my spouse's love life—
He at our new home, cleaning and prepping for our return
A compression sock that hurts so much to put on—
A compression sock that helps her leg to heal
Night four in the hospital spent trying to climb over bed rails—
Day five heralding freedom in the form of discharge,

after she tells the doc she's in no rush to get out
Nonsensical at bedtime, so exhausted from the week—
Clarity the next day, as we go to our new home:
"Portland…" Mom says, when we drive though the city
"It hasn't changed a bit," she adds,
as we turn up the road of my childhood home
"It's so big and blue," she observes after we wheel her seaside,
her eyes tearing up
Afternoon spent watching boats—
Evening spent worrying that she needs to pack
My repeated assurance that we are not going anywhere—
We are home for good.
Letting Go of Expectations, as they say in AA—
Holding on to what's helped before:
my spouse and kids, cousins and friends,
research and advocacy, love and faith.

Somehow, through all the extremes, balance reemerged. After a seventeen-hour sleep, Mom awoke pink-cheeked, hungry, a smile on her face, and I knew in my heart, as her docs in Wisconsin and Maine had affirmed, we had grabbed the window of opportunity and gotten her back where she belonged. Mom was right where she was supposed to be. Look who's boomeranging now!

A Tree in a Forest and a Health Care POA Prayer

If a tree falls in a forest and no one is around to hear it, does it make a sound? According to Wikipedia, this query has been around for quite a while (317 years, to be exact), with its philosophical, scientific, religious, and environmental implications.[83]

Yep, that's what had occurred to me one Saturday in Wisconsin as I waited with Mom at the hospital to have her blood drawn, the third time in five days, because the nurse used her two pokes without success on day one and then entered the wrong order for blood drawn on day two. Mom's doctor had been carefully monitoring her blood for signs of infection after her first hospitalization and blood loss after her second hospitalization—no small feat given the way Mom's fragile veins resisted intrusion.

I was thinking about the fact that Mom didn't remember these attempts, nor would she recall another, even though all three times she had winced with an "Ouch!" charming medical personnel with her good humor and polite "Thank you" as I wheeled her out the door.

The redemption? Mom's appreciative "I don't remember the last time I had a burger!" before happily taking the first bite of her post-blood-draw snack as we sat in the car overlooking Lake Michigan; this had quickly become a tradition.

If a tree falls in a forest and no one is around to hear it, does it make a sound? If Mom has all these experiences, and her memory doesn't record them for later, do they even matter?

A similar phenomenon occurred on a larger scale during Mom's three hospitalizations when she'd undergone various uncomfortable procedures, her dementia taking a beating—ripped-out IVs, unanswered pain, arduous colonoscopy preparation, medicines added inadvertently and dosed incorrectly. Mom had no memory of any of this, and again and again medical personnel remarked on her resilience and good nature. At one point, as the GI specialist breezed in, one of his assistants even quipped, "Well, at least she won't remember..."—true, yes, and also unnerving to hear from the medical team guiding her care.

On the last day of Mom's most recent hospitalization for a clot in her leg, the doctor admitted that the drop in her hemoglobin level indicating anemia might actually have been due to all the blood draws to monitor for blood loss and clotting time. Go figure. Again, despite her clear discomfort while getting poked, Mom quickly forgot afterward, endearing herself to those who cared for her; the nurse who looked after her the first four days even tried to get an overtime shift to see her through discharge.

The redemption? Mom, newly home from the hospital, calling "Terry!" to which I came running so that she could point—"Look at the boat!"—from her new favorite chair.

If a tree falls in a forest and no one is around to hear it, does it make a sound? If Mom has all these experiences, and her memory doesn't record them for later, do they even matter?

Long before I imagined that I would be caring for Mom, I had asked my cousin's spouse, Janis, about caring for her parents, both with dementia. She had said that, while some might wonder why take them to a Red Sox game that they wouldn't remember afterward, she'd learned that it was all about creating moments of joy for them *in the present*. Thank you for that, Janis.

Fortunately, Mom continued to rebound; I wondered if that was due to the fact that, in addition to the excellent health care she'd received, she didn't remember it, so fear of another round didn't hold her back. This made my role as her health care power of attorney (POA) challenging and essential; it's why I remained vigilant, took note, reassured, and advocated. It was why having others step in when I stepped away was essential.

The bottom line? In all the talks Mom and I had about what she wanted with respect to end-of-life medical care, she always came back to "Living is for living." This guided our advocacy on her behalf—balancing giving her a sunny Saturday on the patio, hanging with Cinnamon, with taking her back to the hospital, again, for another blood draw. In every moment, we tried to protect the quality of her days while also maximizing their quantity. Although Mom's DNR provided that heroic measures would not be taken to prolong her life should her heart stop, we were determined to take heroic measures to prolong a life worth living until then.

That's why we got Mom to Maine, even with the risk and uncertainty. That's why we got her to the ER the next morning. That is why I slept at her side on a hospital cot for four nights, even when the awesome Hannah offered to give me a break. That's why, when Mom arose, I settled her in her new favorite chair and let her be, and then, later, gathered her up to go meet her new doctor—for what turned out to be another unsuccessful five pokes with needles of all sizes.

The redemption? That night, as I tucked Mom into the hospital bed we'd set up in her new first-floor room, we hugged and I asked her, "Mom, are you getting what you need from me?" to which she replied, "Yes." And then asked me back, "Are you getting what you need from me?"

"Yes, Mom," I told her truthfully. "I am getting exactly what I need from you."

I'm of the belief that a tree that falls in a forest does make a sound, whether or not anyone hears it. Mom may not remember these moments, some magical, some not. However, we do, and if one day our memories fail, too, I am glad they are recorded here.

This is a prayer I'd written two years earlier, as Mom underwent a bone marrow biopsy and I stepped into the shoes of her POA:

Dear Higher Power,
Please help me to care for Mom,
to stay in the moment with her while getting her the health care she needs,
to keep her safe while supporting her independence,
to collaborate with the boys and all the rest,
to meet her needs as well as those of the others in my life, and
to stay right here, right now, while figuring out what's next.
Thank you for helping us to help her.
Amen

I am so grateful for our time with Mom in Wisconsin and in Maine, and for all the love, support, and encouragement that came our way. Remembered or not, these moments matter.

Step Eleven: I Am Not Alone

Step Eleven: Sought through prayer and meditation to improve our con-
scious contact with a Higher Power, *praying only for knowledge of* a
Higher Power's *will for us and the power to carry that out.*
                              —Al-Anon's Twelve Steps & Twelve Traditions[84]

With Doug back in Wisconsin for another eight weeks to transition his work so he could join us in Maine, I found myself in tears. I was starting to question all kinds of things when I remembered this poem I'd written to help me in parenting:

I Am Not Alone
When I'm feeling anxious and need a hand to hold,
I can hold my own.
Then I'll find my hands are joined in prayer,
and I am not alone.

I used to feel threatened by the words *prayer and meditation*. I didn't know what they meant or how to do them. I was afraid of the silence, of quieting myself enough to listen, and of what would surface if I did. I thought I had to find the right words to talk to God. Although I'd learned the Lord's Prayer when I was a child, it didn't really bring me closer to God. I knew how meaningful the prayer is to others, it's just that I'd learned the words without feeling a spiritual connection. Years later, when I got to AA's Step Eleven, I found a prayer I understood: "Higher Power, I pray for knowledge of your will for me and the power to carry that out," shifting "Here's what I want from you" to "What do you want from me?"

According to the Jesuit priest at the silent retreat I'd attended, "Prayer means raising our minds and hearts to God and talking to God as a friend." I had found reassuring his promise that "God's will is within us." I also found it comforting that the goal of Step Eleven isn't to obtain total and complete conscious contact with a Higher Power, though that would be nice, it's simply "to improve our conscious contact." No matter how foreign or scary prayer and meditation might seem, we can choose to make them part of our lives; over time, they become a natural part of our daily routine.

The best part is that prayer and meditation are available to anybody and everybody, anywhere and anytime. At times of high stress, when it can be most difficult to remember and we feel the drag toward old behaviors and old efforts to control outcomes, the miracle of contact can be most awesome. Al-Anon's *Twelve Steps & Twelve Traditions* tells us that "taking the Eleventh, for many of us, opened the door to 'a new heaven and a new earth.'"[85] That day, feeling alone with Mom in Maine, my spirits sinking, I recalled the above poem and started to pray for direction, which quieted my rising panic and returned me to a place of calm. As they say in the Twelve Steps, "It works if you work it." I can vouch for that.

For Today, a Fresh Start

November 1, 2017, was a great day: Mom became a great-grandma and I a great-aunt. The twinkle in her eyes and the smile on her lips each time I showed her the photos of the sweet little newborn made our recent travails shrink in significance. Like the birth of my niece Rosie had lifted Mom from the grief that had engulfed her when her mom had died decades earlier, the birth of Rosie's child provided an undeniable reminder that each day offers a fresh start, and so I recommitted to these goals I'd set in March 2016, shortly after Mom moved in with us:

For Today:
Serenity
Courage
Wisdom
Speak quietly
Speak truth
Live and let live
Let go and let love
Forgive
Embrace
Celebrate

Ayuh, aka "Do You Even Go to Church?"

One Maine morning, Mom got up and found me on the couch watching Netflix. When I mentioned it was Sunday, she grinned and asked, "Why aren't you at church?" It wasn't the first time I'd been asked about my churchgoing practice, although others, like a mother-of-the-bride upset that I'd been asked to officiate, had been more pointed, as in: "Do you even go to church?"

It wasn't that I hadn't gone to church growing up. I'd been baptized, and I remembered well the fancy spring hats and melted chocolate eggs of Easter morning services. Mom had taught me the Lord's Prayer and, believe me, both my parents had shown me by example the importance of leading a moral life. And, too, there'd been lots of love in my family. It was just that my dad had been put off by what he called "the BS" of organized religion and, by the time I came along, he'd preferred to spend Sundays with family outdoors, walking at the beach and boating on the ocean. I think it had something to do with a girl he'd dated whose parents hadn't approved. Needless to say, it had caught me unprepared when my curious someday-to-be-mother-in-law had asked me about my religion. "Congregationalist?" I mumbled, a question mark at the end, as if she could tell me whether I'd got the answer right. Darcy Wakefield, who bravely wrote about her first year diagnosed with Lou Gehrig's disease, described it best: "Maine Religious," she called it. "They have strong values and beliefs, which they are careful to keep to themselves."[86] *Ayuh*, I thought when I read that, as I liked that approach, even though I was going out on a limb and sharing my faith here, hoping it wouldn't offend.

Later, in my mid-twenties, when I'd begun my own journey to find a happier way, I'd found relief in AA's Twelve Step program, where I conscientiously practiced and developed faith. When Doug and I started having babies, I had experienced spiritual awakening sitting on a stepping stool in the kitchen of our first house, watching our kids interact, tears in my eyes, as I knew with total certainty that a power greater than me was at work. In an effort to educate our kids about religion and to find a church where we felt at home, we'd tried Unitarian, Lutheran, Episcopalian, Methodist, and Presbyterian; we would have tried Congregationalist, too, if there'd been one near. The language had kept getting in the way—I just didn't feel comfortable with any sort of judgment or exclusion in celebrating a Higher Power's love. Yes, I worried whether our kids had enough religion, enough spirituality, enough faith, and whether "we should" take them to church on Sunday. What if, even after all the time we'd spent together in conversation, prayer, and fun, it really did matter that they didn't have an easy answer to the question, "What religion are you?" Ironic that my concern hadn't been about their relationships with God, it had been about their relationships with people.

I'd felt unsettled by a discussion among a group of moms regarding whether they wanted their kids to have a teacher not of their religion; one of the many things I had treasured was our kids learning from people different from me and Doug. And I'd felt relieved after a conversation with the Jesuit priest at the silent retreat where he'd said that, while growing up without practicing faith could explain the void I'd felt, "different religions are all different aisles to the same altar."

One day, on the bus, a kid from our neighborhood had told first-grade Garrett that he wasn't a real Christian because we didn't celebrate St. Nicholas Day on December 6. (Sorry, that wasn't a thing where I grew up.) That night, as we lay in bed discussing what church to attend that Christmas Eve and the notion that perhaps we ought to go to church more regularly, ten-year-old Matt had chimed in, "I like it the way it is." He shared a memory of being in the basement at a church we'd attended for Sunday school, where the teacher had separated him and Garrett, even though Garrett was scared. Listening to Matt recount that memory, I realized it was okay that I didn't want to give our Sundays away. Like

Dad had taught me, I wanted to spend Sunday mornings with our family, without the weekday, workday stress of getting up and out by a certain time. While I respected that attending church might be the best way for some to celebrate their faith and to share it with their kids, it wasn't the only way.

I was deeply grateful the Thanksgiving when Reverend Bill, a retired Methodist minister and our friend Gwyn's dad, baptized our three kids in a kind and respectful way, with Gwyn and her husband, John, as godparents, Gwyn's mom, Jean, and daughter, Grace, as witnesses. The ceremony felt meaningful and spiritual, and would, I hoped, provide at least a partial answer to the questions that might come our kids' way.

My friend Tina, the most well-read person I know, told me once that I might be a Buddhist. That could be; I have a feeling I may be a lot of things. One thing I knew for sure was that I did not want to be a member of a religion based on exclusion, judgment, or fear. When I was honored by the request to help a young couple wed, rather than question why they'd asked for my help, I relied on AA's Step Eleven prayer for knowledge of a Higher Power's will for me and the power to carry that out. *Ayuh,* I thought again. That felt sacred to me. Although it might not sound like it, I was thankful for all these experiences and the diverse ways they'd helped me develop faith—a faith that guided me in all facets of my life; a faith that set me free. So, no, I didn't go to church on Sunday. I did, however, try my best, not without blips, to worship a Higher Power, in word and in action, every day of the week.

Post-DVT Haikus
Deep vein thrombosis,
her leg all swollen and blue,
and we feared a bleed.

On blood thinner now,
filter protecting her lungs,
home to recover.

Compression stocking,
why are you so freakin' tight?
No more blood clots, right?

Noticing the bench,
"I played piano on that..."
she says with a smile.

"Is that Mother's chair?"
I nod at the needlepoint.
"Is she still around?"

"About the baby,
can we make a plan to see?"
a great-grandma now.

Behind her at work,
the builder pounding away,
making our home sound.

Ever resilient,
her eyes as blue as the sea,
a cat with nine lives.

Mom sits with a book,
dog in lap, rocking away...
a smile on my face.

Eighty-five years young,
expect the unexpected,
one day at a time.

"Hot Tamale" and the Blessing of Awesome Caregivers

When I'd prayed for knowledge of my Higher Power's will for me and the power to carry that out, it had come across loud and clear that I was meant to care for Mom as her health and memory declined. It hadn't been quite as clear, however, how I would carry that out in the midst of caring for the rest. Then along came some awesome caregivers, among them Hannah.

I guess it was fitting that, the day after Hannah returned to Wisconsin, having helped us settle Mom in Maine, we lost power for four days, giving me plenty of time to search for words to express our gratitude. During our first two weeks here, with so much in flux, Hannah had taken care of us all, helping Doug ready our new house, taking the dogs for walks, giving Mom all kinds of love, and supporting me, too. When I was trying to figure out whether it still made sense for me to take my long-awaited weekend road trip to see each kid, Hannah had reassured me: "You really need it. I got this." And she did.

I'd gotten to know twelve-year-old Hannah coaching her in softball. An athlete who could play any position, she was the one who'd dive headfirst for a ball and throw it home for the out. At the end of that first season, when I gave each player candy acknowledging their particular strength, Hannah had gotten Hot Tamales for her bold approach. I never anticipated that it would be her, ten years later, who would help me care for eighty-five-year-old Mom.

Over the past year and a half, Hannah had shown up when promised and helped out when the unexpected occurred, like when I had to run Garrett for stitches after he got an elbow in basketball. Hannah had listened conscientiously, asked insightful questions, paid careful attention, and provided top-notch care, all with an upbeat and humorous attitude. She'd been fearless about taking on the unpredictable, nerve-racking care of someone who couldn't communicate reliably about pain or change. Hannah had been a great teammate.

What I appreciated most was how Hannah had acted with kindness and respect. It hadn't been unusual for me to return home to find her and Mom side by side at the kitchen table sharing a meal—Mom's peanut butter and jelly, Hannah's tofu nuggets—or on the couch, Mom rereading a book, Hannah studying for the medical school entrance exam. Hannah had actually gotten to know Mom, asking daily questions about her favorite things and looking through scrapbooks with her. Although Mom may not have remembered Hannah's name or understood exactly why she came to visit, she had enjoyed Hannah's companionship and considered her a friend. When I asked Mom what she thought of Hannah, she said, "She does what she needs to do and that's that. She doesn't fiddle around. She also likes to have fun, too, not to be working all the time. She's easygoing. I just like her."

Hannah, like Samantha and Jen, had proven that AA's Step Eleven works: When I prayed for knowledge of my Higher Power's will, I'd received the help I needed to take care of Mom in Wisconsin, away from her Maine family and friends, while also taking care of the rest, including me (which she'd want me to do). The power in Maine restored, the dust settling on recent change, I was looking for help caring for Mom in our new home. Understanding its importance, I was determined to set up Mom's care above-table.[87] Already, support was emerging—more proof that "it works if you work it," as they say in Al-Anon.

The Joy of Not Caring, aka "Hypersensitive" Me

This may come as a big surprise: It's possible I cared a little too much. Not about Mom or others who had my back, but about those who were more whimsical in their support. In the Twelve Step program, we are encouraged to detach from situations that bring us down. It doesn't mean we have to walk away or stop loving, it just means we need to look within and accept ourselves, to practice self-confidence when others' words or actions hurt us. I wrote this poem at a time like that, in an effort to detach:

Hypersensitive Me

I've been called many things by those who are supposed to know me best:
"hypersensitive," "too emotional," even "nuts."
Sometimes I wonder if I'll ever get to a place
where their words don't cause me pain.
Probably not…that's one of the costs of being:
"hypersensitive," "too emotional," even "nuts."
Here are some things I've realized, moving back to where I'm from:
The more things change, the more they stay the same.
I don't need to be loved by everybody, just by some.
I can choose those who accept sensitivity, emotionality, and even nuttiness.
I can live with the anger I feel at expectations unmet,
the fear I feel at being judged, and the sadness I feel at being rejected.
I can take care of me, even when it's difficult—
exercise, hydration, nutrition, sleep, writing,
friendship, animals, family, faith—
The healing these bring is within reach.
This is the way to take care of me,
not believing what I am told when I am not who others want me to be.

"Hypersensitive," "too emotional," even "nuts"—yes!
With these three things, I've been blessed.

Okay, so maybe this poem was a bit hypersensitive. It was true, though, and something I needed to work on—not fighting how I was wired or letting criticism get me down. That's what detachment is all about. Although I tried to celebrate the joy of caring, there were times when I needed to practice the joy of not caring. Sometimes not caring was the most loving approach.

"Wicked Good"—the Blessing of Old Friends

wicked good *(adj): it means really good*
—www.urbandictionary.com

It was a rainy night, Mom safe and sound at home with Holly, while I ran around the Maine Mall trying to fix my phone, recover my lost wallet, and find suitable undies, after which I stopped in at the convenience store. As I headed to the back corner where the milk and eggs were shelved, the thought came to mind: *I can buy beer!* I hadn't been to that Cumberland Farms since I was eighteen, I hadn't drunk a beer since I was twenty-six, and there I was, feeling like a teenager. I literally laughed out loud.

Sort of like my childhood friends, Kathy and Nancy, had been making me laugh since they'd rescued me and Mom from a dark, electricity-less house by bringing candles, flashlights, and supper from Hannaford. Seriously, I hadn't seen these girls since about the last time I'd drunk a beer (coincidence?), and there they were, giving Mom some love with stories they remembered from knowing her when she was our age. (Little did I know then that it would be Nancy who would show up the morning of Mom's last day, bringing more food, companionship, and light.)

In the push to get Mom back to Maine, my focus had been on Mom and getting her closer to family, on our kids and getting within driving distance of them, on Doug and starting a new chapter of our life, on our animals and transferring them safely across country, and on our Midwest friends and saying sad farewells. I had hoped to reconnect with old friends here in Maine; however, I'd had no idea of the warm, arms-open welcome they would give us. Doug had warned me not to cry until they'd gotten into the house or I might scare them away; that wasn't to be. It was kind of appropriate. They'd known me back before spouse, kids, mid-life stress, and they'd made me laugh then. And now here I was, settling Mom into a new routine, away from Doug and the kids, and in addition to the tears, they were making me laugh, again.

In the past twenty-five years, Doug and I had lived around the world, and I'd made amazing friends who had shared in marriage, parenting, coaching, volunteering, tutoring, and more. They'd known me and sup-ported me. They'd made leaving Wisconsin tough, and I hoped we would stay connected. One thing I'd not done so well in my role as caregiver was make regular time for friends. Don't get me wrong, I loved them; we had each other's backs, whether by text, by phone, or in person. It's just that in the busyness of family life—parenting and daughtering—I hadn't made consistent time to step away to spend regular time with them. I was sorry for that.

When I was young, sometimes I worried about Mom and wished she'd had more lighthearted fun, more friend time. Between working long hours and caring for our family, she hadn't stepped away much, either. I had wondered what she would do when I left for college and her nest was empty; as it turned out, that's when her mom had been diag-nosed with lung cancer, and so that had filled her days. In my current caregiving role, I saw Mom's line of friends, from childhood on—and I got it. They were neighbors, classmates, teammates, wives, athletes, colleagues, travel buddies, kindred spirits; they'd watched each other's kids grow. They'd shared grandparenthood and, in some cases, widow-hood. They were the kind of friends who understood each other's other demands, like the friends I was so fortunate to have. Many of them were the moms of my friends, and I appreciated their opening their homes to me. Many of them still stayed in contact with Mom, through me. Some-time soon, I hoped to have them over for egg salad and iced tea to recon-nect with Mom, and share some more laughs of their own.

Sunday night, as my concern grew about Berry the beagle, usually so rambunctious and increasingly subdued, Kathy dropped in. She offered to hang with Mom while I took Berry to the animal hospital. It was a good thing, as it turned out Berry had a painful pinched nerve. When

I got home, I expected Mom to be in bed, and instead she was dozing contentedly on the couch beside my old friend. The next night, we had a potluck supper at our new home, with more laughs and reconnection. Our beloved field hockey coach, Mrs. Cayer, and a basketball teammate, Biz, joined us, too. Mom sat and listened and afterward remarked what fun it was, which set me to planning a holiday gathering to reconnect with more old friends.

It was my second time in the Maine Mall in less than a week, this time meeting Nancy for lunch at the food court followed by a foray into Spencer's. You wouldn't believe what they sell in the back corner of that store. It was *not* eggs and milk. It made me blush and sent us running, laughing so hard that the back of my head throbbed. I'd have to work on whatever those muscles were. I had a feeling I was gonna need them. There's something about reconnecting with those who knew us and our families way back when—it's wicked good!

Just Plain Thankful
Thanksgiving brunch at camp in Belgrade, Maine.
Mission accomplished.
Their combined 170 years looked pretty damn good.
They may not have remembered where it all started; however these two
—Aunt Joan and Mom—
still enjoyed hanging out together, side by side.
Speaking of Gratitude.

Sweet Dreams, aka Taking Care of Caregiver
In the recent flurry of activity, it had been difficult to find time or insight to write. While there had been plenty of inspiration, I felt too fuzzy to put it into words.

To begin, I was thankful to all who inquired about Mom in those first weeks back in Maine. After a tricky start, she was doing great and enjoying time with family and friends, hence my ability to take a moment and check in on me. A week earlier, I had felt so run down I'd gone to my new doctor to be reassured that my blood and heart were just fine. Neither the Lyme disease that had laid me low several years back nor other tick-borne illnesses were at play, my vitals were strong, and my ticker was ticking, leaving me to wonder, *What's the deal?*

Early one recent morning, as I lay in bed listening to Mom on the monitor, getting up various times to check on her—"new baby syndrome," the OT called it—I realized that disrupted sleep could be the culprit. It's not unusual for people with Alzheimer's to suffer sleep disturbances, so I'd done what I could to ease this for Mom, kind of like when our kids were little: active days, peaceful nights, regular routine, gentle reassurance, a security object, i.e., Cinnamon.[88]

Mom had suffered disrupted sleep since I was a child. It had not been unusual for her to awake around four a.m., toss and turn, doze and dream, worry and fret, until she'd get up, eyes puffy and red. The challenge, these days, was that she could not reliably get herself back to bed, she'd forget that she'd already gone to the bathroom, and sometimes Cinnamon would end up on the wrong side of the door. One night, Mom couldn't get her door open, and another night I'd found her in the dark, light bulb unscrewed from its socket. Hence the monitor at her bedside and my nightly wake-ups.

That weekend was the first since we'd moved to Maine that I actually slept in my own bed, thanks to Doug's awesome paint job during his Thanksgiving visit from Wisconsin, where he was shifting work gears so he could join Mom and me full-time by Christmas. I hadn't realized until I stretched out that, while the sofa across from Mom's first-floor room was convenient for keeping tabs on her, sleeping there, along with moving furniture to and fro, had done a job on my back.

It felt great to be back in a real bed, although it would take some figuring out how to care for Mom from there. When Rosie brought her beautiful newborn to visit the day after Thanksgiving and I watched her swing him, walk him, nurse him, and snuggle him, it reminded me of being a new mom and how, even in the very best moments, it's exhausting. It had always been hard for caregiving me to let down my guard and sleep, which fueled many a late-night round to make sure everything was in order, one more time. Watching my niece reminded me to be proactive in catching up on my own sleep now.

It was not just a matter of having pep in my step so I could participate the way I wanted to today, there was also a long-term incentive I hadn't realized as a new parent. In addition to a variety of risk factors for Alzheimer's and dementia,[89] recent research suggested a link between sleep disturbance during midlife and cognitive decline in late life. As CNN journalist Sandy LaMotte reports, "A few studies in cognitively normal people and one in mice have shown a connection between chronic sleep disruption and the development of amyloid plaques. The research in mice was particularly interesting because it showed that mice who slept well reduced their levels of beta amyloid, effectively clearing the toxin from their brains....[According to] Dr. Rudolph Tanzi, who directs the Genetics and Aging Research Unit at Massachusetts General Hospital...Increasing amounts of evidence indicate that getting at least seven to eight hours of sleep is essential for brain health and function... In the deepest stage of sleep, the brain cleans itself out of plaque and other toxic materials that trigger Alzheimer's disease."[90]

When the kids were little and Doug was traveling, once they were in bed it was hard for me to resist staying up late to paint a room, watch a show, or write a reflection, like I'd been doing since arriving in Maine with Mom. I realized that, in order to care for Mom in our home, I needed to make sleep a priority, for her and for me. Just as counting on the kids to nap so that I could get some rest had never worked, praying for Mom to sleep so that I could sleep wasn't a solution, either. Being strategic about when to catch up on my own sleep—particularly now that I had a bedroom with a door—was key. At least some of the time when I had help, I was gonna have to sneak up to that awesome bed and just shut my eyes. Yes, I'd still get out to exercise, run errands, see friends; however, I'd also try to get some much-needed rest.

In taking care of caregiver, makeup sleep had to be a priority—it would improve the quality of my days and of the care I provided, and I hoped it would help my brain stay healthier as I aged. After a particularly rough night, when Mom came into the kitchen bright-eyed and bushy-tailed, I gave her a hug and asked, "How's my sweet mom this morning?" to which she replied, "Good, I think....How's my sweet...my sweet lady?" Sleepy me smiled as I recalled it had never made sense to get mad at the kids for disrupted sleep, nor did it make sense to get irritated with Mom now. I just had to make a plan to get some shut-eye and stick with it. Speaking of which, time to get some sleep. Sweet dreams!

Step Twelve: Whole, Not Hole

Step Twelve: Having had a spiritual awakening as the result of these Steps, we tried to carry this message to others, and to practice these principles in all our affairs.
—Al-Anon's Twelve Steps & Twelve Traditions[91]

I didn't used to believe in God. In fact, I worried I had God-like powers, that if I imagined something horrible happening, it just might. And I didn't have a clue what *spiritual* meant; I felt a hole in my soul and tried to fill it in all kinds of unhealthy ways.

When I first read the words *having had a spiritual awakening*, I thought, *Yuh, right.* Though I wanted it, I doubted it could happen to me. I was advised to let go of my skepticism. When a guy at an Al-Anon meeting described his Higher Power as the Pillsbury Doughboy, it freed me to open my mind; no disrespect intended, I actually envisioned my Higher Power as a toilet where I could put my pain and confusion and flush it away. Although that may not sound much like "a spiritual awakening," it helped me let go of yucky stuff I'd been holding on to.

Caring for Mom, twenty-five years later, I was spiritually alive and well, and the way I envisioned a Higher Power, like my faith, had evolved. My spiritual awakening meant being present in the moment, right here, right now, with spouse, kids, pets, family, friends, Mom, self—maybe not all of the time, but more and more of the time.

When I started going to Al-Anon meetings and focusing on recovery, I feared it might interfere with relationships with those who hadn't taken the same path. I was grateful that Doug had supported my finding my way. I was also relieved that the program had encouraged me to focus on myself, trusting others to find their ways, too. I'd always felt uncomfortable with those who preached or tried to convince me to see it their way. Back in college, evangelical students liked to knock on my door; their pressure hadn't felt spiritual at all. The Big Book affirms that the Twelve Step program is not the only way to heal; it's just a way that works for many: "We have no monopoly on God; we merely have an approach that worked with us."[92] For so long, I had healed privately, quietly. Now I was finding joy in sharing the healing I'd found and the challenges I still faced.

Here's the wonder of it: I had discovered the Twelve Step program out of concern for loved ones. It had helped me accept that I couldn't control them and needed to focus instead on my own health. In the years since, this approach had worked its way into every bit of my life, transforming, healing, and improving all of it. When I found myself feeling some old, unresolved feelings—feelings I wanted to flush away—I reached out to those I trusted and was lifted, reminding me of how far I'd come since moving away from my hometown in Maine at age eighteen. I may have come back, geographically; however, I was not the same lost soul I'd been back then. Even though being spiritually awake sometimes meant feeling spiritual pain, I was grateful that being open and honest with those I trusted worked. My spirit lifted, I felt again whole.

Helping Mom Manage Her Finances: in retrospect

Shortly before we left Wisconsin, an envelope had arrived from the Maine Department of Corrections containing a check to Mom for something like twelve bucks. At that rate, it was gonna take a while for that jerk to make up for what he'd taken from her.

It had happened several years before, when Mom was still living alone in Maine. She'd started to mention that she couldn't find certain things, including some of her grandmother's silverware. She had blamed herself, saying maybe she'd misplaced them or accidentally thrown them out. We searched without success. Then one day a police officer had knocked at her front door to ask if she was missing any items from around the house. They had caught a guy who'd stolen things all over her retirement community. Turns out the man who'd come to tune up Mom's furnace and "spent an awful lot of time looking at the radiators" was a thief. Mom had described him as a chatty sort when we'd spoken on the phone; in fact, he'd been distracting her while he cased the joint and took her valuables. Mom had gone to a pawn shop looking futilely for her things; he'd gone to jail. It had been a heads-up to the rest of us that Mom was vulnerable. Though it was hard to fathom, some people look for people like her to prey upon. I felt badly afterward that I hadn't called the police when Mom had first mentioned something amiss; however, it had been complicated by the way her memory was changing, leaving her unsure and questioning herself.

Later, when Mom had forgotten to pay her insurance, I realized it was time to step in. According to the National Institute on Aging,

"People with Alzheimer's disease often have problems managing their money. In fact, money problems may be one of the first noticeable signs of the disease."[93] Raising the topic of helping with Mom's finances hadn't been easy, as she'd always been so independent and organized when it came to this stuff, and it had meant acknowledging that that was changing. It had required a series of respectful yet honest conversations about her vulnerability, which she'd forget afterward. Knowing that Dad would have wanted us to protect Mom's financial well-being had helped me persist, even when it felt intrusive.

Although Mom hadn't realized she needed help, she had willingly shown me her bookkeeping and given me access to her accounts. Having run a small business, she had an impressive system in place. It helped me ensure that I didn't leave anything out. At first, I paid Mom's bills and sent her a monthly summary. When she moved in with us in Wisconsin and I saw that it only confused and stressed her, I began doing her bills myself, keeping careful track, so that when and if anyone asked, I could show the care I'd taken to manage her finances.

It is a delicate balance, knowing when to protect independence and when to step in, particularly given *use it or lose it* concerns. Looking back, I was glad we intervened when and how we did, as it spared Mom more loss. Putting a durable power of attorney in place while she was still able had been essential in managing her finances as her Alzheimer's progressed. Helping with Mom's finances was one small thing we could do in the Alzheimer's maze where so much was beyond our reach, which reminded me, once again, of the Serenity Prayer:

> *God, grant me the Serenity to accept the things I cannot change,*
> *Courage to change the things I can,*
> *and Wisdom to know the difference.*

Helping Mom manage her finances had been an important step in giving her care, one I'm glad we took before another loss, despite the discomfort, to keep her financially safe.

Paradiso Found, aka Reversing the Jinx

"This place is jinxed," the carpenter had told me, right after he'd said as much to the delivery guy, just before they realized some lumber was missing from our order. Original walls rotted, replacement windows with too few panes, new doors too short, generator not generating, sewer backed up, painters swapped, tank of heating fuel empty, renovator no-shows, and there Mom and I sat, two months post deadline. In fairness, we'd been forewarned. Two months that had begun with a twelve-hundred-mile move, followed by a third hospital stay, and finished with another amazing comeback—not too shabby for a jinx!

True, my back was a bit sore from sleeping on the couch, and my patience wasn't as patient as it had been at the start, especially when renovations stalled, for a variety of reasons, including "blockbuster" winds.[94] Still, we were getting close. In a week, when family would arrive for Christmas, I hoped to welcome them to an orderly, peaceful home; however, as Thanksgiving had confirmed, we could have fun in construction chaos, too.

In the spirit of doing what I could, I cleaned, unpacked, sorted, cleaned, moved things to and fro, monitored the details, cleaned, communicated, practiced patience (most of the time), cleaned, painted, threatened to paint some more, cleaned, practiced gratitude (most of the time) and enjoyed the carpenters, the view, the time with Mom, and the relief of having her back in her neck of the woods. Although she didn't necessarily remember she was here, she seemed much better than she had since her vision loss last spring.

Highly sensitive to words, a marketing team's dream, I chose Benjamin Moore's Paradiso to paint the floor in the upstairs hall closet. I figured a little blue Paradiso in the middle of our new home might help exorcise the jinx noted by the carpenter. When I told the painter the reason for this choice, he responded, "L-O-L, when we're done, your whole house will be a paradiso." Thank God for humor, animals, friendship, and faith—more than anything, those had kept me on track. Those, and Mom, who was not one bit superstitious and enjoyed the ocean view, even through the scaffolding—she knew paradise when she saw it, even with one eye.

⸎

Looking for the Right Words, in Alzheimer's and Elsewhere

I remembered Mom as being reserved, more a listener than a talker, when I was growing up; she was usually quite careful with the words she chose. At eighty-five, she was more open and direct. Lucky for us, she was generally kind in the words she used, although she sometimes had a hard time finding the ones she wanted.

According to the Jesuit priest at the silent retreat, "Within each of us dwell an angel and a beast," which leads to an internal struggle between good and evil, between creeping on our bellies and soaring like birds. Which part prevails depends on which we feed. His description had reminded me of the value of filling and surrounding ourselves with positive and nurturing language. In *The Four Agreements* (1997), Don Miguel Ruiz says we can cast spells with our words: Negative words create negative outcomes and positive words create positive outcomes.[95] According to Jeffrey M. Schwartz, MD, and Beverly Beyette, authors of *Brain Lock: Free Yourself from Obsessive-Compulsive Behavior*, changing the way we think from negative to positive actually changes the way our brain works: "Change the behavior; create a new groove; get behavioral improvement; and, in time, you will change your brain and get relief from OCD symptoms."[96] When I first heard about Schwartz's work on the *Today* show decades ago, it had given me hope. When I'd looked at the places I'd been stuck, they had been on negative, not positive, thoughts. Maybe if I made positive language a priority, I could actually heal emotionally, spiritually, and even physically.

My spiritual awakening meant realizing in every instance that there was a choice, whether to choose positive or negative language with myself and others. Although I still had plenty of moments of negativity and sometimes said awful things, this awakening had brought me the ability to hear myself, catch myself, and break the spells I'd set with my words so I could cast new, more loving ones. This didn't mean denying the pain or the difficulty, it meant believing, hoping, and having faith.

We don't always know how the words we choose will be heard by others. That's why we listen, we learn as we go, we keep searching for the right words, while we are able, that can heal. And if we ever lose the ability to find those words, we rely on those we trust to help us through. Choosing positive language had transformed every single relationship in my life. The wonder of it was that finding and using a more loving language is something we can all do, right here, right now, to make the world a better place. Amen to that.

The Cherry on Top: Getting Mom Back to Maine

"When we get to Maine…" Mom would say as she sat in our new home, here in Maine.

It wasn't that she didn't like where she was—she was peaceful and content, and her health had improved. She commented regularly on the view and, when I asked if she was happy, she nodded. When I told her we were here to stay, she smiled. When we got out, which was admittedly rare, we drove familiar routes, by the home where she'd raised me and my brothers, the stores where we'd shopped, her work commute of forty years, and the nearby park, where we'd walked together the morning of Dad's funeral.

Old friends and work colleagues came to visit, family stopped by, childhood friends dropped in. I showed Mom a book about Casco Bay and a local map from the atlas that had been in her home, and she regularly scoured photo albums for reminders. Mom may not have remembered where she was; however, she knew her way around our new home and appeared to have no desire to leave. There was no question that, even with its blessings, this had been a difficult stretch. True, we could've stayed in Wisconsin, in our home by the stream "connected to Maine," as Mom would say, and she could've been content. We could've avoided some of the challenges of the prior nine weeks. The thing is, when we strategized about how best to care for Mom, in addition to her doctors' advice, we were guided by all the conversations she and I had had along the way about where and how she wanted to live. I even heard Dad weighing in with his "Don't let the weather change your travel plans."

Mom was a Mainer through and through; given the choice, this was where she'd want to finish, brunching with extended family, reminiscing with old friends, holding her great-grandchild. That Mom didn't remember, though challenging, wasn't defining. Our kids didn't remember the first phases of their lives, yet that didn't stop me from carting them to Maine every chance I got. Mom may not remember her Alzheimer's phase, yet we gave her the best care we could, and that included bringing her back to the people and place that she'd always loved most. I was thankful that we got her back while she could still enjoy the view. And I had to admit that, when Siena stopped by to drop off Edith on her way out for a night with friends, I couldn't have been happier to be within her and the boys' reach. We just needed to get Doug here, too, to make our new home complete.

So when Mom got out of bed and walked into the living room where I slept, to ask, "Where are we?" I put aside my laptop and off we went, to make the most of another beautiful day. In the end, whether this move was for her or for me, or for some blend of us both, to me, as in parenting, it was more about the *we* than the *her* or the *me*. Later that day, returning in the snow from the doctor's office, we passed the dentist Mom had gone to for fifty years and would see the next month for a checkup. After reading the name on the sign, she turned to me and said, "I guess we're home." This was the cherry on top.

Parenting from the Empty Nest Plus One

Waiting for family to return for the holidays, I rewatched Melissa McCarthy's *Spy*. So many f-bombs were dropped that Mom got up and went to bed. Still, it made me laugh out loud, which felt good. The first five minutes, watching McCarthy's CIA-analyst character, Susan Cooper, sit at her desk with her technology, directing field agent Bradley Fine via his earpiece, on a mission to recover a suitcase nuke, reminded me of parenting adult kids, minus the nuke or the innuendo.

Just the week before, I had sat, at midnight, Mom tucked into bed, dogs at my feet, typing away on my computer, proofreading a paper, checking our international cell coverage, and perusing vintage sweaters. Matt liked to joke that I reminded him of James Bond's Miss Moneypenny as I parented from the empty nest plus one, doing what I could from the kitchen table to make life easier for the kids, nineteen, twenty-two, and twenty-four, all into their own cool things—taking finals, traveling abroad, shopping for Christmas. Before Mom came to live with us, I'd done the same for her.

Don't get me wrong, my work wasn't limited to logistical support; there were also the occasional requests for encouragement and/or advice, which, as you can probably guess, I wasn't above loving. I didn't like to think of myself as a helicopter mom so much as a safety-net mom—if a loved one felt like they were falling, I wanted to soften the landing. Of course, I wished none of them had those moments. However, stuff happens.

As I was unpacking a box, out fluttered a scrap of paper from Grammy's book of quotes:

Friendship

The inexpressible comfort of feeling safe with a person, having neither to weigh thoughts nor measure words, but pour them all right out just as they are, chaff and grain together, knowing that a faithful hand will take and sift them, keep what is worth keeping, and with the breath of kindness, blow the rest away.

—Dr. Calkins.

I'd been warned against being our kids' friend. Every time I heard that, I wondered, *Why bother having kids if friendship isn't a goal?* That didn't mean abdicating parental responsibility; it meant building this kind of honest communication, when our kids were little and when they became big. Open sharing wasn't always easy, given how we worry about our kids and want to protect them from what hurts. At the same time, it seemed to me, it was the whole point. Best of all, it went both ways: They could share with us and we could share with them. Although I tried to protect our kids from my concerns when they were little, in caring for Mom I took to heart their honest and loving advice when I shared what was on my mind.

I just hoped I was not called into action to save the day like Cooper or Miss Moneypenny. This might sound a bit far-fetched except that just a week before, Matt had sent me a text from the Amazon, where he was traveling with a friend who'd been there doing research: "Hey just wanted to let you know all's good down here, got sick last night but the medicine…seems to be working. Going to a high ropes course and monkey island tomorrow! Love ya."

I was glad to help where I could and to live vicariously the incredible adventures the kids were having, thanks to technology, even though, as any parent knows, there were challenges, too. And when all three got home for the holidays, I had to admit that, although I felt weary as I waited for the coffee to brew, it was fun listening to them laugh in their room in the wee hours of the night—even better than listening for Santa Claus.

Happy New Year!

Here's a reflection, written a year and a half after Dad died, when our kids were ten, eight, and five, long before I'd ever considered the possibility that we'd one day care for Mom:

December 31, 2003: Happy New Year!

Another year, come and gone. Nothing has changed and yet, everything has changed. A year ago, I resolved to continue my efforts to take care of myself physically, emotionally, and spiritually. It has been a year of growth and joy. In the year to come I resolve to continue my journey toward greater physical, emotional, and spiritual health.

Exercising regularly, eating well, getting to bed on the early side so I am ready to rise early with the kids, financial accountability, continued time for friendship, meetings, writing, reading, prayer, and a place of worship that I may share with my family. I have learned that this is a lifelong process, and I am grateful for that. There will be highs, like whizzing down the snowy slope with my spouse, kids, and dog yelling "I'm free!" as loud as I can. What a wonder to notice and savor the exhilaration, the joy, and the serenity that life offers. There will be the lows, like reading about the family that lost their two-year-old son in a sledding accident just two days later. There will be sadness, anger, and fear, and the anxiety they produce. There will be the gathering of information so that we may make reasonable choices for our kids and ourselves …and there will be the turning over of all the rest. Praying for help and putting our trust in a Higher Power.

In Barbara Cooney's *Miss Rumphius*, a child tells her great-aunt Alice, "When I grow up, I too will go to faraway places and come home to live by the sea," to which Miss Rumphius responds, "That is all very well, little Alice, but there is a third thing you must do…You must do something to make the world more beautiful."[97] I love this tale; I have gone to faraway places, I hope someday to return to live by the sea, and I hope in the meantime to make the world a more beautiful place. What a miracle it would be if all this writing helps others, as it has helped me.

Here it was, fourteen years later: The kids had grown, Mom had settled in, we'd returned to live by the sea, and I continued to seek greater physical, emotional, and spiritual health. Grateful for the many blessings of 2017 and committed to maintaining balance amidst ever-changing challenges, I continued to hope that all this writing would somehow help others, as it helped me. I was eager to make the world more beautiful in 2018. Happy New Year!

Step One: Admitting We Are Powerless Over #fillintheblank

Step One: We admitted we were powerless over alcohol—that our lives had become unmanageable.
—Al-Anon's Twelve Steps & Traditions[98]

JUST BE read the bumper sticker on the car in front of me at Dunkin' Donuts as I prepped for the big storm. What better time than the Blizzard of 2018, with its heavy snow, whipping winds, Arctic cold, and third-highest tide in history, to reflect on the language of AA's Step One?

We

For much of my early life, I felt like I was outside looking in. Involved in all kinds of activities, I'd gotten a certain excitement, pride, and joy out of all the doing, and not much serenity from just being. I'd felt powerful, not free. The way I felt inside hadn't matched the way I presented myself to the world, and I hadn't felt safe in my relationships to really be me —if I'd even known who that was.

What I found when I walked through the door of my first Al-Anon meeting had changed all that: people, of all sorts, sharing their lives, their pain and their joy, their wisdom, their strength, and their hope, with courage and honesty. What "we" shared in common was that we'd been impacted by another's alcohol use. I learned that the details that had kept me in hiding for so long weren't important. What mattered was our shared quest for health and balance, in the midst of the stressful details. What mattered was not how we'd gotten there, it was that we had gotten there. I no longer felt outside looking in.

admitted

For far too long, denial had kept me trudging along, telling the outside that everything was okay. "I'm fine," I'd say, a smile on my face. When the pain was great enough—physical, emotional, and spiritual—I came out of hiding and "admitted" I wasn't fine at all. Admitting is not necessarily all or nothing. For me, it had been a gradual awakening. Once it had begun, there'd been no going back to the way it had been before—maybe for moments here and there, but for shorter and shorter spans of time as I went along.

Having survived so long by not opening myself to the pain I felt, admitting was scary. I feared being overwhelmed with my vulnerability. I found instead that admitting in the context of a loving and accepting community was healing. All around, I found living proof of people who'd "admitted" and found their way through the pain to the joy and serenity beyond.

we were powerless

Admitting "we were powerless" didn't mean we lay down and gave up, it meant we admitted we weren't in control in the way we had thought we were or should have been. These words didn't mean we were victims. They meant we needed to look at what we were fighting to control and why we were doing so, and to take responsibility for what we could do to choose healthier lives.

over alcohol, or #fillintheblank—

While living in Prague in the nineties, I'd attended a weekly meeting that included individuals with various addictions, all of which had brought them to the Twelve Steps. I learned then that the key wasn't the type of addiction, it was the underlying pain, and that the Twelve Steps helped a variety of people, regardless of their addictions. What mattered was that we recognized the unhealthy ways in which we dealt with our anxiety, so we could replace them with ways that worked.

I'd gone to my first meeting because of the pain I felt regarding the alcohol consumption of my loved ones. In subsequent years, I'd become aware of the unhealthy behaviors my own anxiety drove, like drinking too much, trying to control others, dwelling on uncomfortable thoughts and feelings, and checking and rechecking for real and imagined threats. Admitting my powerlessness over the anxiety that had driven these behaviors and applying the tools I'd learned through studying the Twelve Steps had brought me continuous freedom, growth, and relief.

that our lives had become unmanageable.

I'm grateful that my home life growing up hadn't been violent or explosive. I hadn't been abused physically or verbally. My parents had taken wonderful care of me in many ways, which I deeply appreciated, especially now that I was a parent and better understood. I knew they loved me and were proud of me. Still, while things may have looked good to the outside world, something had been amiss in my inner world; the alcohol they'd used to relieve stress had actually *created* stress, at least for me. Caroline Knapp describes *functioning alcoholics* as "strong, smart, capable people who kept drinking—who put off looking at the dozens of intangible ways alcohol was affecting their lives—precisely because they were strong, smart, and capable....High-level functioning stands in the alcoholic's path like a huge road sign, flashing the message that everything is under control."[99] As a result of this kind of drinking, it took me a long time to realize and admit that *my* life "had become unmanageable," too.

Looking back, I could see all sorts of physical evidence of this unmanageability, including bouts of irritable bowel syndrome, a string of unhealthy relationships, and my own alcohol excess. More recent episodes of back and neck pain, stress fractures in my teeth from nightly grinding, another cold sore on my mouth, incessant worry, and general exhaustion and weight gain had reminded me that anxiety continued to affect me physically. When I noted these signs that my life was becoming unmanageable, it helped me to stop and look at how I was dealing with stress and to choose a different way.

In caring for Mom, as I worked to maintain a manageable life in the face of all I couldn't control, I appreciated the reminder to admit where I was powerless, as it helped me to focus instead on the places where I could make a difference. Although I couldn't change the course of Mom's Alzheimer's disease, I could impact the quality of her days. Hence, it was oddly reassuring when I asked her at dinner, the weather raging outside our door, "Mom, do you like where you're living?" and she responded, "Good building, good people, what's not to like?" And then, to my curious, "Do you know where you are?" she smiled and answered, "Heaven."

HALT and Let in the Love

With hurt feelings that kept me awake and were hard to release, concern for loved ones who were struggling, too, and another UTI causing Mom heightened agitation and sleeplessness, free time and clarity had been scarce since ringing in the new year.

I'd learned long ago, in Al-Anon, that when we feel irritable or unreasonable, we need to HALT—it may be that we're Hungry, Angry, Lonely, and/or Tired. When anxiety started to build, expressing itself in the most obnoxious ways, this acronym prompted me to pause in the midst of the busyness and take care of myself and others—to eat, to hydrate, to vent, to pray, to connect, and to rest. Rather than letting my mind take off on another intellectual (crazy-making) analysis of my angst, HALTing restored peace of mind. This wasn't meant to minimize the brutal realities of depression, anxiety, addiction, Alzheimer's, or anything else; this was the reminder I needed in the midst of those challenges to pause, assess, and change what I could, to bring relief.

Hungry: HALTing had come in handy in caring for the kids, too. One morning, way back when, leaving Maine after a visit with Mom and Dad, two-and-a-half-year-old Matt, sandwiched figuratively and literally between his siblings, had started to whine. He'd wanted his jacket unzipped and he'd wanted it zipped, too; I couldn't get it the way he wanted. Getting frustrated because time was ticking and we had a flight to catch, I bribed, "When you stop whining, you can have your cocoa." Then I remembered to HALT: I gave him his cocoa and Cheerios and—voilà!—he quieted and began to eat. In my rush to pack, I'd saved breakfast for the car and he'd been hungry. Jacket zipper forgotten. Obvious, no? However, the obvious wasn't always easy to discern when whining was escalating in the backseat.

Angry: I recalled an Al-Anon meeting years before when an attendee said she had never really felt angry, and she wondered if it was okay to do so. I could relate: I had rarely felt anger for the first twenty years of my life; instead I had a lot of stomachaches. In recovery, I felt a lot of anger—as my twenties could attest. I knew what it felt like to "stuff it" and didn't want to do that anymore, so I went to the other extreme: If I felt it, I expressed it, without much grace. In my thirties, as I settled into parenting, my approach had changed again; I became better at feeling anger and then choosing what to do with it. The urgency I'd felt before became more manageable. It had been nice to feel anger without judging myself, to vent it—exercising, hitting a pillow, yelling in my car when I was all alone—and then to choose appropriate actions to address its causes. This approach had worked in parenting, too. It wasn't so easy to raise kids who were encouraged to express their feelings; sometimes it all erupted at the most inconvenient times. I was convinced, though, that dealing with anger and other uncomfortable emotions directly was essential to our health. Although we couldn't prevent our children, or ourselves, from feeling painful emotions, we could help them, and ourselves, to respond in ways that worked. By offering outlets for anger and other feelings, words to express and options for action, we could set them, and ourselves, free.

Lonely: Oddly, at those times when I most needed company, I would isolate. Then, as my loneliness built, negativity would creep in, which, of course, only furthered the distance I felt from others. HALT reminded me that when I heard myself whining, what I really needed was to be heard and acknowledged, held and comforted. Once I realized this, I could ask for what I needed. I could find this connection with others by opening up to it, praying for it, writing about it, calling a friend, reaching out to Doug and our kids. I used to think it was wrong to ask the kids to help me this way, that they'd feel responsible for my happiness. Then someone at Al-Anon had suggested that our kids *want* to help us when we're sad. What hurt them was feeling helpless; letting them help— the old "I need a hug"—was not only okay, it was empowering. And it taught them how to ask for what they needed when they heard themselves whining. So if it wasn't hunger or anger, the next thing I tried was connecting, by words, by touch, in prayer, in presence—whatever was possible in the moment.

Tired: When I looked back at my life as a parent, I could see that my lows were linked to sleep deprivation (there'd been plenty of that) and my highs to catching up with myself (which took intention and attention). It had been when I was exhausted that I tended to mix it up with Doug at bedtime, the last thing either of us needed. I finally learned to avoid that trap by repeating "Less talk, more sleep" over and over to myself until I'd fall asleep, instead of staying up to argue. Almost always, I'd awake the next day with no need to further discuss whatever had felt so pressing the night before. This seemed obvious when we looked at our kids. When they were tired, they fell apart. They'd do all the things that challenged us, and if we could just see it as a sign that they needed sleep rather than react to it with our own tired responses, we could give them what they really needed. Less talk, more sleep!

Just as it had helped me to better care for me, Doug, and the kids, HALT also helped me to better care for Mom. We kept a regular routine to try to minimize unnecessary stress. If we noted her a bit off her game, we HALTed to address the obvious, which Alzheimer's could keep her from communicating. And if HALTing didn't work, we got medical help, as in her case that often meant another infection was brewing.

As I cared for Mom, I happened upon several lists at dailycaring.com that confirmed the importance of HALTing to care for ourselves as we care for others.[100] As one post put it, "Caregivers are at risk because they put caregiving duties first and tend to ignore the symptoms of stress-related problems...putting your own health last leads to severe chronic stress, serious health conditions, and poor lifestyle choices."[101] HALTing to care for ourselves when we are caring for others is crucial, even when it's inconvenient.

That first winter back in Maine, I HALTed big-time with Doug and the kids, so that we could ski. The fun meals, open sharing, together time, healing laughter, and uninterrupted sleep restored me so that back at the kitchen table in the early morning, Mom still asleep in her bed, I wrote this reflection, remembering that this, too, was how I HALT. I was deeply grateful to our caregivers Jessica and Karly for stepping in and providing loving care for Mom that allowed me to step away so that I could return ready to take on the day and whatever came next.

I could learn a thing or two from Mom. After breakfast, she sometimes went to her room "to get ready for the day." When I'd peek in, there she'd be, back in bed, singing Jimmie Davis and Charles Mitchell's "You Are My Sunshine" to Cinnamon. Sometimes HALTing means putting our own feet up; sometimes it means taking a moment to learn from others who are doing just that.

Step Two's Coming to Believe

Step Two: Came to believe that a Power greater than ourselves could restore us to sanity.
                    —Al-Anon's Twelve Steps & Twelve Traditions[102]

As I've mentioned, my spiritual awakening had been gradual and life-changing. Coming to believe in a power greater than myself had been no small thing. However, my prior efforts to handle things myself had left me anxious and depressed, obsessed and compulsed, trying harder than ever, and suffering more and more deeply, convinced that I was falling short internally, not that I could find help externally. Though I had wanted to believe, I hadn't known in what to believe. It was when I finally let go of worrying about what to believe in and instead made the decision to believe in something, anything, outside of myself, that I'd begun to heal. This had come slowly for me, at first fueled by pain, later reinforced by joy, especially when we had kids who brought me the undeniable knowledge there had to be something greater than me at work.

Caring for Mom, I saw this power greater than myself everywhere I looked—my spouse, our children, our pets, extended family, neighbors, friends, nature, Mom, her caregivers, and more. If "insanity is doing the same thing over and over again and expecting different results," as I'd heard in Al-Anon, then sanity comes through trying something new. For me, this something new meant taking AA's Step Two and choosing to believe in a power greater than myself, even when that was difficult—like learning a left-handed layup. I remember well the summer I was fourteen and set my sights on that—it had felt so awkward, dribbling with my left hand, until, after much practice, it finally clicked and I never looked back. When I "came to believe," it brought amazing and immediate relief. When angst started to creep back into my life today, as it did from time to time, Step Two was still there for me, reminding me of the way back to sanity.

"Pardon me…" Mom, rebounding from another UTI, interrupted politely, "can you help me?" When words failed her, she led us to her bedroom and pointed at the recently hung mobile, a Christmas gift in honor of the geese in our backyard in Wisconsin.

"Why are they just floating there? Why have I never noticed them before? Why don't they do something?" she asked. When my attempt to explain didn't soothe her, I took the mobile down and put it in a drawer. Later that night, Mom asked me to take down the SNOW POND sign that hung above the painting of camp, too. Then, thanks to the Alzheimer's, she promptly forgot being unnerved in her room and fell asleep. It helps to believe someone we trust can take our worries away.

Thank You for That, aka an Attitude of Gratitude

Between kids asking universal questions and Mom asking confused questions, my anxiety sometimes climbed. At one of those moments, I got a text from Hannah: "Hoping you find some time for peace…What are you doing for you?"

I thought about that and realized that one of the ways I cared for me, in the midst of all this, was by trying to practice an "attitude of gratitude," as I'd heard it called in Al-Anon. Like seeing the cup half full, an attitude of gratitude means counting our blessings, even when we are barely hanging on. It doesn't mean that we deny our pain or pretend that everything is okay, it just means that we take a moment in the middle of it all to give thanks for whatever we can. This, in itself, transforms. Practicing an attitude of gratitude had helped me drift off to sleep on many a restless night.

While I used to have to practice gratitude purposefully, recently I'd caught myself doing it without intention. It helped that I had Mom showing me the way:

One night, before family arrived for the holidays, I was tuckered out from all the preparations. When I rued that I wasn't going to have our new home set up to welcome the kids, Mom said, moments after forgetting the word *boat*, "They won't care about that. They'll just want to get here, get outside, and scramble around." Thank you for that.

Another day, stuck on the question of why I'd moved Mom back to Maine before renovations were complete, I asked her if she was getting what she needed and, amidst the loud and smelly building going on around her, she looked out the window, nodded at the blue, and asked me back, "How can you complain about that?" Thank you for that.

Too, after a recent week when Mom was having a hard time sleeping at night, I had to coax her into bed after a nap-less day. As she lay there wide-eyed, I said, "Mom, I'm sorry you are feeling confused right now," to which she responded, quietly, "Well, I don't want to feel too sorry for myself because then it'll make others feel too sorry, too." Thank you for that.

Then, another night, when nineteen-year-old Garrett asked her, "What is a nice thing to do for a stranger?" Mom answered without hesitation, "Have a conversation with him, ask him about himself…Wouldn't you like that?" He looked at me and smiled. Thank you for that.

Finally, when Mom noted Doug's absence and I explained he was golfing with friends down south and had asked me to join him for a couple of days, she chimed in, "Go for it.…Why stay around here and do all the work?" To my "Will you be okay without me?" she declared, "I've made it this far; I think I can make it through that." Then came the twinkle in her eyes and the smile on her lips. "Cinnamon and I may just stay in bed." Thank you for that.

In caring for Mom, I was especially appreciative of the wisdom and support I received from so many different places, including Mom—although she might have forgotten a thing or two, she still exemplified the life-changing impact of an attitude of gratitude. Thank you for that.

Sandwiched—Caring for Mom While Caring for Kids

That winter, our first back in Maine, our empty nest plus one became an empty nest plus two. It was awesome having Garrett back home as he figured out what was next. Having seen firsthand the impact of Mom's Alzheimer's and other health concerns, he was generous in lending a helping hand while also hanging out with her.[103] He knew just the song to get her dancing. There's plenty of literature about the challenge of being part of the "sandwich generation"—i.e., taking care of our kids while taking care of our aging parents.[104] It's a big job with plenty of stress. There's no question I had sleepless nights worrying about loved ones on both sides. At the same time, hanging out at the kitchen table with my mother and son, wearing sunglasses as they basked in the glow of the HappyLight I'd bought to brighten the short winter days, I had to I admit, it was pretty cool, too.

Happy Easter!

It had been a while since I'd found time to write, and I missed how it helped me to find balance. As a jump start, I thought I'd look back at a journal I'd kept years ago:

April 17, 2003, Easter Rebirth

It had been ten months since Dad had died and feeling low, I emailed Mom, asking her about all kinds of things, including how he had felt about me. Although I felt embarrassed, self-centered, and insecure doing so, I needed to know. I knew Dad loved me; he was dutiful in his support of me and committed to visiting me all over the world. However, I feared that somehow, on an emotional level, emotional me had let him down.

Mom called me immediately and deliberately answered all my questions. This is some of what she said: Dad was proud of me. He never liked it when Mom and I argued—that was not a reflection of what he felt about me, that was about his desire for harmony in our home. Although Mom and Dad knew we kids wanted more from them in the way of words, that wasn't their way; they never intended us to take that negatively, it just wasn't how they were brought up. I felt a flood of relief when Mom added that Dad knew I was devoted to him. I felt forgiven.

The following Easter Eve, as the kids and I read Aileen Fisher's *The Story of Easter*, I was touched by the conclusion that, "the message of Easter is always the same. It is the joy and celebration of the belief that God's love is stronger than death."[105] Mom's response to my questions had made real for me Dad's love, almost a year after his death, and reaffirmed for me that that love lives on.

I was thankful as I read this reflection, fifteen years later, with Mom's memories of Dad depleted, that I'd taken what felt like a scary leap and that Mom, usually so private and reserved, had given me exactly what I'd needed in return. I was grateful, too, that these days I could sit at Mom's side, no words necessary, secure in the knowledge that she felt my love and that it was the emotionality I'd once felt sorry about that now fueled me as I provided her daily care. Amen.

When Meds Are a Mess: in retrospect

On International Women's Day, this one back in Maine, as the hubby and I sat at the hospital waiting for the surgeon to retrieve the filter he'd placed in Mom's inferior vena cava to keep the blood clot in her leg from traveling to her lungs, I distracted myself by writing this look-back at an issue that initially alerted me that Mom needed me to step up. As mentioned before, I am not a medical professional, so the following is simply a sharing of my experience in caring for Mom.

For Mom's eightieth birthday, we'd taken her on a bucket-list trip to the Galápagos Islands. I knew she'd been nursing an injured hip; however, our first night as layover roommates, observing Mom handle her medicines, dropping some on the floor and leaving others untaken on the dresser, caught my attention. After a fascinating week learning about survival of the fittest, we knew something had shifted: Mom had still been a gamer, ever ready for the next adventure; at the same time, her forgetfulness had been undeniable.

When I called my sister-in-law Nancy, asking her to meet Mom at the airport in Boston, Mom said tearfully: "You must think I'm getting old." That was the first time of many that I had to make calls to try to keep Mom safe; six years later, I still had to remind myself to breathe. According to authors Robert B. Santulli, MD, and Kesstan Blandin, PhD, "the care partner will usually review the relationship she had with the afflicted individual, prior to the illness. Part of her anguish comes from the awareness that her relationship with the loved one has now changed, forever."[106] Bingo.

We'd made the adjustments we could (me in Wisconsin, Mom in Maine), hiring caregivers to set up the pill minder, check that Mom was taking her pills, and help out where she'd allow. In addition to calling Mom twice daily to check in, I communicated regularly with Mom's helpers, by voice and text, monitoring updates and concerns. Thanks to them, Mom continued to live on her own another three years after the Galápagos trip.[107]

Then when Mom came to visit for Thanksgiving, she was tired and loopy. I discovered an expired bottle of sleeping medicine among her toiletries, "to be taken as needed." I wondered if she'd been taking them unknowingly, which prompted a call to her doctor in Maine, who had no idea of her memory change or difficulty managing meds.

When Mom came to stay with us that winter, I kept the pill minder where she could get to it. After she double-dosed herself one day, Siena suggested I put it out of reach. My concern for Mom's autonomy sometimes challenged my role as her caregiver. I still saw her as Mom, even when she did not (these days she called me "my sweet friend"). She had been so organized, efficient, independent, and accomplished—sometimes my effort to give her the respect she deserved left me fretting adjustments obvious to others. I appreciate Doug and the kids and the awesome caregivers who spent enough time with Mom to know her well, to let me know what they saw, and to make sure she got her meds when I was away.

So here's what I learned when it came to keeping Mom's medicines straight, in addition to the fact that expired *to be taken as needed* sleeping pills are a red flag.[108]

To start, I had to figure out what medicines Mom was taking. That meant completing the necessary paperwork to allow me to communicate directly with her doctor. As my role in her care grew and I became her health care power of attorney, I was able to accomplish more: asking the doctor to review her meds, many of which she'd been taking for years. He cut out some that were no longer appropriate and reduced the dosage of others to suit her aging metabolism.

These days, at the start of all Mom's appointments, I handed over a summary of her health concerns, with a list of medications and health care providers (see Medical History Summary in Appendix). It spared Mom not being able to answer questions and offered a sense of her health right from the start.

Along the way, I learned to pay close attention when a new medicine was prescribed; every person is unique and what helps one may not help another: Aricept, a medicine intended to slow memory loss, had actually shut Mom down, impacting other cognitive strengths that helped her through. What a relief when it was discontinued and Mom's spark returned.

We had also seen that the more people involved, the more the opportunity for blips in care. During Mom's various hospitalizations, miscommunications had led to confusion about the appropriate dosage of prednisone, hesitation about her need for pain relief, and inconsistency regarding which blood thinner to use—the night team continuing heparin despite the day team's concern it was causing an internal bleed.

In addition, after her second hospitalization for an intestinal bleed, Mom had been discharged with an extra blood pressure prescription. When I asked her regular doctor about it, he said it was repetitive of another medicine she was on; when I checked back with hospital staff, I learned it had been prescribed in the hospital *in place of* the one usually used and unintentionally included in her discharge instructions.

Pain relief is especially challenging when caring for those with dementia who struggle to communicate when they hurt. After Mom's first hospitalization for ruptured diverticulitis, we'd been sent home with a bottle of morphine to use, as instructed, at our discretion (which I'd done just once). At that point, Mom had been unable to swallow pills, so we had to squirt liquid antibiotics into her mouth and crush tablet meds in applesauce. I thank the kids for having taught me how to deliver medicine through clenched teeth.

As most over-the-counter pain meds were tough on Mom's kidneys and digestive system, these days it was Tylenol as needed. If that didn't work, it was back to the doctor we'd go, as there was usually something brewing that required their attention. And, even though a medicine may have worked along the way, that could change. The tramadol that had alleviated Mom's bursitis a year before now left her awake at night, scared, confused, hallucinating; the Bactrim prescribed to treat a recent UTI had left her covered in hives.

Also, while some medicines made sense to address a health crisis, they didn't make sense long-term: While the prednisone prescribed after the stroke in Mom's eye had protected the sight in her other eye, it had hindered her ability to fight off infection—within a matter of weeks she'd landed in the hospital with ruptured diverticulitis and five months later with an intestinal bleed. The 80-milligram start dose had since been tapered to 7.5, mitigating apparent side effects.

The blood thinner for Mom's deep vein thrombosis had to be closely managed as well, with regular runs to the Coumadin clinic to check blood level, which swung with diet changes and antibiotics, requiring regular dosage modifications. With the clot's successful resolution, the filter could be removed and the Coumadin discontinued to reduce the risk of another internal bleed.

We were thankful that Mom had received excellent health care that had helped her to survive a series of medical declines so that she was alive and well and enjoying life back in Maine. In each of these instances, I was glad we were present to witness, to ask questions, and to advocate. As Matt noted, "The point is to never apologize for being vigilant for the people we love, especially when it comes to their health care." I hope he remembers that!

Two years earlier, newly diagnosed with Alzheimer's disease and discussing the need for help, Mom had told me earnestly, "I don't like the feeling that people are trying to control me." As her Alzheimer's progressed, Mom had continued to inspire with her resilience, good humor, and spunk. I was grateful that, these days, she accepted help without taking it as an affront and in a way that allowed us to give her the care she needed here in our home, while also enjoying the time that we shared. Thanks to that, the caregivers who kept Mom company while I stepped away had become dear friends, and kept coming back.

What Is Basketball?—aka Caring for Me

"What is basketball?" asked Mom as I handed her the evaluation I had just brought home from a women-over-fifty basketball camp. Just a few days earlier, when I left for the Not Too Late overnight camp, she'd said with a smile, "I want to come, too!"

So when my friend Darlene texted "Blog?" after my three-month summer silence, I thought Mom's question a good place to start. This reflection is less about caring for others and more about caring for me, which I'd been told again and again was essential.

What Is basketball?

Mom played in college, back in the days of special rules to keep girls cool, calm, and collected. She was a guard, which meant she got to defend, rebound, dribble a couple of times, and pass down-court. Pre–Title Nine, she was fiercely competitive and enjoyed beating the boys on the playground.

She was there later for Larry Bird in the Boston Garden, my brother Dave and me, and then Siena and Garrett, too. Even when she couldn't remember the comings and goings and needed to hitch a ride in a wheelchair, Mom loved being in the gym and cheering on her grandkids. Although I wished she could come to the women-over-fifty camp with me, I needed that time away, sleeping in a dorm, connecting with other women, and re-finding my balance by playing a game I'd always loved.

What Is basketball?

I learned basketball in the driveway with Mom, Dad, and Dave—two versus two we'd play, followed by soft-serve at Red's Dairy Freeze. Then came my first team in middle school, playing with childhood friends I still have today, as well as summer camps with my cousin Margie. I'd start out homesick till Margie's posters of Chachi from *Happy Days* and later Nancy Lieberman from the WNBA, along with her other shenanigans, distracted me from missing home so that I could focus on improving my game. Margie (who went on to play Division One) was consistently the MVP and I the "tries hardest." Big surprise, right?

In high school, basketball was one of three sports I played. I remember practicing the drills I'd learned at hoop camp under the summer sun, alone in the driveway, coaching young athletes on Saturday mornings, managing the stress of tryouts and preseason practice. And, too, there were the aching knees and lunchtime ice baths, the camaraderie of team spaghetti dinners, the pregame listening to Pat Benatar's "Hit Me with Your Best Shot," the butterflies as we took the floor, the squeak of the shoes, the sweat on my brow, the mouthful of Bubble Yum, my coach yelling "Perk!" (my nickname back then), the thrill of competing (including a win over our rival Gorham!), and showering up afterward before watching the boys play. Most of all, I recall the support of our parents, the respect for our coaches, the love for my teammates, and the sadness when the seasons wrapped.

What Is basketball?

Later, basketball meant finding a place to play: It was college and law school intramurals, competing on an all-male teachers' team in Guangzhou, China, where we made it to the championship, the occasional game of Horse, and a church basement in Wisconsin with a bunch of moms.

Then came a Fisher-Price hoop when Siena was two, coaching when she was ten, managing her teams after that, watching her experience what I had, with her own new twist. Standing on the sidelines required a whole new set of skills: sharing my knowledge where helpful, encouraging her to work through the challenges, cheering her on, helping her keep fed and hydrated, her uniform clean, and driving all over the Midwest and New England—even the summer I had Lyme disease—grateful for every moment we shared, thanks to this game. In a blink, basketball meant traveling to and from Maine to watch Siena's college games, sporting Polar Bear gear, staying with Mom and taking her to games, and, when I couldn't, watching the action on the computer and looking for Mom in the stands—and a highlight: the yearly mother-daughter game. I appreciated from afar the challenge, the heartbreak, the determination, the pain, the elation, the excitement of being part of the team and the sadness when each season ended.

Then came a whole new layer, when the boys started to play. Matt had decided to focus on golf when he realized that his passion was out on the links. The tallest now, he had a killer three. Garrett, whose devotion to basketball had been complete—endless hours dedicated, teammates who became best friends, coaches who were great mentors, more busy summers traveling to and fro, a charity started to renovate a public court he discovered during a family vacation in Turks and Caicos, a YMCA job coaching kids from Angola and elsewhere. I felt such intense gratitude for the opportunities and growth basketball had brought him. And, throughout all of the above, rebounding—hour after hour—in support of our kids going after their dreams.

What Is basketball?

Then came my bucket-list trip, not long after Doug took his fourteen-hundred-mile bike ride from California to Colorado. Five years before, I'd gone to dinner with a high school teammate, Biz—and she told me about an over-fifty basketball camp. This year, back in Maine and looking for ways to rejuvenate sandwiched me, I signed up. For a while, it looked like the camp might be canceled due to water damage in the gym. I must admit feeling relieved—maybe it would be easier on all if I just stayed home. When the camp was resurrected, and I ran my uncertainty by my family, they didn't let me off the hook. Garrett took me to the gym to beat me into shape. "You got this, Tarb," he reassured. Given Mom's ups and downs, I wasn't sure till I signed in on day one that I would actually get there. Day two, when Mom's caregiving fell through, the hubby stepped up, making sure I didn't turn tail and run. When I shared my concerns at lunch, my new teammates reassured me, reminding me of the importance of taking care of me.

It was an eye-opening and inspiring four days—playing with women fifty-two to seventy-nine, from all walks of life, sleeping in a dorm room, getting to know my suite mates, being coached and letting someone else tell me what to do (so rare and so appreciated), playing with my awesome teammates, practicing new and old skills, listening to a variety of experts share their knowledge on yoga, strength and conditioning, defense, the game. Then came the tightening calves, a sharp stab when I V-cut, my foot puffy and blue, the trainer diagnosing a bone bruise and sprain. I appreciated her kindness and direction, even as I felt the sadness and apology of missing out, and the honor of sitting beside one of the seventy-plus-year-old Pioneers, injured, too. My foot screamed in pain as I drove two hours home afterward. Showing Mom my evaluation, as I had when returning from camp forty years prior, to which she asked:

What Is basketball?

Recognizing this was not my last chance, that it's never too late to go back to the things we love, I had sat out the rest of the camp, icing, compress-ing, elevating my foot, soaking up the love of my teammates, the respect for our coaches, and the appreciation for all the athletes. When we were instructed to line up, I was the second youngest of these fierce women, who played with grit and grace, determined to heal from injuries that had gotten in their way, so many with their own caregiving stories to share.

Earlier in the camp, the dribbling coach had said, "You're only as strong as your biggest weakness," encouraging me to dribble harder—two balls at once! Her words resonated, giving me reason to keep working on me, on the court and off. The orthopedic doctor and physical therapist were helping me to correct the weakness in my foot (likely from a college ankle break, when I slid into home plate) to get me back on the court ASAP.

What Is basketball?

Simply put, it was just so much fun, and I'd only just begun.

FALLING

I'm deeply grateful for the support that softened our return to Maine—of new caregivers and old friends, as well as various conversations, like the one with my mother-in-law, Millie, that affirmed the commitment to maximize the quality over the quantity of Mom's remaining days. As Atul Gawande writes in *Being Mortal*, "We witnessed for ourselves the consequences of living for the best possible day today instead of sacrificing time now for time later."[109] In many ways, this season of Mom's care in our home could be considered the most beautiful, as her leaves changed color and began to fall. It was a time of learning new skills to care for her as her physical needs intensified, things I never knew I could do, being present in a new way, as first I held on and then I let go, like the little yellow leaves that have kept finding me since.

What follows is different from before, when caregiving focused me and I felt so spiritually connected. It turns outs that grief, like dementia, is nonlinear, too. The feelings of loss continued to hit me—fast, slow, up, down, all around—sometimes when I least expected, making it hard to process, to reflect, to find words. I struggled to find the humor and fun, the discernment and connection, that had helped me through before. Even now, it's hard for me to read what I wrote during that time.

When I began my two-year course at the Chaplaincy Institute of Maine, I did so, in part, because of the ways I thought it would complement caring for Mom; I had no idea I would complete my studies while caring, instead, for our adult kids, brought home by COVID-19. Like they had after Dad died almost two decades before, the kids provided love, support, and plenty of distraction as I worked through my loss, not alone, but with others grieving in their own ways, as well. As put by my faculty adviser Lisa in *Arriving Here: Reflections from the Hearth and Trail*, "Summer's abundance will soon be gone, but autumn will be full of gifts, too...."[110] Falling is all about those last moments spent with Mom and the moments since, when I've continued to find her, at my side, still stretching together toward the autumn sun.

〜✳〜

Dear Higher Power,
Thank you for your patience with me and
for all the beings past, present, and future
you share with me to show me the way.
You keep reminding me I am not alone.
When I most fear losing Mom,
you bring me more love, from unexpected places.
Even when I isolate in pain, the dogs are always here.
If I keep my eyes open, I see that you keep sending the love.
I feel bad about "me, me, me" in this world at this time—
Please help me to help others, so it can be bigger than that.
Thank you, Higher Power.
Thy will be done.
Amen.

〜✳〜

Simple Kindness

I was meeting with Erica, the new counselor I'd found to help with the stress. When I described feeling off-kilter, she offered this metaphor:

Caring for Mom in Wisconsin, I had found a deliberately constructed balance—supportive family, trusted caregivers, reliable medical care, and my own life of tutoring, friendship, exercise, and writing. We'd found a routine that worked. Taking the show on the road, to reassemble in Maine, was like putting all those essential pieces in a cup, shaking it up, and dumping them on the table, hoping for a sense of order.

As Erica put it, each time we rebuilt some stability, something would come along and bump the table: a health blip for Mom or one of the animals, adult kids and a spouse in transition, carpenters gone AWOL, comments that felt unsupportive and even critical, an abscessed tooth and other medical concerns of my own. Even as I counted our blessings, I sometimes wondered if I had what it would take to see caring for Mom through.

Then, noting the one-year anniversary of our return to Maine, I was struck by all the simple, and unexpected, kindnesses we'd received along the way:

The late-night nurse easing my guilt that third hospital stay; my Wisconsin friend Megan sending her prayers via text; childhood friends Nancy and Kathy bringing light in a storm; Mom's secretary, Val, meeting us at the Lobster Shack for lunch; a stranger giving me a ride home as I walked in the cold rain; Mom's new doc appreciating her resilience and validating our approach in her care; longtime neighbors enthusiastically welcoming us back to the lake; Midwest friends warmly welcoming us back as visitors; Mom's longtime friend Helen offering reassurance and support; basketball teammates reminding me how to play; incredible caregivers going beyond taking care to giving love; my tutoring friend Darlene reminding me to write.

I appreciate all these kind souls, and more, who'd lit our path, even when they didn't have to—how would I ever have done this without them?

It had been a wild twelve months, and finally I felt myself letting out a long-held breath. In addition to Mom making it back to Maine and recovering from the DVT that came with her, the various health concerns that had peaked while we were still in Wisconsin had quieted, so that she had enjoyed a relatively pain-free and peaceful year, including six weeks at camp, her favorite getaway. I appreciated each moment Mom could sit by the window, Cinnamon in her lap, enjoying the world around her. Thanks to all the simple and unexpected kindnesses that had helped me as I had helped her, the pieces were starting to fall into place.

⌒⚓⌒

Making Peace with Mom's DNR: in retrospect

"Your job really boils down to protecting your Mom's dignity," Doug had commented along the way. His words rang true in terms of keeping Mom clean, helping her communicate, reducing her anxiety and the behaviors it provoked, and also helping her to live out this life the way she would have wanted if Alzheimer's disease hadn't gotten in the way of her ability to make decisions for herself. As the Alzheimer's Association puts it, "All end-of-life decisions should respect the person's values and wishes while maintaining his or her comfort and dignity."[111] Easier said than done.

I'd never heard of a DNR (Do Not Resuscitate order) when it was first mentioned to me, shortly after Mom came to live with us in Wisconsin. My friend Barb, whose mom's Alzheimer's had been more progressed than my mom's, advised me on one of our first walks to make sure we had Mom's legal affairs in order. Fortunately, Mom already had a living will and health care power of attorney in place; she didn't have a DNR. When I talked it over with my siblings, they thought it consistent with what she would've wanted, given her health concerns.

At our next appointment, I asked the doctor to address the topic. He explained that, without a DNR, emergency personnel must do whatever they can to try to restart the heart and breathing. Some people didn't want this because of the risk of broken ribs, punctured organs, brain damage due to oxygen deprivation, and dying in the hospital. The doctor added that there was no gentle way to do CPR. He also explained that having a DNR would not prevent other appropriate medical treatments. In that context and speaking directly to him, Mom said that a DNR made sense.

As soon as the doc left the room, however, Mom turned to me and asked, "What was that all about?" When I repeated the conversation we'd just had with him, Mom asked me what I thought. I told her I wanted to make sure I understood her wishes on the matter. We talked it over and she came back to the same decision: "It makes sense." By the time the nurse returned to get Mom's signature on the necessary paperwork and attach the DNR bracelet legally required in Wisconsin, Mom had already forgotten what it was for.

"Please don't tell the kids. I don't want them to worry," Mom said that night as I tucked her into bed. When I asked her what she meant, she answered, "That the doctor said I will be dying soon." I drew in my breath and reminded her of that day's DNR conversation: that there was no indication she'd be dying soon and that we were just trying to understand what she wanted regarding treatment if her heart should stop. We rehashed the pros and cons, and she again chose a DNR: "There's no point to living if you're not really living," she said.

Over the next several weeks, each time she noticed the DNR bracelet encircling her wrist, Mom asked me what it was for, and we cycled through the DNR conversation again. It reminded me of when the kids were little and full of "What's that?"s and "Why?"s, and Mom's advice: "You know, you don't have to explain things to your kids as much as you do." Some might wonder why I didn't just put the kibosh on Mom's repetitive concerns and distract her with other things—I guess that's not my way. Plus, I, too, was trying to find peace with the bracelet attached to her wrist. In truth, it felt like the DNR discussions were breaking my heart. Those repeated conversations highlighted Mom's inability to choose for herself and doing so for her felt like making a decision between her life and death.

"Where's happy Terry?" asked Doug in the midst of all this, and Siena observed, too, that I seemed continually sad. Their concern prompted me to think about what had helped me address other anxieties in the past: naming the source of my fear, doing research to better understand its likelihood and ways to reduce it, making a reasonable plan of action, and turning to faith to ease residual stress (shout-out to Bernie, my Wisconsin therapist, who'd suggested this strategy to help me address parenting fears).

Plain and simple, I feared doing Mom harm; I was losing sleep with the thought of her heart stopping and denying efforts to restart it. How could I tell Siena, or anyone else, not to attempt CPR if the need arose? It had felt like giving up. Which brought me to my research.

What kind of life did Mom want from here on out? What were the odds of saving her life via CPR if her heart were to stop? How could I love her and care for her, and know I'd done all I could, and still support a DNR? Looking for guidance, I read, and reread, carefully Mom's living will and health care power of attorney, and I listened closely to her comments. Each time she inquired about the DNR bracelet on her wrist, I took note.

"Women in my family live a long time," Mom had said. She hadn't seen herself as sick—she had no memory of her health challenges or Alzheimer's diagnosis, or talking with the doctor about the implications of a DNR. When I re-explained its purpose, she hadn't liked the idea of making a blanket decision about future care and preferred to have her doctor decide her care based on the current facts—"What if I'm the one to beat the odds?" she asked.

I followed Doug's suggestion and put the information about the DNR in writing, to help anchor Mom's thoughts. I explained, again, that in the absence of a DNR, emergency responders were legally required to perform CPR and/or intubation, no matter the situation, and that having a DNR wouldn't affect other appropriate medical treatments. Each time through, Mom came back to what I'd come to consider the governing principles in her care: She didn't want to be sick or in pain; she didn't want to be in a coma hooked up to tubes; she didn't want to be "in an institution around other ailing people"; she didn't want to be a burden or cause others to worry; she wanted to know what I thought on the topic; and she wanted to be with Cinnamon.

"Living is for living," she'd say. "I've had a good life, I've hardly been sick; it would be a shame to spend the last part of my life sick." One night, after another round on this topic, Mom told me she trusted me with her well-being and knew I had her best interests at heart.

To better understand the impact of CPR on elders, with various health concerns and dementia, in addition to listening carefully to Mom, I'd also done my research online:

According to the Family Caregiver Alliance, "When a person is in failing health from a serious and progressive illness, the heart and breathing will ultimately fail as a result of that illness. In such a circumstance, there is little chance that CPR will succeed at all. Any success will be temporary at best, because the person's weakened condition will soon cause the heartbeat and breathing to fail again."[112]

Ethicists Kevin M. Dirksen and Neil S. Wenger note that, "Studies of CPR performed on individuals 85 years and older who suffer cardiac arrest in a community setting show that few—perhaps 4 in 100—survive to leave the hospital, and the majority of these 'survivors' are moderately to severely neurologically compromised...treatment is nearly always burdensome, including being attached to life-sustaining machines."[113]

Michael Gordon, MD, concludes, "Of particular importance when it comes to such discussions and decision-making, the evidence is quite compelling that in the very elderly, especially those with multiple pathologies and experiencing dementia as part of their collection of chronic medical conditions, the results of CPR are particularly dismal."[114]

Still uncomfortable with the DNR decision, I called the friendly facilitator of the Alzheimer's support group I attended. Sitting in my car,

tears running down my face, I told her about the DNR, Mom's ongoing questions about the bracelet she wore, and my own heavy heart. She
helped me see that what I'd been grieving was giving up on trying to save
Mom should her heart stop. It wasn't that I wanted Mom to live forever; it
was that I didn't want to let her down.

As I processed all the above—Mom's words, my research, the conversation with the support group facilitator—I finally realized that there was
a difference between giving up and letting go. I'd been confusing the two,
which led me to this prayer:

Dear Higher Power,
Please help me to take heroic measures to love and care for Mom,
to help her continue to live healthy and well—
not to prolong the time when she is failing and unwell.
Please help me to never give up, and also to let go when the time comes.
Please help me to honor Mom while she is alive, and also when she dies.
A DNR—natural death—is the right choice—it's a choice Mom has made.
It's a choice I agree with.
It's a choice that hurts and relieves.
It's a choice I need to respect.
Please help me to find peace with Mom's DNR.
Thy will be done.

In the three years since getting the DNR, Mom had undergone a
series of health challenges and life-saving treatments. Having a DNR had
meant that when we sought care, or called 911 for help, we would start by
informing medical personnel that Mom was an elder with Alzheimer's
disease, a variety of health concerns, and a DNR. It also meant that when
we left Mom in another's care, split-second decision-making would not
land on them. Through all the ups and downs, Mom's heart had kept
beating. I appreciated that, among other things, moving to Maine had
meant the DNR bracelet was no longer legally required, so that, these
days, it lay quietly atop Mom's jewelry box, collecting dust, out of sight,
out of mind—Mom's, at least.

Death is like birth in that we cannot predict when or how it will play
out; we can, however, choose the approach we hope to take, and I had
come to appreciate the freedom the DNR promised from intervention

that would only prolong Mom's pain and suffering. I also found comfort in a newer acronym: AND (Allow Natural Death), which, according to Susan M. Matthews, PhD, "does not mean that physicians are to stop treating illnesses a person needs help with, such as pneumonia, a heart attack, or a fractured bone. It means only that if the heart should stop: do not administer CPR and do not connect a ventilator."[115] I had made peace with the fact that taking heroic measures in Mom's care meant making sure she finished in a way consistent with her words and spirit.

"Will you take care of me forever?" Mom asked me as we went through our morning routine, getting ready for another day.

"I'll do my best, Mom. I'll do my best," I assured her, understanding that one day, taking care of Mom forever would mean letting her go.

⌒∗⌒

"Excuse Me"—Saving Face and Alzheimer's Disease

"Excuse me...are you planning on working today?" Mom asked from across the gate, after making her way gingerly out the back door to find me on the porch. It reminded me of the way she would have busted an employee who was sneaking a cigarette with a coworker on the loading dock, back when she ran a paper box factory.

I had just sat down with Doug so that he could tell me about brunch with Garrett. We'd planned to bring Mom along; however, her back had spasmed, so I'd sent Doug off, tucked her back into bed, and cleaned house instead.

Two things of note:

1. Doug's good-natured response when I bowed out of breakfast and again when I jumped up to help Mom upon his return. I appreciated the ways he joined me in her care. We'd gone straight from parenting to caregiving, no pause in between, and still, most of the time, he was at my side, helping me keep perspective.

2. Mom, previously resistant to asking for and accepting help, now welcomed and even requested it. This made it much easier to care for her than before; as a result, she had a healthier and more connected life, thanks to the awesome caregivers who had become her friends, most recently the upbeat Diane and unflappable Lesley.

Not only did our wonderful caregivers address Mom's changing needs, adapting as her daily ups and downs required, discovering new and unique ways to engage her, they also treated her with respect, concern, and kindness. I was brought to tears later that day when newly engaged Jessica invited Mom to her wedding-dress fitting. That she met Mom during this phase hadn't kept Jessica from becoming Mom's friend—joining her in the present with vigilance and playfulness—maintaining Mom's health and enriching her days. Perhaps because our caregivers could not compare who Mom was today with who she'd been before, they met her where she was, without the history that could get in the way.

"Excuse me…are you planning on working today?"

When Mom couldn't hear my reply, I glanced at Doug with a rueful smile, got up from where we sat, motioned Mom back inside, grabbed her hearing aids from her bedside table, and met her in the kitchen, where I asked: "Mom, do you know who I am?"

"No," she replied, narrowing her eyes at me as she tried to cipher it out.

"I'm your daughter, Terry. I don't work for you; however, I'd love to help you."

Mom looked at me, widened her eyes, and twirled her index finger at the side of her head.

"Will you still be my daughter?" she asked with her contagious smile.

"I'll always be your daughter, Mom," I answered, giving her a hug before sitting her down for her second breakfast of the day.

This interaction coupled with the wedding-dress invitation reminded me of the notion of "saving face" I'd learned when I taught in China; it allowed others a way to retreat from a difficult interaction, whether it be an altercation, a miscommunication, a mistake, or some other awkward spot, to preserve their sense of dignity and hold their head high. I don't believe Mom saw Alzheimer's disease coming; by the time she was diagnosed, she was beyond grasping, and remembering, its significance. This was a blessing in that she would have hated the threats of losing control, becoming a burden, and forgetting the people she loved. I do believe, though, that it would have eased Mom's mind to know that, even now, she was making new friends, bringing them and us joy, living a life of humor and grace, and inspiring the rest of us to do the same.

In Mom's Words

When I thought back on a lifetime with Mom, fifty-four years and counting, I recalled her words. As reserved as she was, the ones she chose stood out:

~ "Put a smile on your face, and you can do anything"—when I faced any challenge, big or small.

~ "I kept trying, till I got my girl"—explaining the gap between my brothers and me, and the miscarriages she overcame to give me life.

~ "I miss him when he's gone"—tearfully, at the front door, as my dad left for another work trip.

~ "Don't let her put too much makeup on you"—as she handed me an iced tea while I got ready to walk down the hill to wed by the lake.

~ "We drink to relieve stress"—when I expressed concern about her and Dad.

~ "You're so emotional, you don't make sense"—the Christmas I pointed out that their pre-gaming martinis was just the activity causing friction between them and us kids.

~ "Go for it"—when I told her we were considering moving to Prague, with our newborn first child.

~ "I don't think you need to talk with your kids so much"—by phone, after a visit, the kids under age five, when I suggested she and I communicate more.

~ "I don't know why I keep crying"—the Mother's Day visit after Dad had died the month before.

~ "Your dad knew you loved him"—when I asked her several months later, by email, if I'd let him down.

~ "You'll never guess what I did today....I bought land and I'm going to build a house and paint it red"—a year later, when she decided to sell our home of forty years and look forward.

~ "Letting your kids express themselves, even when they fought, you helped them be close; my brother and I never had that chance"—another Wisconsin visit, the kids in their teens.

~ "I don't like it when he talks to you that way"—stomping away in a huff, after Doug made fun of my cooking skills in the kitchen at camp.

~ "Guess what I did today....I took a refresher course and the instructor passed me with flying colors"—when my brothers and I urged her to retire her car keys.

~ "I don't want to be a burden"…"I don't want to worry the boys"… "Don't tell the kids the doctor says I'll be dying soon"—after her Alzheimer's was named.

~ "I trust you with my health, Terry—you understand it better than me"—when she settled in to live with us soon after.

~ "Will you be coming to camp this summer?" again and again, and again, then and now.

~ "Who are you?"—regularly, these days, particularly when I returned from time away.

~ "Maybe I don't remember because you never talk to me"—one night, when I reminded her I am her daughter.

~ "Have fun"—when I told her I was leaving for Florida with my husband and kids.

~ "Stay there and enjoy.…I'll wait till you get back"—when I called home to check in, Jessica rousing her from sleep on the couch, as she battled another UTI.

~ "Aren't we lucky?"—her most constant refrain, as far back as I remember, repeated these days, a smile on her face, as I tucked her into bed and kissed her good night, like she used to do for me. I hoped to hear this one again real soon.

I recalled Mom's words, like salve to my soul; even the ones that had stung when delivered, these days felt like love.

∞

High Fives All Around—We've Got This

Back when I was an at-home parent of three little kids, my cousin Margie (a PhD in leisure and recreation management) had noted the challenge of finding recreation partners in my role: My schedule was unpredictable and my free time limited, as was that of potential friends.

I treasured those pals I eventually found during my twenty-two years in the Midwest, pals who helped me step away from daily life and cut loose—whether it be a weekend in Madison, a game of tennis, breakfast at the Wooden Goose, a cup of coffee at Fiddleheads, or a walk with the dogs around the neighborhood—you know who you are.

There had been many times, my kids now grown, when I'd been in a grocery store and noted a young parent, kids in tow, and resisted the urge to offer a high five—"You've got this," I'd say, if I didn't fear overstepping. It's strange that, in those activities in which so many of us partake, sharing parallel highs and lows, we sometimes feel alone.

Caring for Mom in our home as Alzheimer's took its toll, I was ever grateful for the support of Doug and the kids, our caregivers—who tended me as they tended her—childhood friends finally within a stone's throw, adult friends from afar, new neighbors I was getting to know, the animals, and Margie, who knew me first and treated me to a Florida getaway during which I kept an eye on Mom by phone, another UTI roaring through. Even with all the love and support, there were days I felt gassed, moments I felt isolated; when I stepped away, Mom's well-being stayed on my mind and it was difficult for me to relax—"remote caregiving" Margie tagged it, after our time down south.

"You gotta get back to basketball," she said. "Knowing you, Perk, it's the one place you ain't thinkin', you're just doin'." Margie would know— we played a lot of basketball together growing up. It was true, playing basketball was the one place my mind was free from daily concerns and I didn't think about Mom's care, except when others kindly inquired. Playing with women ages fifteen to eighty inspired and rejuvenated me; it helped me rethink my excuses and believe I could age differently than Mom had.

In support of a member facing a recent cancer diagnosis, her team handed out bracelets reading: NO ONE FIGHTS ALONE! Every time this reminder on my wrist caught my eye, I was honored, humbled, and hopeful. Running errands and thinking of this fierce, kind, and resilient athlete, sending prayers and positivity her way, I pulled into Dunkin' Donuts for an afternoon pickup. To my surprise, the guy in front of me bought my cup of coffee. It was the high five I needed. So, on this sunny spring day that promised gentler days ahead, I was cognizant of the many challenges we all faced that could leave us feeling isolated and alone, and I sent out high fives all around—we've got this.

⌒⋆⌒

RIP, Little Bunny—Processing Grief and Finding Meaning to Help Us Through

Recent research suggested several potential contributors to the development of Alzheimer's disease: *the herpes virus,*[116] *chronic periodontitis,*[117] *stress,*[118] not to mention *lack of sleep.*[119] Oh, for the love of God; based on my four cold sores since ringing in the new year, the gums that bled when I brushed my teeth, the worry that sometimes got the best of me, and the nightly wake-ups, the research didn't bode well for yours truly.

It has been said by those with a lot more smarts than me that one of the hardest parts of caring for a loved one with Alzheimer's, in addition to subsisting on a lot less sleep, is adapting to the constant trail of losses, big and little, with neither time nor space to grieve them. According to the Alzheimer's Association, "Alzheimer's gradually takes away the person you know and love. As this happens, you will mourn him or her and may experience the different phases of grieving: denial, anger, guilt, sadness, and acceptance. The stages of grief don't happen neatly in order. You may move in and out of different stages as time goes on."[120] At the same time, Mom was still here, and we owed it to her to greet each day with as much sunshine as we could muster, and to embrace who she was, right here, right now.

"When your number's up, your number's up," Dad had liked to say back in the day. It had helped him cope with the what-ifs of making decisions that could mean life or death for younger Marines in his charge back in the 1950s Southeast Pacific. *Good grief!* I'd think, sitting beside him at the dinner table. What if that was what it all came down to? Dad's "When my number's up, load my dinghy up with gin and push me out to sea" had been sort of what we'd done when sepsis shut down his organs and we circled around him as the machines keeping him alive were unhitched. It had taken me years to accept that we'd done the right thing, even though it was what he'd clearly instructed in his living will. These days, as I made decisions affecting Mom's well-being, I saw the allure of Dad's fatalistic approach. While it didn't exactly fit Alzheimer's long goodbye, the humility, surrender, and acceptance it requires did.

To celebrate my turning fifty-five, Doug and I went on a bike trip in North Carolina with my cousin Beth and her spouse, Janis, whose beloved sister died unexpectedly on day two. After their departure, I thought nonstop about the brave faces they wore as they ate breakfast with the rest of us and then filled our water bottles before they flew north to gather and to grieve. The pair displayed humor, strength, and poise as they encouraged the rest of us to ride on. As I continued into the headwind, I considered the places I was stuck, and where I'd like to find their grace and grit. I realized that some of the losses I'd been grieving in caring for Mom were for things that had never even existed and it was time to let them go. Of course, if it were easy for me to let things go, I probably wouldn't have been the one in charge of Mom's care.

When Siena left for college eight years earlier, I'd stumbled around for a month, lost, before remembering Susan Jeffers's Whole Life Grid, which I describe in "Part Two: Springing." When I'd made my (get-my-act-together) grid, that time around one of my nine squares had been Helping Others, so I had volunteered at the local humane society to clean the small-animal room. When one of the rabbits got her nose bitten off by another, I helped nurse her back to health. Fretting that her tendency to pounce defensively at anything coming her way could get her into trouble when she became available for adoption, I brought Patty Noseless home. She made the move with us from Wisconsin to Maine to celebrate turning eleven, a ripe old age for a bunny who'd almost died at three. Several days after returning from our bike trip, I discovered Patty sprawled out in her cage. Even when death from old age was expected, it could be hard to accept.

That afternoon, as Doug dug a hole in the backyard, I panicked. I told him to hold on while I ran Patty to the vet to make sure her heart had really stopped. When I passed my new neighbor, Mandy, a retired nurse, at the top of the hill, I rolled down my window and asked, "Do you have a stethoscope?" The next thing I knew, we were standing at her dining room table, where she carefully confirmed she could not hear a heartbeat. When she offered me the stethoscope, my own heart was so loud I couldn't hear anything else.

"Are you sure?" I asked as I stood in her front hall, cradling Patty's orange shoe box.

"Yes, I'm sure," she answered tenderly, decisively.

When I pulled back into our driveway, Doug was leaning on his shovel, waiting patiently. I petted Patty's silky coat one last time and wrapped her in my fuzzy outer layer. We buried her below an azalea he had bought to remind us of the blooms we'd enjoyed on the bike trip.

According to David Kessler, who helped Elisabeth Kubler-Ross adapt her five stages of dying to the process of grieving, "Meaning is the sixth stage of grief, the stage where the healing often resides."[121] Writing was my attempt to find meaning in what challenged me most. After a sleepless night—Mom up eleven p.m. to four a.m., organizing—I skipped playing basketball to get some rest. Thanks to our caregiver Karly, I awoke two and a half hours later, eager to write. I was so embroiled in Mom's care, I sometimes lost sight of the big picture. Looking at the losses of the prior month, I could see that it was in sharing our experiences that we find humor and strength, and build connections with those around us, connections that lift us up and help us through.

The afternoon we buried Patty Noseless, I texted Mandy my sincere thanks.

"RIP, little bunny. Glad I was here," she replied.

"Next time I ask you if you have a medical device, feel free to say no," I responded, to which she replied, "I don't do defibrillations or circumcisions."

Even in grief, I laughed out loud. I'd shown my true colors and she had welcomed me in. I had no idea then that she'd be the one I would call in the middle of the night, several months later, to help get Mom off the floor and back into bed. While I still wasn't sure about Dad's "number's up" approach, I was glad I wasn't in this alone.

⌒∗⌒

This One's for You, Mom

Click! On went Mom's light.

Moments later, I heard her rattle the stuck latch on her bedroom door. As she banged the door with her cane, I clambered down the stairs with my groggy head and torn hamstring.

Mom smiled as I opened the door. I took her hand and led her to the bathroom, where she asked, "What do I do?"

I gave her an assist and, while she did her business, let Cinnamon out to do the same. When I returned to the bathroom, Mom greeted me with a chipper, "Good morning!"

"Mom, it's the middle of the night," I replied.

Mom furrowed her brow and asked, "Why are you up so late?"

My eyes crossed and rolled to the back of my head—actually, I smiled and got her back to bed.

I was grateful for the layers of support as I cared for Mom in our home. Still, in the middle of the night, I sometimes panicked. How long could I keep this up?

I did my best to take good care of me while caring for Mom—eating well, staying hydrated, finding humor, meditating, praying, getting overnight help, and stepping away to walk the dogs, spend time with my spouse, kids, and friends, go to counseling, do physical therapy, do yoga, and play basketball.

Stepping away for longer periods was not easy. During the twenty-five years I'd spent parenting, I could count on one hand the number of times I'd done so. Once, I had tried, to attend Doug's work event in New York City, our nursing four-month-old in tow, and we'd returned home to our two-year-old's cryptic "That's what David wore" when Doug went in to check on her in his boxers. When I mentioned this to the babysitter our neighbor had so highly recommended, she denied there had been any visits from her boyfriend, David, while we were away. I stuck close to home and the kids after that.

Caring for Mom was similar in that stepping away required a lot of planning and a leap of faith; it was different in that, this time around, I had a spouse who'd waited a long time for my undivided attention and adult kids who needed me, sometimes, to cut loose. As Siena said during a recent family getaway, after a day sitting on the beach beside me while I texted with caregivers back home about another UTI, "I know you worry about your mom and want her to be okay; well, you're *my* mom, and I worry about *you*."

A couple of months later, as I prepared for a trip to Albuquerque to play basketball at the National Senior Games, Mom suffered another round of worrisome symptoms, addressed by her doctor the day before I headed west. I was deeply grateful for his reassurance, for the women who would care for her in my absence, for Doug asleep at my side on our six a.m. flight, for our kids who always have my back, and for my teammates and coaches who welcomed us, cheering when we boarded the plane. If she could, Mom would have cheered us on, too.

Father's Day in Albuquerque

And so I spent Father's Day a long way from home, in the University of New Mexico's basketball complex, participating in the 2019 National Senior Games. For four days, my team competed, in pool and silver bracket play, to ultimately win gold. It was an honor to play for team

Phoenix, who'd worked toward this for years, and it was a relief to pour all of me into something other than Mom's care. I was thankful that you can't play basketball and text at the same time. I knew Mom was in good hands, allowing me to give my all to this incredible experience. What I hadn't anticipated was that, focused on basketball, I would feel Mom's presence in the most positive sense: as she used to be, before Alzheimer's, commenting on the game, calling out the refs, watching with pride. Mom would've gotten a kick out of seeing me play at Nationals—and I felt her there with me.

Dad was there in spirit, too. He wasn't the player Mom had been—he'd quit in high school when he tired of warming the bench—still, he'd loved the game and watching us play. That Father's Day, sixteen years since he'd passed, I heard him heckle when I missed my foul shots, laugh when I threw my elbows, and cheer when I backed someone down. When one opponent said to another, "What are you supposed to do? She has sixteen pounds on you," I held my tongue, though Dad would've cracked up at the reply I thought of later: "It's a scientific fact: Muscle does weigh more than fat." At the end of the day, Dad would've counseled, "Don't worry about what's over and done. You can't change that. Ice your aches and get ready for what's next." So that's what I did. Beyond all else, Dad would've been impressed by the scrappy, skilled persistence of my teammates and appreciative of the calm, knowledgeable approach of our coaches, though he'd definitely second-guess the refs.

I'm grateful that, when I looked to the stands, I saw Doug, Siena, and Garrett. The kids, players too, offered their own great advice: "Trust your coach and teammates," "Focus on three things you can control," and "Have fun, even when it's hard." How lucky was I, for all this support? Not to mention all the dedicated Maine athletes and fans cheering each other on. Talk about support. The day after Father's Day, when I noticed the eighty-five-year-old, and older, men playing on a neighboring court, I imagined Dad mixing it up in that group. What I wouldn't have given to see his killer hook shot one more time. Too bad I hadn't got that gene; Dad's hook shot, in addition to his insights, sure would have come in handy.

Never Too Old to Play Basketball!

The Sunday our carpenter's eight-year-old kept me company while he varnished the floors, she made herself right at home, playing with the animals, coloring Mom's coloring books, and assigning me a walkie-talkie to stay in touch: "Terry, Terry, are you there, Terry? Over." When she asked me why I was limping, I explained that I'd hurt myself playing basketball, to which she exclaimed: "Women your age don't play basketball!"

"Judging from your injury, maybe she's on to something!" added her dad when I mentioned this to him. Externally, I chuckled; internally, I gave the pair the stink-eye.

Honestly, though, how could I take offense? Until the summer before, when I'd attended the basketball camp, I'd had no idea the level of competition I would find. The last time I'd played "competitive" basketball, my kids were little and I was in a church basement with a handful of other young moms, playing pickup and not keeping score. When that didn't give me a place to swing my elbows, I'd given it up.

It was true, the senior basketball players I met had fought through their share of injuries. To my torn hamstring and mother's dementia, they each had their own obstacles to overcome. Those obstacles, however, hadn't stopped them from showing up, working hard, pushing themselves, taking risks, and preparing to compete at the national level, all while wholeheartedly supporting one another. While the level of skill and experience varied, the love of the game united. It was a blast to practice Tuesday nights with younger players who tested us and older players (the seventy-year-old-plus silver-winning Pioneers) who inspired us. And it was fun to have coaches invested in helping us improve. One of the things I liked most was that when our whole group, ages sixteen to seventy-eight, scrimmaged on Saturday mornings, it was all business on the court and hugs and high fives off the court.

I was proud to have played at the National Senior Games, where I was one of 13,712 athletes over age fifty to compete.[122] Here are bits and pieces of what I experienced:

~ Doing my best to ready Mom and the animals for my absence—turning over their care with a prayer as I pulled out of the driveway, the sun just coming up;

~ Setting foot in the Dreamstyle Arena—chills up my spine when I looked down at the court in the Pit, before registering with the other senior athletes and donning my ATHLETE badge;

~ Getting up early to catch the shuttle with my coaches and teammates—like the freshman on the varsity team, unsure what to expect and eager to add value;

~ Warming up exactly as my physical therapist had advised—hoping that one of the many salves handed out at registration would loosen me up;

~ Testing my healing hamstring and adapting my play, by necessity, to that ominous tweak in the back of my leg—determined to play with my injury, not be my injury;

~ Being part of a team and the camaraderie that comes with this—getting to know coaches and teammates better on and off the court;

~ Playing hard while also appreciating the women on the other side: When another forward helped me up with a "You all right, mama?" I replied, "Yes, I am....You all right, mama?" and we shared a laugh and a hug, which we followed later, as we shook hands at game's end, with a "Nice job, mama"..."You, too, mama";

~ Off the court, so much of what I did required a gentle touch—what fun, on the court, to let that go, and try to frustrate opponents with physical play;

~ Looking into the stands to find my cheering family—it had always been me on the sidelines, offering pep talks to them, and now the roles were reversed;

~ In between games, icing, hydrating, eating healthy snacks, taping my leg for extra support, and running, again, through my pregame warm-up—no time to fret about Mom;

~ How good it felt, at day's end, sweaty and tired, to stretch, ice, shower, and meet the team for a meal—getting to be a kid again;

~ Feeling such pride in my team—a scrappy, persistent crew that shot the lights out and knew where to find each other on the court;

~ Winning gold—my team had worked for years to earn this, and I was grateful that, a year in, I got to be part of it. How lucky was I?

It was an honor to be one of 130 Maine athletes to attend the National Games and to be one of the women basketball players, many of whom I recognized from last summer's camp. Having observed Mom's health challenges as she'd aged, watching women ages fifty to ninety play basketball gave me hope.

I got news for you, kid: You're never too old to play basketball!

On the Edge, aka Re-finding Balance in Caring for a Loved One with Alzheimer's Disease

After all that, it was little wonder that I was about to unravel. As we got out of the car and approached the South Rim at sunset, I felt eager. Then the Grand Canyon's expanse opened up in front of us and I went weak. When Garrett stood on a rock wall between it and us, spreading his arms, I didn't feel like I could fly; I felt like I could crash. And so I did, emotionally, at least.

It could've been fear for Garrett's safety. It could've been anger at Doug's standing by. It could've been a genetic shout-out to Mom's fear of heights. It could've been exhaustion after the seven-hour car ride following all that basketball. It could've been the nagging pain in my injured leg. It could've been the line I constantly walked, in caring for Mom, trying to maintain balance between helping her be safe, sound, and happy and sometimes just wanting to let go, be free, and fly away. Whatever the mix, it left me breathless, faint, and panicked. I stepped away to gather myself; however, it wasn't to be. Over the next couple of days, the shit hit the fan. I fell apart.

I'm grateful Doug and Garrett gave me space while also bringing me along, in my less-than-charming state. I wanted to hide and, at the same time, I didn't want to miss out. Soon enough I'd be back home, taking care of Mom, unable to join in spontaneous adventure like the twenty-mile bike ride we took along the rim. Thankfully, the bike grounded me so I could get close, witness the beauty, feel the relief, and enjoy time with the guys, my hurts slowing me, not benching me.

Caring for a loved one with Alzheimer's is a long haul. In ways, I felt like I'd been caring for Mom since I was a kid: hanging around (because I was little) when she got uptight about the details of life, helping Dad support her when her mom died and she was wrecked, then walking her out of the hospital, blinking into the bright April afternoon sun, the afternoon we turned off the machines keeping Dad alive. It felt like I'd been blinking into the sun at her side ever since.

Our relationship had evolved. After decades apart, the ten years after Dad died had reunited us. I missed that Mom fiercely. I also missed the Mom who'd held me in her arms when I was a kid, tucked me into bed as I'd grown, had my back when peer pressures got me down, and been at my side later, during times of difficulty, even when she'd disapproved. When Mom had come to live with us in Wisconsin three and a half years before, I had lots of empathy for her and zero personal experience with Alzheimer's disease.

Since Mom's first diagnosis with mild cognitive impairment and, really, the onset of symptoms prior to that, it had been a constant squinting into the light, searching to understand, to make sense, to alleviate, to address, to grieve in private and to enjoy in public. This was still Mom's life, after all, and I firmly believed if we couldn't celebrate her today, we weren't meant to care for her tomorrow.

Which brought me to the sad reality that Mom had stopped recognizing me. It had been a relief, in a way, because it brought a certain freedom. When I stepped away, she no longer constantly asked for me. And we had incredible caregivers who met her where she was in any given moment, with love and respect and without the sense of loss that could get in my way.

Sometimes, though, I felt so worn out, so tired, that I didn't know how long I could keep this up. Even with excellent help, I spent most nights listening for Mom's wake-ups and most days filling the gaps, trying to bring her my A game when I had others who needed me, too. I did my best to suck it up and get it done, to make the best of it. I appreciated Mom's resilience, scrappiness, and wit; I soaked up the moments we connected with love. I was grateful for the time she was at peace, Cinnamon at her side.

Stepping away, however, like I had for Nationals, gave me time to feel the vastness of Alzheimer's—like when I stood at the edge of the Grand Canyon, exhausted, I sometimes felt overwhelmed, like I could fall right in. Then I'd get a good night's sleep, the love of Doug and the kids, the support of friends and caregivers, a new path would appear, and I'd find myself eyes wide open, looking into the depths, a smile on my face, able to see clearly again.

In frank and painful talks with Garrett after my Arizona meltdown, he expressed concern for my well-being and asked me to consider other solutions to Mom's care. So that summer, during valuable caregiving hours, Doug and I visited memory and nursing care facilities. Although I felt like I was abandoning Mom just walking through the doors, it was reassuring to learn about options, to have a backup plan, and to better understand the costs and benefits of the daily commitment we were making to Mom's living with us. I also increased overnight help—shout-out to Karly! The realization that I needed more predictable sleep was nothing new; however, the commitment to deliberately scheduling it was.

Not a whole lot had changed in caring for Mom since I'd stood at the Grand Canyon's edge in June, yet I felt more informed, more equipped, more supported, and more rested. Although at times I was still blinking into the setting sun, my balance had been restored. With the residential care options better understood and with Sharon added to care for Mom so I could get to Saturday morning basketball, I was back to taking it a day at a time and feeling grateful for the moments we still had with Mom, here in our home.

⚬⚬⚬

Here's to You, Ainty Jono

My aunt, whom I affectionately call Ainty Jono, and Mom, whom my cousin Margie affectionately calls Ainty Loro, had a lot in common.

Both were born in central Maine in 1932. Both liked to compete with the boys on the playground. Both lost their dads, whom they looked up to, at a young age. Both left Maine to go to college in Boston and returned to Maine to be close to their moms. Both wed, raised three kids, and welcomed others into their homes. Both enjoyed cocktails and late-night laughs. Both were practical, courageous, ambitious, loyal, and dedicated to people and causes they held dear. Both were avid athletes and sports fans who led on and off the field. Both hit eighty in style and then adapted to life with Alzheimer's disease. Both continued to display humor and grace, even as Alzheimer's took its toll. Both had kids dedicated to their care.

I have so many great memories of Ainty Jono from as far back as I can remember to the last time I saw her, dancing me across the activity-room floor. Ainty Jono was an independent woman who loved her sweets and knew how to have fun. It was her we went to when we wanted a "yes." She had a strong voice, grounded in compassion, and the willingness to do the hard work necessary to make positive change, like founding the first Girls Club in Maine. Her sense of fairness benefited people of all ages and fueled friendships with those who shared her politics and those who did not.

Ainty Jono took ownership of her future as she aged, moving into assisted living because she thought it the best choice. Even then, she brought the sense of adventure that had landed her the job with Governor Muskie in the 1950s—sneaking off with her Waterville friends to grab a bite to eat and hitching a ride from her Thursday driver to shop in her hometown of Augusta.

None of us know exactly how to do this job: caring for elders as they forget who they, and we, are. Even with the similarities, each of our caregiving stories is uniquely challenging and beautifully unique. I marvel at the care Beth and Margie—and their spouses, Janis and Marisa—gave Ainty Jono, doing their best to honor her wishes and her spirit while loving her without holding back. And I'm deeply grateful to all who supported them in doing so along the way.

That August, we laid Ainty Jono to rest. Each time I thought of her, my lips smiled as my heart ached. I am so lucky that this sweet, funny, intelligent, feisty woman was my aunt and that her daughters and their spouses are part of my village. I hoped we could see Mom through her journey here on this earth with the steady, patient, and brave approach that had helped them see Ainty Jono through hers. I'm thankful to them for showing me that it could be done.

Here's to you, Aintie Jono. May you rest in peace. Better yet, dance on.

A Bushel and a Peck: i.e., Transitioning to Hospice Care

That fall, Mom began sleeping more, eating less, and forgetting how to use the toilet, walk, and even swallow. It became increasingly challenging for her to communicate. Given the ups and downs of the last several years, I was unsure whether she would bounce back or was entering a new stage in her Alzheimer's disease. Just that spring, her doctor had said she was doing so well she could live another ten years, prompting me to enroll at the Chaplaincy Institute of Maine (ChiME), which seemed a forward-thinking complement to caring for her.

After a midnight fall, Mom was admitted to hospice, after two prior referrals when she hadn't met Medicare qualifications. I appreciated Beth and Janis for helping me know it was time. At first, I felt relief. Finally, we had in-home medical help. We were provided a phone number to call any hour of the day or night, for any reason, medicines to address discomfort of various kinds, access to a nurse who came twice a week to check in and advise, and the support of a social worker, a nondenominational chaplain, and a CNA who assisted with hygiene. I felt reassured that continuing to care for Mom at home wouldn't mean unnecessary pain or suffering, that I would be taught the skills required to keep her clean and comfortable, and that, if needed, there was a hospice house where she could go for her final days.

On visit one, the nurse said it looked like Mom might have started the dying process. On visit two, finding Mom by her favorite window, the nurse said that it could be that, instead, Mom had reached a new plateau—battling back from another UTI combined with the midnight fall. The nurse's uncertainty confirmed the confusion I felt in understanding Mom's health status. I appreciated the opportunity to talk with her about the challenges of existing in this *limbo*, as she called it, and making sure we continued to give Mom top care while respecting what she'd want, according to her living will and expressed wishes.

There were plenty of moments after those first two nurse visits when it seemed Mom's condition was deteriorating, as well as others when it seemed she was holding steady and maybe even improving: One Sunday morning she sat with our nephew Eben and his new wife, Lucy, marveling at their wedding photos with an "Isn't he handsome!" when she saw him all dressed up; then, late one night, she sat up on the edge of her bed, unassisted, for the first time in a month! One night, after months of not knowing who I was, she asked for me by name. I'm so glad Doug encouraged me to get out of bed and go to her—"This could be a last," he said. Mom's face had lit up when I went in to kiss her good night. I had thought our Alzheimer's journey called on us to take it a day at a time before; now that practice was more important than ever.

For so long, caring for Mom, we'd guided her through a daily routine to promote good moments. Getting her up, helping her to the bathroom, aiding her hygiene, serving healthy meals, keeping her hydrated, giving her medicine, spending time with her in activities she enjoyed, observing any changes, getting her needed medical care, helping her to get good sleep, and keeping her safe from potential threats. Simply put, we were loving Mom up in an active way, as her Alzheimer's and other health challenges took their tolls. Now, with the obvious decrease in Mom's wakefulness, appetite, thirst, mobility, hygiene, and continence, and the wisdom and support of our hospice team, we were modifying our approach to better meet her needs. Mom's care was less about guiding her through a daily routine and more about following her lead, offering the above opportunities while respecting any resistance or expression of pain, and doing our best to keep her comfortable. Our daily rhythm varied more than ever, depending on what she was up for. We were doing our best to love her through—letting her sleep, making the most of wakeful moments to offer nourishment and hydration, keeping her clean and dry, and paying close attention to the needs she expressed, without words.

As we entered this new phase, bolstered by my studies in interfaith chaplaincy, I was determined to encircle Mom in love and positive energy—caring for her evolving needs while helping her feel whole. As mentioned by author Maggie Oman Shannon, "Catherine of Siena wrote that 'perfect prayer is achieved not with many words but with loving desire....Everything you do can be a prayer.'"[123] Thanks to what I was learning at ChiME, this is how I approached Mom's care. This meant staying closer than before, which presented its own challenges to my health and balance; I appreciated the support of family, caregivers, friends, pets, and hospice. Without it, I couldn't have been as present in these moments at Mom's side.

As author Judy Flickinger puts it, "When done well, end-of-life care will affirm a dying person's life and our own as well. What else could be more important if the body cannot be cured? Our greatest gift then becomes our willingness to be in the presence of the dying person, empathetically as well as physically. While we are with them, we can listen and enter into the unknown with them. This goes beyond the words we speak to them. It has more to do with being with them rather than doing for them."[124]

Caring for Mom in our home and sleeping with my ear to a baby monitor, I'd known she was in a good place when I'd awake to hear her singing Frank Loesser's "A Bushel and a Peck" to Cinnamon, the same affectionate refrain she'd sung to me when I was a child. At the end of a particularly tough day, during that last stretch, when I sang Mom this song, she opened her eyes and smiled at me. I am deeply grateful that, even though caring for Mom as she approached death was not easy, I got to do so, and that, even when I felt alone, I wasn't.[125]

⌒✳⌒

Notes Stored on My Phone: During Mom's Home Stretch, Unblogged (brackets added later)

Yesterday Mom was accepted to hospice and I felt immense relief—as Mom's recent rise of pain doesn't mean I have to move her elsewhere. During the night, though, in addition to immense relief, I felt a whole mix of other emotions, too.

Sad

Tired

Worried

Unsure

Afraid

Start with Gratitude

Set boundaries

Walk the dogs

Gather info

Pray

Sounds like a game plan to me.

Goals for her

Sacred circle

Safe landing

Poop.

The following several weeks we let her lead/she stopped eating, drinking, getting out of bed. I used morphine only when she was really in pain [i.e., when she got up]. PT continued to come as did hospice nurse and CNA 2 x a week. Mom was clearly slowing down, going inward, and nurse consistently told me how peaceful she was. I had more moments of clarity with her during this period than I'd had in a long time....It was hard to stand by as she stopped eating etc. I learned how to change her in bed, watch for sores, bathe her, etc. It felt like a sacred thing I was doing for her. I sat at her side a lot. She'd open her eyes and make a face at me and close them again. She was mostly with eyes closed. I felt like she was contemplating—moving closer to the Divine...Sometimes she got mad at me cuz it hurt—like when I had to roll her to the side to clean her....One day though she actually opened her eyes and told me I was doing a wonderful job.

The nurse told me that the most likely way she'd die was of infection/either UTI or pneumonia from aspirating food. We were on the lookout for signs of that. My family was away for the holiday weekend. It was mostly me and her with a couple of breaks when I stepped away to walk the dogs, shower, etc. [thanks to my brother, my niece Holly, and our caregiver Lesley, who I found massaging Mom's still hands with moisturizer] it really was a beautiful weekend. Friday the nurse had said her vitals were still stable, she seemed peaceful, not in pain. During the course of the weekend, I thought she was shifting though I wasn't sure....I thought she might bounce back....Friday night she even ate a pb and j sandwich! She mostly slept peacefully. I slept in a cot at her side.

I'd had Karly lined up to help Monday night so I could sleep and I canceled her cuz I just didn't wanna step away. I kissed [Mom] good night at ten, and at three AM I was lying there and she asked "could you come over here Kim?" or maybe Tim [her brother]. She'd been breathing funny at bedtime and I was worried about her so I had medicine ready/I gave it to her when she told me she needed help with the pain. I called hospice and spoke with the nighttime nurse who instructed me how to use the medicines to address her pain. Mom continued to express discomfort so I did all I could/using the meds, singing to her [until she shushed me], doing a visualization [of jumping in the lake at camp], etc., etc.—it was intense. Much like childbirth. I was just totally focused on her. Telling her she did not need to stay in her body where she hurt. She didn't need to try to control it, she could leave it, she could be free. As sky started to brighten I turned off night-light and put up shades. She had sort of a spasm, some coughing spells, a gurgling sound, and then deep gulps for air and turned toward window. Then she was still and there were tears on her cheeks. I had my arm on her. After a bit I looked at my phone and it was 6:56. I found out later the sun rose at 6:54. I think that's about when she died. At 7:05 I texted Doug. It didn't seem real. I wasn't sure she was really dead. I called hospice and nurse came over later, around 8. She said when someone like Mom dies in hospice, they attribute it to natural causes.

Looking back, when I think about what I witnessed and her history of clots, I wonder if she had a clot that stopped her heart. Cuz it was really so quick and intense, in the whole scheme of things. I really felt like she was trying to stay and trying to go. I'm so glad I was with her— all the animals were with us, too. And I did not feel alone [thanks to my spouse and kids, and sister-in-law Heidi, for all the texts].

It's just hard now—it's a lot to process and I hope I did what she needed and that she felt my love all the way through. I sort of knew that however it played out, when Mom's life came to an end, I'd wonder if I'd done enough for her, made the right decisions, shown her my love. After all it's my over-the-top responsibility that led me to care for her these past years. I wanted to walk her out of this life, and I'm so grateful I could. And I suspect focusing on this lets me avoid the bigger reality, which is the loss.

> *Last night as I lay in bed, my thoughts racing,*
> *I was hit with the loss I feel.*
> *For so long I've been pacing myself...*
> *all at once I missed every mom I ever had.*
> *The one my aunt Joan told me never put me down...*
> *The one that wore red lipstick for Saturday night date nite with dad...*
> *The one that told me to put a smile on my face...*
> *The one that waited up late at night every time I flew in late...*
> *The one that hurt when her own mother died...*
> *I'll get through—I owe it to her, I owe it to my husband and kids...*
> *I'm so grateful I was with her and could ease her way*
> *even as it will take me time to sort through every last moment.*

[This next paragraph I found on my phone was me, starting to process Mom's death and not quite ready to share.] Mom did not like funerals, nor did she care for sad eulogies given by teary family members. And she most definitively did not prefer obituaries that read "she passed away after a long illness surrounded by family." She preferred to keep things upbeat and practical. In fact, when we packed her up to move with us to Wisconsin, I found a file in her bottom desk drawer labeled "funeral arrangements," which we followed to a T (thanks to my brothers). When I started to help Mom with medical decisions, she said again and again, "Living is for living." That's exactly what she did, right up until the end. She also said, "I've spent most of my life healthy, it'd be a shame to spend the last part sick." Well, it wasn't until the last several hours that she expressed pain and asked for my help. She was so brave, the way she marched out of this life and on to whatever's next.

Rereading these notes, I wonder whether they're too much to share. Then I look up to spot a bald eagle perched on the ledge outside our window…a reminder to be brave, to have confidence, to have faith, to be free.

⌒⋆⌒

Grief and Belief: in the Four Weeks Since Mom Passed On

Mom died at dawn on Tuesday, October 15, 2019—two years from the day we'd gotten her home to Maine. The best way I could describe my experience in the four weeks afterward was that it felt like a kaleidoscope—a constant whirl of memory and emotion turning over and over in my mind, like colorful pieces of sea glass, mixing and remixing in an ever-changing pattern:

A lifetime of memories embodied by the photos we'd arranged, the friends and family that had gathered and grieved, and Mom's sweet little Cinnamon, who was joining the rest of us in a whole new way…

A tumult of emotions—disbelief, relief, dread, curiosity, fear, gratitude, guilt, respect, anger, happiness, sadness, love…up and down and all around…

It was like I knew where Mom wasn't; I was just not sure *where she was.*

When Doug, our pets, and I had left Wisconsin two years earlier to get here and prepare for Mom's arrival, we'd had no idea the winds that would ensue.[126] Almost as relentless was the storm that hit the week after Mom died, taking down trees and cutting power,[127] so that the minister came here to sit in Mom's chair and write her service, aided by the generator we'd bought after that first wild storm.

Even though Mom had been on hospice for five weeks and I was with her when she died, I still struggled to accept it. As the minister put it,

when I told her I feared burying Mom alive: I'd taken care of Mom's physical being for so long, it was hard for me to let that responsibility go—my
brain hadn't yet caught up with my heart. I just couldn't believe it. As my
grieving brain tried to adapt, I found comfort in the loving condolences
we received from people I knew as a child, friends we made living away,
and those we'd met since returning to Maine. I also appreciated the hospice nurse's reassurance that Mom had been at peace, here in our home,
and that her death, with the animals and me at her side, had been consistent with how she lived, making the most of each moment.

In late September, my college friend Dina had asked, on the way to
her car after spending the night, if I'd given Mom permission to die. I'd
been uncertain how that would go, given Mom's confusion and memory loss. Plus, I hadn't been sure what Mom believed about the afterlife.
She'd always been more focused on living. I decided to go for it, hoping I
wouldn't upset her.

"Mom, do you believe in Heaven?" I asked the next time I caught her
aware.

"Sure," she responded with a nod.

"A lot of people are waiting to see you there," I said. She smiled.

"When you go," I added, "I'll be okay, Mom."

"Thank you," she said, looking me in the eye.

The day before Mom died, two weeks later, I asked if she was excited
to see her parents.

"Yes," she answered clearly. "I hope I see them soon."

I realize how lucky we were that Mom lived to be eighty-seven and
that, after decades living thousands of miles apart, we got to spend her
last four years together, two of them back in Maine. Still, I missed her, all
eighty-seven years of her, beyond description. It was like she was everywhere and nowhere, here in our home. For the first time, there was time
and space to grieve the loss we'd experienced, before and after Alzheimer's disease. It was a lot.

Then, at fifty-four, our beautiful friend Terry T, who lit up the basketball court and made us all feel special, died too. Terry T was filled with
courage and grace and, even in the midst of battling cancer, had reached
out to me: "Sorry about your mom," she'd texted, "but I know, because
I believe, that she is at peace." To honor Terry T, I also chose to believe.
In grief, I'd forgotten that was an option. As I just typed those words—*I*

choose to believe—the kaleidoscope in my brain began to slow and I felt more at peace. Thank you, dear Terry T, for showing me the way. Peace be with you as well.

⌒∗⌒

Remembering to Breathe: i.e., Taking Care of Ourselves During the Holidays

I stood on the side of the pool, in a line of swimmers, butterflies in my stomach. When I heard the signal, I dove. My body glided through the water and came to rest. Despite moving my arms and legs back and forth with increasing gusto, I couldn't get back to the surface. My chest tightened as I began to ache for oxygen. Unable to resist any longer, I inhaled deeply.

With the disrupted sleep of Mom's care, dreams had been rare the past several years. What a relief to awake and realize I wasn't under water, I was in our warm bed and I'd been holding my breath. When I inhaled, it was fresh air I got. It reminded me of the minister's advice the day of Mom's funeral: "Remember to breathe."

I must admit that the very next day after my underwater dream, Thanksgiving, the minister's advice escaped me. After a morning turkey trotting and an afternoon cooking, we gathered 'round the feast we'd prepared and took rambunctious family selfies for my in-laws. When we sat down at our kitchen table to eat, I felt the air swoosh right out of me as I was hit by Mom's physical absence. The laughter quieted as I voiced my pain. I sat there awkwardly afterward, fearing I'd killed the festive vibe. It's common knowledge that this time of year is hard on those who grieve. As captured by www.grief.com, founded by author David Kessler, "Since holidays are for being with those we love the most, how on earth can anyone be expected to cope with them when a loved one has died?"[128] It's one thing to know this; it's another thing to know what to do with it, when family time is precious and grief can flare in unexpected ways.

"The holidays can bring about a wide range of emotions," writes Amy Morin. "You might feel joy, guilt, and sadness all within a few minutes. Allow yourself to feel those emotions without judging yourself or thinking you should be happy or you shouldn't be laughing."[129] Wait a second: I didn't need to beat myself up for feeling upset instead of feeling thankful?

I was grateful to Doug and the kids for pulling me back to the surface, again, with their patient pause, Thanksgiving prayer, comforting looks, gentle reassurance. In the five weeks since Mom's death, they'd reminded me to take care of myself. I was trying—sleeping (hence the dream), exercising, sharing my feelings, and showing up for the activities that had helped me maintain balance while I'd cared for her. In an interfaith chaplaincy class, our instructor, Patricia, likened the aftermath of sudden life change to a box of dominoes flung up in the air and crashing to the floor, spread out all over—nothing in its place or as it was. She noted the value of pausing in that disarray, rather than rushing to reorganize or pick it all back up, as we might find that we don't need all the pieces we'd had before or that reorganizing them makes sense. This resonated with me as I sat there fighting the urge to lie down on the floor among her helter-skelter dominoes.

The question was, how do we manage our dominoes, flung across the floor, during these holy days that call us to gather to celebrate gratitude, peace, and joy? According to Tish Harrison Warren, an Anglican priest, the answer may be found in the weeks leading up to Christmas: "To practice Advent is to lean into an almost cosmic ache: our deep, wordless desire for things to be made right and the incompleteness we find in the meantime."[130] I appreciated Warren's reminder, on a broader scale, "to look long and hard at what is cracked and fractured in our world and in our lives. Only then can celebration become deep, rich, and resonant, not as a saccharine act of delusion but as a defiant act of hope." Ah, hope.

When I shared my Thanksgiving mix of love, laughter, joy, distraction, sadness, guilt, and loss with the hospice bereavement counselor the Monday after, she reassured me it was normal and reminded me of the importance of letting my feelings out and doing my breathing exercises in those intense, unexpected moments of grief.

"What do you mean by 'doing my breathing exercises'?" I asked.

She explained that, when she feels heavy of heart, she finds a quiet space (like her car), thinks of a comforting time or place, and breathes deeply in and out—at least five times, ten if needed—until she feels her sorrow lift.

It's okay to count our blessings, even as we grieve. I'm grateful Mom lived eighty-seven years, that I got to care for her the last four, that I was at her side when Dad died and when she died, too. I'm also grateful for how she taught me to put a smile on my face and carry on. I'm grateful, too, for the unending love of Doug and the kids. And I'm grateful for the time to grieve the many losses that came before and after Mom's Alzheimer's diagnosis, all the losses I held in so that I could focus on helping her live. It was time to let those losses, like my breath, in and out. During Mom's home stretch, I'd been intentional about protecting her sacred space. I needed to be that intentional now, about creating sacred space for externalizing my grief. In addition to making space to mourn, I needed to start with the most basic act: remembering to breathe.[131]

On a retreat with ChiME, two months after Mom died, I took a long walk by myself in the woods. Before returning for the afternoon art project, I flopped down in the fresh snow. I lay there, looking up at a tall evergreen that reached up to the blue sky (the blue Mom loved). I breathed in and I breathed out, deliberately, five times. It felt so good I decided to go for ten. Then I moved my arms and legs back and forth, back and forth. As I stood up carefully, to preserve my snow angel, I felt renewed and refreshed. I headed back to class, sending out lots of healing love, grateful to those who'd supported our family along the way, and hoping that all who needed time and space to mourn in the midst of the festivities would find it, and, at the very least, would remember to breathe.

⟳

Pep to My Step—The Emotional Toll of Caring for a Loved One with Alzheimer's Disease

I was standing at the front of the line trying to pay for our food, and I kept dropping things. Then I saw Mom come out of the restroom and walk toward a table of strangers. They looked at her blankly as she sat down. She scanned the group, stood back up, and turned toward me. I went to get her and she met my eyes with relief. I noted a fresh bruise across the bridge of her nose, as if she'd been smacked by a door. When I asked what had happened, she touched her face gently, answering, "I can't remember." Flooded with tenderness and concern, I awoke. I'd cared for Mom for years from afar and then in our home. I'd been with her, trying to ease her way, when she'd died three months earlier. I understood that nothing was perfect and I'd done the best I could. Still, especially after a dream like that, I wondered, *Was it enough?*

Over the holidays, Siena and I watched Lulu Wang's *The Farewell*, in which grandma "Nai Nai" is diagnosed with terminal lung cancer. Her family visits her in China under the guise of a wedding, keeping her diagnosis from her so that she can live out her days fully. When her granddaughter, raised in the United States, urges the family to tell the truth, her uncle says, "In America, you think one's life belongs to oneself. But that's the difference between the East and the West. In the East, your life is part of a whole. Family. Society... You want to tell Nai Nai the truth because you feel too much responsibility carrying it. If you tell her, then you don't have to feel guilty anymore. We're not telling her because it is our responsibility to carry this emotional burden for her."[132]

This scene reminded me of caring for someone with dementia. While U.S. law requires health care professionals to follow a certain etiquette to protect individual privacy,[133] the lines shift when a patient can't remember their own health care history, understand diagnoses, or make decisions. As Mom's POA, that job had fallen to me. The result was that Mom had gotten to live in the moment, through the ups and downs, while I, and others, had carried the emotional toll of caring for her, at her most vulnerable, as Hannah put it, when we didn't have answers or know what to expect.

I'm grateful for the many ways others helped me through that first holiday season, and the aftermath of carrying this toll, in addition to just plain missing Mom:

~ My friend Brieanna inviting me to a Blue Christmas service for those who were grieving and putting her hand on my shoulder when they read my parents' names, while her husband, Nick, took care of the little one;

~ My in-laws, Cliff and Millie, sitting on either side of me at our holiday celebration, after she put a blanket on me, as I fought a virus that had laid me low;

~ Our niece Ali encouraging me to have the Christmas Eve gathering that Mom used to host and family showing up with food and gifts;

~ Siena helping me cook a feast of Mom's favorites: macaroni and cheese, meatloaf, and chocolate pie, which actually jelled;

~ Garrett filling my stocking with thoughtful gifts meant to brighten my post-caregiving days;

~ Matt inviting me out for a lobster roll, something I used to enjoy with Mom;

~ Holly's now fiancé, Albert, asking, with genuine interest, about what was next for me;

~ Driving around my hometown with childhood friends, reminiscing; and

~ My sister-in-law Heidi putting her arm around me as I cried on her shoulder after I woke up from the dream described above.

There were moments when I actually felt the return of pep in my step. I still had bouts of stark loss, like my first night alone in our home since Mom had died. I also had moments of sweet relief, that Mom suffered no more. To ring in 2020, I'd gone through the photos on my phone her last four years with us. Seeing the good moments that preceded her last ones had made my heart glad. I resolved to keep it simple: sleep, hydration, nutrition, exercise, writing, gratitude—I hoped taking better care of me would make me physically healthier while my heart continued to adapt to this post-caregiving phase. I had no idea that a pandemic would bring our adult kids and their animals back home to work and to study. I was just grateful for the time Mom had had, after a long life of hard work and worry, to enjoy the view and connect with the beings around her. It was the best gift we could give her and, even with the emotional toll it sometimes still took, it was the best gift she could have given us, too.

Speaking of Pep in Her Step—Cinnamon's Getting Hers Back, Too!

I knew we were in good shape when I'd awake in the early morning light to hear Mom singing to her little canine caregiver, whose attention never wavered, even as it required her to adapt from walking partner, to therapy dog, to lapdog, to watchdog.

Mom had grown up with dogs and raised us the same way. She and Dad had chosen otherwise once their nest emptied, in favor of freedom to come and go. After Dad died, Mom had moved north and retired; she made new friends and spent summers at camp. Still, we had worried about her being lonely.

"I'll never by choice ever live alone," Mom had written in the summer of 1953 while Dad was at sea. Fifty-six years later, we'd found her a cockapoo, reminiscent of her childhood cocker spaniels, to make sure of that.

Mom had chosen the name as soon as she saw the first photo. We agreed that Cinnamon would live with us in Wisconsin until she could sleep through the night and relieve herself outside. With our pets and kids, their friends and all the ball games at the local park, the pup had quickly learned to interact with beings of all shapes and sizes.

Mom couldn't wait to meet her, so she paid an unexpected visit to the Midwest. It was love at first sight. When the time came, Mom took Cinnamon back to Maine, where Cinnamon quickly broke all the rules. She sat on the living room furniture, begged (successfully) for treats, and slept in Mom's bed. Mom had begun sleeping in late because "Cinnamon didn't want to get up."

The two became inseparable. They walked three miles a day, enjoying the attention they received from the neighbors. Mom brought Cinnamon to one grandchild's college graduation and another's college softball games. They watched the loons at camp. They visited us in Wisconsin. After her early months in the van with me, riding around town in an airplane carrier, Cinnamon would hop right in when Mom got out the blue pet carrier.

"Isn't she good!" Mom would exclaim, wheeling her proudly back and forth.

Every time Mom prepped to fly west to us, she put Cinnamon on a diet to meet the weight requirement; to this day, Cinnamon loves frozen green beans.

Mom also trained Cinnamon as a therapy dog, taking her to the local nursing home and college campus to relieve others' stress. When her brother, Tim, became ill, Mom took Cinnamon to see him at the VA. When her neighbor faced a cancer relapse, Mom took Cinnamon to visit her every day, too. Cinnamon had helped Mom show up for others in tender times, and then had helped Mom process the grief that followed.

When Mom's own health started to shift, a hip injury curbing their to and fro, Cinnamon's greetings became more vigorous, like she was trying to alert me. Constantly at Mom's side, watching her every step, barking at her to signal it was time to eat or go to bed, the little dog worked overtime.

One day, as they were headed to the groomer, Cinnamon took off on a busy street and Mom fell trying to get her back. With another winter approaching, I had worried that Mom might forget Cinnamon outside, get stuck outside herself, or slip on the ice trying to retrieve her. So I was relieved when the pair came to live with us so we could look after them. I counted on Cinnamon to help Mom adjust to life in the Midwest. As long as the two were together, they were content.

While the belief that a pet would be a good companion for my widowed Mom had brought us Cinnamon, little did we know the continued quality of life she'd help us provide as Alzheimer's and other illnesses took hold. When Mom lost the sight in her right eye, curtailing the reading she enjoyed, Cinnamon filled in the gap, enjoying the extra petting that came with free hands. That first scary hospital stay, when Mom's dementia had become "severe," I got permission to bring Cinnamon to visit, and Mom came out of her shell. The next hospitalization, I didn't wait for her to unravel before bringing Cinnamon in. When Mom was hospitalized upon our return to Maine, the nurse even invited Cinnamon to stay overnight.

It makes sense that pets of all sorts have been shown to benefit people with dementia, reducing anxiety and depression and improving daily behavior and nutrition.[134] In fact, according to Anne-Marie Botek, "Alzheimer's service dogs can be trained to assist their cognitively impaired handlers with a variety of daily tasks, including alerting them when a stove is left on, identifying their car in a crowded parking lot, and directing them to their house if they get lost while on a walk."[135]

Although Cinnamon hadn't been trained as a canine caregiver for someone with dementia, she figured out what the job required. She would get me if Mom got up at night or needed help during the day; she did her best to keep Mom happy and safe. As Mom's world became smaller and smaller, so did Cinnamon's. If I offered her a walk, alone or with the other dogs, she flat-out refused. If separated from Mom, she'd wait nervously by the door. Even when Mom had forgotten who I was, she remembered her "little pal."

When Mom lost her mobility and her attention drew inward, Cinnamon stayed near. It had taken one "Ouch" from Mom when Cinnamon jumped on her bed for Cinnamon to adapt to sleeping on the floor. That's when I got Mom a stuffed Cinnamon look-alike.[136] With the coming and going of the hospice nurse and CNA, Cinnamon shifted to watchdog mode, barking with each new arrival before resuming her post at Mom's bedside. Mom's last weekend, Cinnamon looked on as I removed the commode and wheelchair, no longer necessary.

I worried that when Mom died, we might lose Cinnamon, too. She had been so forlorn and, at almost eleven, not young. Mom had been the center of her universe. For a while there, Cinnamon had quietly watched and waited. She'd been grieving, too. Then, somewhere during the weeks following Mom's death, Cinnamon had reset her sights.

I appreciate this sweet little dog for taking such good care of Mom and now us. It's like all the love we'd given Cinnamon in her puppyhood, she gave to Mom during their life together. And now, all the love Mom gave her during that time, Cinnamon is giving back to us.

These days, Cinnamon curls up at my side to sleep, hops up on Doug's lap to snuggle, pounces on our cat to roughhouse, scampers with our dogs to play. And when she sees me get out the leashes, she's first in line to go for a walk, speaking of pep in her step!

⌒⋇⌒

COVID-19 Staying at Home—Finding Guidance in Parental Wisdom

Maine governor Janet Mills had issued a stay-at-home order, to take effect the next day and hold through April, making exceptions for shopping for necessities such as groceries and medicine, going to jobs deemed essential, and exercising outdoors, as long as we stayed six feet from people outside our households. Mills warned, as reported in the words of Tax Axelrod, "drastic actions are needed to blunt the spread of the coronavirus, which has already infected at least 303 Mainers and killed five."[137] Since our household's work was not "essential," we would do our part by working from home, taking care of each other, and supporting others from afar.

Seeking order to my whirling thoughts and feelings, I started with the facts. As I pecked away at my keyboard, flanked by dogs and cats, Garrett, twenty-one, sat at the kitchen table, watching his college counterinsurgency class remotely; Siena, twenty-six, and her classmate were sequestered—one in Mom's bedroom, the other in my study—Zooming their veterinary rotations, white coats set aside; and Matt, twenty-four, sat at our dining table, glued to the screen he brought with him when he was instructed to work remotely. After five months empty, our nest was full.

A month earlier, when I still thought Zoom was a seventies kids' show, not an online meeting space, I'd been working on a blog post for St. Patrick's Day, to mark the five months since Mom's death and to share one of her favorite sayings: "Aren't we lucky?" By the time St. Paddy's

Day rolled around, however, with coronavirus disease 2019 (COVID-19) wreaking pain and suffering around the world and increasingly here in the United States, the mention of luck seemed insensitive, if not preposterous.

There were moments, when nothing seemed as it was and everything seemed newly tenuous, when I wished I could check in with Mom and Dad. "Have you ever experienced anything like this?" I'd ask. "How did you get through it?" Then I'd close my eyes and think of them, and certain phrases would come back to me, bringing guidance and relief.

When I was young and wanted an answer *now*, Dad's "We shall see" drove me nuts. As COVID-19 concerns had continuously escalated, with frightening predictions and increasing restrictions, these three words offered solace. These times of uncertainty called on us all to focus on what we knew instead on of what we didn't—not easy in the midst of fear and loss. More than ever, I appreciated Dad's reminder to resist panic and await clarity, practicing patience in the meantime.

"What's the bottom line?" was another Dad go-to, referring to the net profit or loss at the bottom of a financial statement. Although his direct, no-nonsense approach made sense given his background as a Marine, it didn't feel all that affirming to teenaged me, who wanted to mull over all the details, real and imagined. I recognized now that Dad might not have meant to shut me up but to help me simplify: to peel away the layers that obscured and find underlying truths. These days, *the bottom line* was that, while COVID-19 threatened us all in various ways, according to the CDC it appeared to be most dangerous to older adults, people living in nursing homes or long-term-care facilities, and those of any age with serious underlying medical conditions.[138]

One morning, I awoke remembering Mom's "Living is for living"—repeated every time I asked her for direction in her care. This phrase had not only helped me make health care decisions for her once Alzheimer's interfered with her ability to do so, it had also helped me to carry on in the months following her death. Mom's words reminded me, in the pandemic's early days, to resist acting grumpy or uptight, to put a smile on my face and find little ways, within our household, to live life: helping our son's girlfriend set up April Fool pranks, stepping outside to take in the sun, snuggling with a pet, making the most of these moments with the kids, humoring Doug when he got antsy. It also meant cheerfully greeting all I met on my runs, from the recommended six feet, and thanking parcel deliverers, grocers, caregivers, and more, for their courage and commitment. *Living is for living* meant letting go of the pull to fear, trusting we would find our way through, and preparing for the time when we could step back into the world and help it heal.

I had been with Mom when she'd drawn her last breaths. Right down the home stretch, when she was still communicating, it hadn't been unusual for her to say, "Aren't we lucky?" It had been a theme for as far back as I could recall. We'd even had a collie named Lucky. I had thought that having luck meant I shouldn't complain, until a counselor pointed out: "Even if you have good things in your life, it's okay to express your pain."

When it comes to caring for a parent with Alzheimer's disease, there's plenty of drawn-out heartache and loss, which we shelve so we can show up and provide care. It's hard to hold vigil, day after day, no idea how long it'll last, what challenges will come next, and whether, in the end, we'll be able to help our loved ones die in a way that is peaceful, protects their dignity, and feels like love. COVID-19 added a whole new layer to Alzheimer's and dementia care. According to James Ellison, MD, in an interview with Tanner Jensen, people with dementia face unique challenges that put them at risk: They might forget to wash their hands, cover their coughs, or keep their distance; they're less likely to recognize and communicate symptoms; they tend to be older; and efforts to communicate about COVID-19 precautions could be more upsetting and confusing than helpful and preventive.[139] In some cases, providing the best care even meant staying away to curb COVID-19 spread. I deeply empathized with all who could not get to their loved ones due to quarantine, and I respected the ways they tried to manage care and stay connected from a safe distance.

Keeping vigil for a loved one with Alzheimer's disease had been the biggest challenge I'd faced yet, and still, thanks to the way Mom had raised me, I knew I'd been lucky to get the chance. I finally understood that her "Aren't we lucky?" had never meant to minimize pain, it had been her way of practicing gratitude for the blessings:

~ I'm grateful that, even when Mom had no idea where we were going, when Kenny Chesney sang "Everything's Gonna Be Alright," she'd ride shotgun beside me, tapping her fingers and bobbing her head, a smile on her face;

~ I'm grateful for the circle of others that helped me keep vigil for Mom, so that I could maintain my balance—a balance that would help me after she died;

~ I'm grateful that, even once she no longer recognized me, when I tucked her into bed at night, with a kiss on her forehead like she used to give me, Mom still felt lucky;

~ In this time of immense and indescribable challenge, I'm grateful to all who went out in the world to provide medical care, law enforcement, emergency response, access to groceries and medicines, caregiving, leadership, and support so that the rest of us could lie low;

~ I'm also grateful that we had safe shelter and access to clean water, food, and toilets, recognizing this was not so for many the world over;

~ I'm grateful for technology that may have once felt isolating and now helped us connect; and

~ I am grateful that Doug and the kids were here in our household, still safe and sound.

In memory of all those who inspire us with the ways they persevere, let's do our best to be patient, to simplify, to live life, and to count our blessings, even as we grieve our losses. Wherever we can, let's help each other through and give one another something to celebrate.

Laughter in Grief—Showing Up the Best We Can and Finding Hope Amidst Loss

It had been eighteen years since Dad died at sixty-eight. I missed him, and I appreciated the ways he visited me still, like the passionate, airy, almost wheezy laugh I'd catch escaping from deep in my chest—which sounded like his. "Give it a good six months and you'll have one hell of a time," said Fred, my parents' longtime camp neighbor and friend, after Mom's service the prior October. Seeing that I was catching myself laughing again, it looked like Fred had been on to something.

Who knew, six months before, what spring would bring? I had thought the challenge was to process the loss I felt after caring for Mom. As I tried to do my small part to flatten the COVID-19 curve by staying at home, I grieved, too, for the worldwide pain and suffering the pandemic wrought. Mentioning laughter was not meant to minimize this, it was just a lot better than fixating on the broken tooth I also attributed to Dad's genes. As David B. Feldman, PhD, puts it, "Grieving appropriately means allowing ample time to remember and feel the loss as well as embracing occasional opportunities to distract ourselves and regroup."[140]

As a kid, I loved it when Dad told me one of his Douglas the Rabbit stories at bedtime. It was probably no coincidence that I'd married a Douglas of my own. When our kids were little, I'd tucked them into bed at night with Douglas the Rabbit stories, too, taking Dad's Douglas out of the woods and off the farm and into our neighborhood and schools. There had always been curiosity, natural beauty, risk, connection with others, and returning home, at the end of another adventure, safe and sound. One of the ways I had grieved Dad's death was by writing down and illustrating the story he'd told, followed by three more that I'd created, celebrating memories of my own and our kids' youths. When efforts to publish *Douglas* had proven unsuccessful—apparently, he wasn't the only rabbit out there—I tucked away the copies I'd made, thinking someday I'd share them with the grandkids. I'd also given Mom a set of the books, which she kept on her living room table. Later, a friend invited me to read these books to her second grade class in Milwaukee, where I encouraged the kids to make up their own stories and color their own illustrations. And then my niece Holly took *Douglas* to an orphanage in Tanzania, sharing her version of his adventures with the children living there.

The last year or two, living with us, Mom, always a voracious reader, had begun to pick up *Douglas the Rabbit* more and more, until it became a regular thing. On the eve of her death, I sat at her side while she looked at one of the books—the original that Dad loved to tell. By then Mom wasn't eating or drinking, mostly sleeping and, in her wakeful moments, going on adventures with Douglas, her facial expression peaceful and focused. Little had Dad known, when he made up those stories for us kids, that someday I'd share them with my kids; little had I known that the stories I'd written to remember him after he died, and to share with my kids, would someday entertain Mom when she could no longer get out of bed.

Sometimes, in the moment, we cannot see the big picture. We just try to do the next best thing. For me, after Mom died, that meant showing up for the things I'd put in place to keep me balanced while I cared for her. Six months into this new world, it meant doing my best to stay healthy and well, our house full with new care to be given, continuing chaplaincy classes and bereavement counseling online, providing service by phone and email, and recommitting daily to exercise, spiritual practice, and writing. And, too, doing the next best thing included laughing, from deep within, when the opportunity arose. My dad loved to laugh. I got that from him. That laughter was coming in handy these days, with our house full of adult kids, their pets, and their computers—"safer at home."

～

Celebrating Mom—Grateful for Grief, Belief, and Relief

I was taking a quick shower when I was hit upside the head with this thought: *What if there's something I gotta do to get Mom into Heaven?* Still dripping, I called the hospice chaplain to set up a visit, which had never occurred because Mom died the next morning.

"There's no reason why your mom's flight into her next dimension wouldn't include a direct flight to Heaven. Really. Try to let that one go. See how peaceful she is? She knows where she's going...." Heidi had texted as I sat at Mom's side later that night.

"Just know she is always with you and forever thankful for all you did. She will throw you signs that she's there. She probably already has...." texted Kathy, my childhood friend, soon after Mom died.

"By the time she gets through the celebration of her new life in Heaven you will be there with her. Time is a blink where she is," added Megan, my Wisconsin friend.

The love and concern underlying these words comforted me. However, after so much time together, knowing right where she was, here in our home, Mom's physical absence was stark. Spiritually, I wanted to believe she was in a better place, I just didn't know where that was. Writing this, with seven months' practice under my belt, things were shifting—I was less focused on where Mom wasn't and was finding comfort in the places I found her. It was getting easier for me to acknowledge certain happenings as more than just coincidence:

~ Mom's weathervane, which Doug had installed in our yard where she could see it, blown over by the strong wind following her death, reminding me of the upside-down thumb she'd regularly hold above her head whenever he was near, to give him the razz;

~ the day I went to Mom's old neighborhood and her friends took me out for lunch and it just so happened the gelato flavor of the day was pistachio, Mom's favorite; and

~ there was the afternoon of Mom's visiting hours:

As part of my first-year curriculum at the Chaplaincy Institute, I'd been assigned Brenda, a graduate, as my mentor. When we planned to hike in the woods, I had no idea it would be in the midst of making photo boards of Mom's life. I kept our appointment, figuring it might do me good to get out for a bit. When it turned out that, in addition to the weathervane, the recent winds had knocked down tree limbs, closing the road to our designated meeting spot, I headed instead to a nearby park, where Brenda had left her car. Crossing paths at the gate, we began to walk; when we paused in conversation, I noticed we were standing within view of the bench dedicated to Mom's best friend, Carol, where Mom and I had sat the day of Dad's funeral almost eighteen years earlier.

"It's like your Mom is sitting right here," said Brenda, indicating the space between us as we sat on the bench. Just then a bright yellow leaf blew up, fluttered back and forth, and settled there. We looked at each other, our eyes wide open, with an unspoken *Are you seeing what I'm seeing?* As I walked Brenda back to her car, she mentioned the word *synchronicity*—which lexico.com revealed afterward was a term coined by C.G. Jung that refers to "the simultaneous occurrence of events which appear significantly related but have no discernible causal connection."[141] The next day, following Mom's service and burial, I walked into the restaurant where we were gathering to celebrate her life. The first to greet me was Jessica, who wrapped her arms around me and gave me a much-needed hug. As she stepped back, she smiled and pointed at my neck. I looked down to find another bright yellow leaf clinging to my scarf. Even in my grief I felt Mom's love.

I am grateful for the countless reminders ever since that Mom is still near: the lasting love of her caregivers, including Cinnamon; the special birthday dinner—a collection of her favorite dishes—planned by Garrett; the lobster rolls and nightly phone calls, once shared with Mom, now shared with Matt; Siena, amidst her online pandemic veterinary rotations, pausing to make herself a healthy meal, like Mom would do; the blue sky, chirping birds, wind on my face, the grit and optimism of all

Mom's grandkids; and the determination I feel to remain positive, even in these uncertain times. That Mother's Day, the first since Mom's death, I felt grief, belief, and relief. I was thankful for all the memories and messages so readily available, when I opened to them, and for the understanding that missing Mom wasn't an *either/or*, it was an *and*. I felt sad *and* I felt glad, just like she'd want me to.

Mom's Birthday, Another First

As Mom's birthday approached, I felt apprehension; I wanted to celebrate her life, yet the grief felt unpredictable. Before COVID-19, I had signed up to swim the Tri for a Cure that day, raising money to fight cancer. I'd invited the Maine Senior Women's Basketball crowd, also participating in Terry T's memory, to our house for a cookout afterward. Then the triathlon went virtual and the day opened up. Doug and kids away, I decided to go to camp.

"Your Mom lives on in you....Going to camp allows her to go there, too," said my classmate Willa when I mentioned my trepidation. In the nine months since Mom had died, I'd had plenty of reminders of her absence and her presence; I'd found peace, even happiness, sitting in her favorite chair. During quarantine, Mom's bedroom became a favorite place to Zoom, giving it new purpose that Mom would have loved. Going to camp to celebrate Mom felt different from staying at home. If Mom were a place, she'd be camp. This would be my first July 19th there without her physical presence at my side.

When we had opened up camp in May, there had still been cookies in the cookie jar from the previous August when I'd planned to bring Mom back for a September stay. As I cleaned every nook and cranny, getting ready for summer 2020, camp served up rapid-fire memories spanning almost a century. Looking across at my grandmother Gum's neighboring porch, I envisioned my mother-in-law, Millie, playing ukulele, Mom and the grandkids posing for a photo on the big rock, me in my wedding dress surrounded by bridesmaids, Dad waiting at the back stairs to walk me down the hill to the lake, family dinners culminating with Gum's delicious pies, Margie and I sneaking Grandpa George's ice cream treats while he snored in his chair, Mom eating breakfast with her brother, Tim, excited to turn twelve.

I was grateful to the kids and animals that pulled me through Memorial Day and stayed on the following week to make new camp memories. I must admit it was a relief to join in freely without worrying about Mom—we swam, canoed, walked, bird-watched, all activities that she loved. Every time we caught sight of a vibrant blue jay somewhere near, Siena would glance my way and smile at the flash of blue: "Hi, Lala" (the nickname she'd coined for Mom way back when).

This time around, for Mom's birthday, it would be just me and the animals. I resisted the temptation to fill the time with projects like painting the trim (which Mom would have done) or writing a reflection (which eats up hours), opting instead to be present for whatever came, a practice Mom had perfected in her later years, dementia easing her concerns. Saturday was a beautiful summer day with heat bugs, sunshine, and visits—the first with Jessica, the second with childhood friend Kate, and the third with Beth and Janis. All knew Mom at different phases and I felt the love—drinking coffee on the deck, revisiting childhood memories, kayaking with the loons. That night, after a quiet evening, just me and the animals, watching *Anne with an E* and working on a puzzle my sister-in-law Jennie had sent, I climbed into my childhood bed and was hit with immense, profound, and gripping loss.

Matt, checking in from a cross-country trip, suggested I go down to Mom's room and lie in her bed. That's where I wept without holding back. Since Mom's death, I'd circled round and round the various aspects of grief. Lying there in Mom's bedroom at camp, I let it all out. What I felt, loud and clear, on the eve of Mom's eighty-eighth birthday, was sadness. Not denial, guilt, anger, or unfinished business. I felt loss, pure and simple. Then came a flood of Love—above all else, Love.

After a while, I went back upstairs to climb into bed, the animals trailing me. The next time I opened my eyes it was four a.m., the sky pink. When I awoke again several hours later, I felt calm and purposeful. I drank our morning coffee on the deck, with the childhood photo albums Mom had faithfully kept, looking for answers to questions I wished I'd asked, questions that had arisen since her death. I texted my discoveries to Margie, Doug, and the kids, pausing late morning to make blueberry pancakes, Mom's favorite, and later, to jump in the lake.

Early afternoon I packed up and headed south, back home for an afternoon run by my childhood home, followed by dinner with Doug and Garrett. Although I still missed Mom, I felt renewed. "On the other side, in that place of deepest exhaustion enmeshed with sorrow, there is more than just a cliff of sadness and loss," writes Edie Thys Morgan, who lost her mother to Alzheimer's, too. "There is this beautiful and unexpected gift—an opposite shore, where the person you've loved so much for so long is waving back at you, exactly as you hoped to remember her."[142]

Although I didn't find the answers to all my questions that birthday morning as I scoured Mom's albums, I did find Mom, as she'd always been—scrappy, delicate, beautiful, strong, brave, resilient, organized, accomplished, devoted, and true. I was grateful for the writing I'd done along the way, describing our life together in real time—with lightness and love amidst heaviness and loss. And I was even more grateful for the records Mom had kept, capturing her life in real time—with lightness and love amidst heaviness and loss—providing a way for me to spend time with her now that she was no longer here, at least physically.

In her later years when I'd ask for direction in her care, Mom would answer, "Living is for living," leaving the details to me. Looking at seventeen-year-old her the summer of her dad's sudden death at camp—"an accident," she called it in her later years—and following her as she marched forward into a life spent pushing the boundaries, I understood that her approach wasn't just a way to deal with aging, it was the way she handled her early losses and carried on. Mom had taught me, by example, to put a smile on my face and keep marching, like I was doing now, trusting that, between that and finding safe places to put down my smile, I'd live life, too.

So on Mom's birthday morning, pausing to look back at her life as she'd captured it, I got Mom back. Like Morgan says, "I do miss my mom, every single day, and especially in times like these when all you want to hear is the reassuring sound of your mom's voice, from anywhere. But I've got the next best thing. I get to miss my mom exactly the way she would want to be missed." Returning to camp later that summer, this time with a full house, Mom was there, in all the ups and downs of our rambunctious pandemic family life. Sitting in her bedroom, where Doug and I now slept, I saw our adult kids whipping a football back and forth just outside her window. When I looked beyond to the lake, I heard Mom's "wind's comin' from the north today," and I sent back a silent *I love you, Mom*, to which she responded, clear as a bell,

"I love you too....Aren't we lucky?"

❧

Labor of Love: Another Take on "Caregiver Burden"

On Labor Day, we returned to camp for one last 2020 stay. While Memorial Day, honoring fallen soldiers, marks camp's opening, Labor Day, celebrating American laborers, marks camp's closing. This weekend had always been bittersweet, with its unique blend of lasts—morning pancakes loaded with blueberries, midday swims chilled by the wind, evening barbecues accompanied by family and friends, and nighttime games started by Kick the Can and finished with Ghost in the Graveyard—all sprinkled with chores from Mom's lengthy list.

Labor Day itself would begin with neighbors gathering to help pull out docks and then share coffee, doughnuts, and lots of laughs and good wishes for the year ahead. While I well recalled Mom's upbeat anticipation as we opened in May, I remembered, too, her heavy sadness when we closed in September. This time around, having survived Memorial Day and birthday firsts without Mom at camp, I decided to postpone end-of-season chores so I could be present with all who came to share these last summer moments, which were not to be squandered during this pandemic time.

"I don't want to be a burden," Mom would say, adamantly, as she aged and we talked about the future, before we knew it would include Alzheimer's. This had become a guiding principle as Mom's needs grew and I took on a larger role in her care, sometimes wondering if I was up to the task. To honor her concern, I had made sure to take time away to nurture my health, my interests, and my other relationships. I was grateful for the Higher Power that had guided me through, along with all the amazing beings that helped us, too. I also appreciated how Mom's worries had fallen away so that, together, we could just be, not just do.

Moving away in my twenties had helped me establish much-needed boundaries and focus on the health of myself, Doug, and our kids. Al-Anon and counseling had helped me become more present, spiritually and emotionally, and not to look to alcohol to alleviate stress. I'd learned from witnessing Mom's grief that finding healthy ways to deal with loss was key. I was glad I had kept coming back to camp with Doug and the kids, fostering their connection to my favorite place and nurturing my adult relationship with Mom. And I was so thankful that camp remained a place we could go to spend time together now, almost a year after Mom's death, and feel close to her and all the rest, in all the best ways. I understood that, although those last summer moments felt finite, they were really infinite, in the scope of lives that overlap.

Labor Day afternoon, after everyone else had left, leaving just me and two of our dogs, I spent several hours doing the laundry, covering the boat, taking down the flag, moving some things around, packing other things up. It felt sacred, the quiet time to reflect, back and forth, back and forth, one task leading to the next, the dogs waiting patiently in the open car. I could have asked for help before everyone left; however, I hadn't wanted the summer vibe to end. As Matt put it when he texted me midafternoon, concerned he'd ditched me even though I hadn't asked him to stay, "Thanks for hosting us all this weekend….It's like camp is back in its prime." Mission accomplished.

Picking up quietly after the weekend fun was exactly what I needed. Mom was with me every step of the way, I realized, as I stored the canoe paddles behind the bathroom door, like she used to. By the time the dogs and I drove down the camp road at dusk, my back tired from the to and fro, my head tender from the frozen turkey that had slipped from the freezer above as I'd cleaned the fridge, I better understood Mom's recruiting the rest of us to address her end-of-season to-dos. It had eased my departure, knowing that others would finish the heaviest work and Doug and I would return to do the final cleaning and closing, though I still turned back to make sure I'd shut the shed door.

On Labor Day weekend a year before, a shift in Mom's health had kept us from camp. Although I didn't even recall closing up in the midst of the hospice stretch that had followed, I did recall those last rays of summer sun and the way we'd stretched toward them together as fall arrived. Sometimes what looks like a burden is actually an opportunity to heal.

∞

Grief and Guilt: A Year Later, and the Magic of Froot Loops, Barking Dogs, Yellow Leaves, and Blue Jays

Caring for someone with Alzheimer's disease is a long and mysterious journey. Mom has had such highs and lows along the way, even now, I'm not sure where we stand. So I need to suck it up, do my best, drop a

*"Froot Loop!" where necessary, keep caring for me, take it one day at
a time, trust I can see this through, and thank God for all the kindness
coming our way, from hospice, family, caregivers, teammates, and friends.*
(Fall 2019, just before Mom died)

Years ago, when Siena was in middle school, I coached her fast-pitch
softball team. One hot summer day, I had an idea for lifting the heads
that were hanging low after an early-morning loss. I knew firsthand that
dwelling on our mistakes, on and off the field, prevented us from making
the most of the opportunities that followed, so I encouraged the team to
own our errors with the phrase "Froot Loop!" and then get ready for the
next play. Although I didn't recall how the tournament turned out, I did
remember having more fun after that huddle and, thereafter, having a
G-rated way to capture those post–flub-up moments, a playful reminder
to "shake it off" and "keep our heads in the game."

When it comes to caring for someone with Alzheimer's disease,
losses are spread out and many, and the situation is ever-changing, so
there's lots of opportunity to mess up. There's also lots of opportunity to
learn. I'm so grateful to all who taught me the skills to adapt to Mom's
evolving needs. Dropping a "Froot Loop!" here and there wasn't meant
to minimize the challenges; it was intended to put a smile on my face and
keep me in the game, ready for the next do-over. It helped me own my
mistakes, learn from them, and keep giving the best care I could.

One night, I climbed into bed at the end of a long day to the realization that it had been a year to the night that Mom's health had slipped.
I felt a pang of the guilt that had gripped me after she died. *I'm so sorry,
Mom*, I thought. I get that Mom's "number was up," as Dad would have
put it; still, I was hit with the what-ifs, which prompted one last round of
online search: While no two end-of-life situations are the same, "the guilt
is inescapable" writes R.M. Vaughan;[143] "a common wing man of bargain-
ing," guilt is part of the grief process, adds Christina Gregory, PhD;[144]
and "the actual grief process looks a lot less like a neat set of stages and
a lot more like a roller coaster of emotions," says David Feldman, PhD;
"It's important to remember, however, that death has medical and physical causes—causes that aren't our fault or, usually, anyone else's."[145] It followed that, after a period of coming to terms with things, my guilt had
resurfaced.

I was grateful for the many times Doug had reminded me of the dedicated care we'd given Mom to help her stay happy, healthy, and safe, even though we couldn't prevent the inevitable. Especially with the way the COVID-19 pandemic threatened elders and complicated their care, I deeply appreciated the fact that I'd been with Mom all the way through. Way back when, when Mom had first come to stay with us, I had learned about *pivoting*: a strategy to interrupt negative thoughts by asking "What do I want?" and focusing on that instead.

What do I want? I want to honor Mom, I want to keep my balance, I want to have fun and appreciate each day, I want peace and closeness with my brothers, I want to be healthy. I want to look to my Higher Power as a source of infinite love and grace. I want to be real. (Fall 2016)

As the anniversary of Mom's death approached, the crisp fall weather was full of reminders of her move to Wisconsin to live with us five years before, our return with her to Maine three years prior, and her hospice stretch here in our home a year ago. While I wanted to be aware of the world around me, the emotions within me had a life of their own, and I was tempted to get busy, to distract myself, to shut down the part that hurt. When it came to the moments before Mom died, "Froot Loop!" seemed glib, even disrespectful. Then I came across the above journal entry about pivoting and I decided to try that approach instead:

What do I want today? I want to forgive myself for the mistakes I made along the way. I want to celebrate Mom's life and the time we shared, I want to let the grief I feel bring her closer, not get in the way of my carrying on, I want to forgive myself that she died in my care, and to accept it's a choice she and I made together. (Fall 2020)

A week before, I'd attended an online workshop, "Reconnecting with Nature" with Susan Howe, as part of my second year at the Chaplaincy Institute.[146] At the end of the day, we participated in a healing hand-washing ritual. Right off the bat, I felt my emotions well up, so I turned off the camera, for privacy. As I immersed my hands in water, the hands that cared for Mom in the most sacred way I knew, the hands that couldn't save her despite all the love I'd felt, I began to weep. In the blink of an eye, our dog CJ was there, barking wildly at me. I couldn't quiet him, so I sat down with him on the floor, letting him lick my hands. Suddenly he stood at attention, head tilted, eyes glued on something outside the window. I followed his gaze to discover, in the upper branch of a tree, aglow with the afternoon sun, a chipmunk nibbling away. I'd been aware all day of that tree, loaded with golden leaves, reminiscent of the yellow leaf that had followed me a year ago, right after Mom died.

As CJ and I sat there watching the chipmunk munch away on another leaf, a blue jay flew down and landed on a nearby branch. This summer Siena had noted that each time she spotted a blue jay at camp, it felt like a visit from Mom, "Lala" to her. *Hi, Mom,* I thought.

I'm deeply grateful for "Froot Loop!"'s and pivoting, for healing rituals, barking dogs, yellow leaves, blue jays, and even grief, and for the many ways they reminded me to stay present so that I could feel, learn, catch my breath, and then dust myself off and get back into ready position so that I wouldn't miss what came next. On Saturday, as we returned home from a hike, Siena spotted another blue jay, this one perched in a tree at the top of our street. We looked at each other and smiled, understanding that Mom was still right here, with us. We just needed to be available to the moment, the best we could, to still be right here, with her.

⤫

Walking with Mom: Year Two, in Grief and in Joy, Too

It had been twenty months since Mom died in our care, and the time had come to weave together the wisps left in her wake.

When I'd enrolled at ChiME two summers before, I had done so because it was something future-oriented that I could do at Mom's side. Little had I known that those first weeks would coincide with Mom entering hospice care and that I would learn about chaplaining grief while actively grieving myself. I was grateful for all the love and support I'd received that had helped me stay the course and heal.

In the year since, busy with interfaith study, service and internship requirements, and a pandemic full house, my grief had shifted. Looking through photos, making a book of family recipes, sorting through Mom's things, sharing in safe places, and sprucing up Mom's room for my in-laws, I was more settled in the present than pulled to the past. I was relieved that, when I woke in the day's first light, homesick for my parents, I could feel the loss without it engulfing me.

Mom used to insist she didn't want her obituary to read "died peacefully in the circle of family and friends," nor did she want one of us kids eulogizing her—"Too sad," she said. Nonetheless, that's pretty much what we'd done, in a stretched-out sort of way, surrounding her as her memory, cognition, and mobility had changed, keeping her happy and safe the best we could, her granddaughters and niece sharing poems she'd chosen and memories they cherished at her funeral, a celebration that would have made Mom's heart sing, even with the tears that were shed.

Mom had said it herself, when asked about her wishes regarding medical care: "I've spent most of my life healthy, it'd be a shame to spend the last part sick." Even though her Alzheimer's spanned years, she had many beautiful moments during that stretch, and even that last six weeks, when we did our best to follow her lead. The hospice nurse who stopped in twice a week had reassured me later, when I worried whether I'd done enough, that Mom got the death she had sought, cognizant to the end, communicating what she needed, not dragging on once the pain set in.

While the joy of caring for Mom in our home, even with the challenges, had been undeniable, especially given her natural cheer, it had taken me longer to sort through the challenges of those last six weeks. With enough time to soften the memories of Mom's last moments, I could see the truth in the observation shared on parentgiving.com that "when your parent is dying on [her] own terms, death can be a beautiful time of bonding and mending."[147]

Eleven days before she died, I'd been writing in my journal when Mom opened her eyes, looked over at me, and asked, "Are you happy?"

"Yes," I answered. "Are you happy?"

"Yes..." Mom said. "Aren't we lucky?"

I realized, more than ever, with all the elders separated from their loved ones during their last stretches due to COVID-19, how lucky we'd truly been, to be together, side by side, all the way through. That's not to say there weren't moments with which I still grappled. Mom died the way she lived, like Hannah had predicted she would, the intensity of that last night, just her, me, and the animals—hospice guiding us by phone—reminding me of childbirth. As it turned out, I grieved the way I lived: As Mom slipped into the beyond, all the emotion I had shelved while caring for her hit me upside the head.

I never felt so sure about my mission here on earth as when I was raising kids. I had known my role, and even when it felt like mission impossible, I hadn't questioned it; I'd just questioned how to maintain balance while filling it. The four years caring for Mom had required similar twenty-four/seven attention. Again, my mission, while not easy, had been clear. Even with the incredible caregiver support we received and our commitment to stay positive and find joy in Mom's days, the process had sometimes kicked my butt and I had wondered how long I could keep it up. As with parenting, each time I thought we'd found a groove, something would shift and we'd have to find it again. As with parenting, when Mom felt pain, confusion, joy, peace, I felt it, too. As with parenting, I just did the best I could, hoping I had what it took to see it through.

In grief, "some people find themselves wondering, 'Who am I without my loved one?'" says Feldman. "People often define themselves by the roles they play in close relationships....Grief takes time because it entails accepting the loss of these roles and redefining ourselves....It's important to take comfort in what is stable and use this as a 'home base' from which to build new faith in who we are."[148]

I felt undone when Mom died, the grief front and center. When Dad had died sixteen years earlier, I processed my grief while attending to three young kids, as well as Mom, suddenly widowed. When Mom died, our kids grown and launched, I had time and place to mourn. I was grateful for the things I'd put in place to reduce caregiver stress: playing basketball, working out with my trainer Tia, and going back to school. I'd done my best to keep showing up, like Mom would have done. Little did I know that that which I'd put in place to help me care for Mom would help me care for me, afterward.

As it turned out, our nest, empty for the first time in almost three decades, filled back up five months later when our adult kids and their animals moved home during the pandemic, which had helped me step back outside of myself. When we moved eighty-five-year-old Mom back to Maine from the Midwest where we'd raised our kids, I had thought we were leaving our family home behind. I never expected our new home here, in Maine, to become a home for our kids. Now that they were all headed back out into the world, I was grateful for all the memories of Mom, intertwined with all the memories of them.

"The goal of grief work," says David Kessler, cowriter of Elisabeth Kubler-Ross, in a recent podcast, "is to remember that person, or that relationship with more love than pain, in time, at your own pace."[149] I was grateful that, more and more, the moments that reminded me of Mom, and Dad, too, made me smile, even when they also brought tears. A year before, opening camp had felt like ripping a Band-Aid off an open wound; this year, opening camp felt like putting on my favorite cozy paja-mas—or, better yet, diving into the cool fresh lake after a long hot day.

One foggy morning this past winter, I was skiing with Siena and Hannah, without poles, in challenging conditions, when I found myself deep in thought. I had hated ski school when I was little because it sepa-rated four-year-old me from Mom, my favorite teacher. When a wrong turn landed us on the steep Narrow Gauge trail, it was Mom who talked eight-year-old me down, bit by bit, fending off the speedy teens who cut too close. I felt torn in high school when skiing with friends meant leaving Mom alone on the hill. A decade later, Mom had taken care of one-year-old Siena so I could ski with Doug. Another decade later, after Dad died, Mom had taken us kids and grandkids to ski for the holidays, coaching Garrett on the bunny slope. As these memories came one after another, I found my balance in the heavy snow, feeling the thrill of the cold, fresh air and the icy, downward slope, knowing Mom would be—Mom was—happy for me. She was right there with me, which put a huge smile on my face beneath the pandemic mask.

This past June, as I stood on the stage of the outdoor chapel at Ferry Beach State Park being ordained as an interfaith minister, I recalled Dad saying that, had he not become a lawyer, he would have wanted to be a psychiatrist or a minister because he liked to listen to people's stories. I heard and felt Mom's presence in the birds singing way up in the trees and the gentle breeze on my face. I felt the pieces of my story settling into place. Recently I was asked what ordination by the Chaplaincy Institute of Maine means to me. It means I survived Mom's death and kept show-ing up afterward, in a way that she would want. It means I modeled for our kids how to keep growing, even when it's challenging and there's rea-son to pull back. It means I'm prepared to take what I've learned here to wherever I'm called next.

When we brought Mom back to Maine and she landed at Maine Med with a life-threatening blood clot, I had questioned the decisions we'd made to get her back. The afternoon she was discharged, Doug and I wrapped her in a blanket and rolled her to the shore of Casco Bay. The sun shining down on her, her eyes opened wide, tears had streamed down her face, and she'd said, her voice full of wonder, "It's so blue." In that moment, I knew beyond a shadow of doubt, we had gotten Mom back to her home—physical, emotional, and spiritual, too.

Mom died two years to the day of her return. The following spring, a facilitator of my bereavement group wrapped up an online meeting with Carol Staudacher's: "The life ahead of me consists of many paths. I choose those that fit with what I know to be right and true in my heart."[150] For the longest time, I had thought it was *we* who had gotten Mom home to Maine; these days, I realize it was the other way around: It was Mom who had brought us home to Maine.

AFTERWORD

I had no idea what lay ahead when I wrote:

A Love-Filled Apology to My Family
Monday, April 2, 2012

To Garrett:
I'm sorry for the times I've lost my temper with you.
I love you, inside and out.
I hope you know that
I see you in all your glory and
I am grateful that you are my son.

To Matt:
I'm sorry for the times I was too busy to stop, look you in the eyes, and listen.
I see you, I hear you—and I'm proud of you.
I noticed the times you saw me stressed, and
gave me a hug, calming words, reassurance.
I see the miracle that you are and I thank you for sharing your gifts with me.

To Siena:
I'm sorry for the times I held on too tightly.
I look at your graduation photo on my desk—
wild-haired, blue-eyed summertime beauty—
a smile that changes everything.
Thank you for smiling at me and setting me free.

229

> *To Doug:*
> *I'm sorry for putting you last, again,*
> *for being too busy, too tired, too needy,*
> *too aware of your absences and our differences,*
> *for taking you for granted and wanting more.*
> *Thank you for what you have shared with me—I love you for that.*

Much has changed in the decade since. Garrett, then an eighth grader, is a college graduate; Matt, then a high school junior, is a software engineer; Siena, then a college freshman, is a veterinarian; and Doug, then working his butt off at his career, is mostly retired. I had no idea, then, that together we would care for Mom as Alzheimer's disease took its toll—speaking of being busy, tired, and needy!

When I decided to write this book, I anticipated that rereading the reflections I'd written would be tough. However, unready to turn my attention elsewhere, I decided to go for it. I was pleasantly surprised when I reread what I would come to call Wintering, Springing, and Summering, and I enjoyed the opportunity to revisit our family life, before and after Mom came to live with us. Falling, however, felt different; it hurt, and I realized I was still processing Mom's last stretch.

So how is it that, when I awoke on October 15, 2021, the second anniversary of Mom's death, I was unprepared, even apologetic, for the intensity of the sadness I felt? Leading up to that day, I had tried to face the unresolved by sharing photos, notes, and texts from Mom's last weekend with my counselor, Erica. I had hoped that would help me heal, like scraping away old cells to let new ones grow. Then, the night of October 15th, I actually told Siena, "I don't know why I'm crying," echoing what Mom had told me in the wake of Dad's death years before.

Even as I talk the talk, I'm still learning to walk the walk. "Grief is an individual journey, and there are no rules to follow (forever, in my case, and maybe in yours, too), so there's no point in judging yourself or others for not 'getting over it' swiftly enough," writes mirabai starr, offering words I need to hear when I wonder whether it's time to just move on. "When someone is brave enough to speak of our loved one, it can be such a relief," starr continues. "For a moment there is another being to help lift and carry the great weight."[151] In addition to providing relief, sharing fuels me to stay the course.

There's no question that, over the years, I've relied on writing to help me through. When the kids were little, I wrote as therapy; as they grew, it provided me a place to create and strategize; caring for Mom, it helped me to find meaning; during my time at the Chaplaincy Institute of Maine, I came to see writing as a sacred practice; and at a recent online workshop featuring Reverend Sarah Shepley, I learned it's a way I self-regulate in response to trauma.[152] I'm just now recognizing the trauma I experienced those last hours with Mom—even as I would not have missed them for anything, I am still hoping I did enough. More than anything else, Mom would want me to be at peace. I am grateful that this book has given me a place to revisit, re-feel, reflect, and heal—essential steps in the caregiving path. Writing restores me to sanity, even as tears run down my face.

Today, the kids remaking their ways in the world of COVID-19, what stands out is that—despite my tendency to wish I'd done more—*gratitude, reframing, and faith* have seen me through. In that spirit, in place of a love-filled apology for the places I've come up short, I offer a love-filled thanks for all the ways my family has rescued me from losing myself along the way.

When I finally shared the notes stored on my phone during Mom's last hours, admitting my fear that I'd failed her, Erica asked what Mom would want for me now. When I blanked, she prodded: What would I tell our kids if they were in my shoes? She encouraged me to give myself the same:

To Me:
I trust you.
I love you and I know you love me.
Thank you for taking care of me and walking me all the way through.
I know you did the best you could with what you knew.
My wish for you now is to let yourself be free.
And just know, I'm still right here in spirit, riding shotgun with you.

When Dad died, it seemed like every time I got in the car I'd hear Joe Nichols's "The Impossible," which is exactly how it felt to carry on without him. When Mom died, fifteen years later, the song I heard, again and again, was Selena Gomez's "Lose You to Love Me," which captured the next big challenge. As I write these words, I see signs that I am on the right track:

Officiating summertime weddings that make my heart glad. Visiting Matt at his new home down south and being fully present for our time together. Forgetting to light the luminary that Hospice of Southern Maine had sent to honor Mom's memory the night that Garrett dropped in unexpectedly. Sharing a wrinkle-nosed smile with Mom's caregiver Jessica's baby, Jack. Expressing, on the second anniversary of Mom's death, my sadness to my sister-in-law Heidi and then to Doug, who after all these years, finally got it right: taking me by the hand, no words offered in an attempt to alleviate it.

And then there was the weekend, two years from the day of Mom's funeral; this time around Siena and Hannah took me to pick pumpkins and decorate Mom's and Dad's graves. When Garrett joined us that night for homemade apple pie, we all hung out, in the kitchen, together, laughing so hard that I cried, like Mom used to do. Even as I felt pain that made me want to run and hide, I stayed.

Even after all this, there is much left unsaid, more stories to tell, additional lessons to share, new medical research to consider. I offer instead *the bottom line*: Even when we are determined to focus on the joy of caring, there is no denying its burdens. The time has come to let them go, to unburden. Living is for living, after all.

♡

COMMUNICATION TOOLS

When I realized that changes in Mom's memory and cognition were interfering with her ability to share medical concerns with health care providers, my sister-in-law Nancy recommended I write a **Medical History Summary** to offer at the start of each appointment. This summary also helped me communicate with caregivers and family members who stood in for me. Reviewed and updated regularly, this tool became essential as health concerns developed and history became more complicated. I kept it in a folder with power of attorney and Do Not Resuscitate papers that we could grab as we headed out the door for medical attention. It proved invaluable in preventing relevant information from falling through the cracks.

I also created the following lists of **Household Information, Daily Care**, and **Additional Concerns Meriting Special Attention** which I shared with caregivers when I hired them and then reviewed when I left Mom with them. These helped ensure consistency and quality of care. Mom's **Daily Care** and **Additional Concerns Meriting Special Attention** evolved with time. At first they were meant simply to familiarize caregivers with her daily routine. With time, they became crucial in ensuring that we were all on the same page and that Mom was getting what she needed. For a while, they helped us lead Mom through quality days, and then, as we moved to her hospice stretch, they became a way to ensure we were letting her lead us, as we noted the signs that would help us with pain management. These guides also helped us track hydration and nutrition, as well as toileting and hygiene, and any changes and concerns.

It is important to ask caregivers to record their daily observations, and to make time to check in, encouraging questions and brainstorming strategies, to ensure a smooth shift in care. This is also a great way to acknowledge and support one another on the caregiving team. This is hard work and we need each other.

Medical History Summary for (Patient's Name)

Dear: **Date:**

My name is: **Relationship to Patient:**

I have been appointed power of attorney for:
We made this appointment with you today because:

I offer the following information, in the hope that it will help with today's appointment.

Current observations
(symptom, date noticed, how treated, any change or pattern):

Ongoing health concerns being monitored
(condition, date, description, treatment, provider):

Allergies:

Medicine list (name of medicine, dosage, purpose):

Other recent health concerns
(condition, date, description, treatment, provider):

Prior health concerns
(condition, date, description, treatment, provider):

Other concerns
(describe anything else that could be relevant with respect to care):

Household Information

Our Address: **Home Phone:**

How to contact me while I'm away:

Any other special instructions:

Important Contact Information (name, phone number, address)
Local police (non-emergency):

Doctors (area of care):

Pharmacy:

Veterinarian:

Helpers:

Neighbors:

Plumber/electrician:

Groceries/food delivery:

Trash removal:

Snow removal:

Other relevant utilities (account number):

Security system (passcode):

Extra key:

Other helpful information:

Daily Care — date:

Today's Goal:

Special Concerns:

Daily Guidelines:

Time	Activity (with specific instructions)	Caregiver name and notes
	Wake-up ritual (toileting, hygiene, dressing):	
	Medicine:	
	Breakfast:	
	Bathing:	
	Snack:	
	Recommended activity:	
	Lunch:	
	Medicine:	
	Quiet time:	
	Snack:	
	Recommended activity:	
	Dinner:	
	Recommended activity:	
	Snack:	
	Medicine:	
	Bedtime ritual (toileting, hygiene, dressing):	
	Wake-ups:	

Additional Concerns Meriting Special Attention

In case emergency care is called, please make sure to tell them
(hospital request/instructions):

DNR and other medical instructions:

Pain relief:

Mobility concerns:

Communication concerns:

Hearing aids (extra batteries?):

Eyeglasses (extras?):

Fluid intake:

Dietary restrictions:

Recommended activities:

Movement reminders:

Anything else that could be helpful (pet care, appointments, etc.):

Caregiver observations, concerns, recommendations (regarding pain, confusion, agitation, mobility, balance, energy level, vision, bleeding, rash, swelling, bedtime, wake-ups, toileting, bed-wetting, etc.):

TOPIC LIST

Health Concerns
Advocacy:

Alzheimer's Disease and Dementia—Assessment, Implications, and More:

Changes in Eyesight—Retinal Stroke and Temporal Arteritis:

Coronavirus 2019:

Hospitalization:

Pet Therapy

The Twelve Steps of Alcoholics Anonymous:

NOTES

PREFACE

1. For a comprehensive guide to caring for someone with Alzheimer's disease, based on personal experience and over 100 interviews, see Patti Kerr, *I Love You... Who Are You? Loving and Caring for a Parent with Alzheimer's* (Flemington, NJ: Along the Way Press, 2010).

INTRODUCTION

2. Tara Bahrampour, "Changing 'the tragedy narrative': Why a growing camp is promoting a more joyful approach to Alzheimer's," www.washingtonpost.com (2/21/2019).
3. Arnold Mindell, *Dreambody: The Body's Role in Revealing the Self* (Sigo Press, 1982), as discussed in: Gregg Levoy, *Callings: Finding and Following an Authentic Life* (New York, NY: Three Rivers Press, 1997), 87.
4. Lisa Steele-Maley, Interfaith Minister, *Without a Map: A Caregiver's Journey through the Wilderness of Heart and Mind* (San Antonio, TX: Turning Stone Press, 2018), x.

WINTERING

5. In addition to monthly support meetings and 24/7 telephone help, the Alzheimer's Association, www.alz.org, provides comprehensive information on all sorts of topics as they relate to Alzheimer's disease and other dementias. I also found helpful information at www.healthline.com, www.mayoclinic.org, and www.webmd.com.
6. To learn about the progression of Alzheimer's disease, as described by Barry Reisberg, MD, see "What Are the 7 Stages of Alzheimer's Disease?" www.alzheimers.net.
7. John Green, *The Fault in Our Stars* (Dutton Books, 2012), 260.
8. For a book that took me a while to open, and then changed my life, see John Bradshaw, *Healing the Shame That Binds You* (Deerfield Beach, FL: Health Communications, Inc., 1988). Bradshaw's work describes the lasting impact of hurtful words and offers strategies for choosing healthier messages to tell ourselves, and others.
9. See Melody Beattie, *The Language of Letting Go* (USA: Hazelden Publishing, 1990). This book of daily meditations helped me look inward

to figure out how to make the changes I sought, rather than waiting for others to do so.

10. See William Strunk Jr. and E.B. White, *The Elements of Style* (New York: MacMillan Publishing Co., Inc., 1979). Even now I turn to this guide recommended by my eleventh grade English teacher, Mr. Conroy, to figure out tense, among other things.

11. For information on central retinal artery occlusion (CRAO), see Kierstan Boyd, reviewed by Robert H. Janigian Jr., MD, "What Is a Stroke Affecting the Eye?" www.aao.org (10/14/15).

12. Al-Anon Family Group Headquarters, Inc., *Al-Anon's Twelve Steps & Twelve Traditions* (Virginia Beach, VA: Al-Anon Family Group Headquarters, Inc., 1981), 19.

13. See Mayo Clinic, "Sed rate (erythrocyte sedimentation rate)," www.mayoclinic.com (8/10/2021).

14. Paula Spencer Scott, *Surviving Alzheimer's: Practical Tips and Soul-Saving Wisdom for Caregivers* (San Francisco, CA: Eva Birch Media, 2018): another book I wish I'd had from the start of our caregiving journey.

15. Paula Spencer Scott, "7 Ways to Save Your Relationships from Caregiver Stress," globalag.igc.org (New America Media, 3/17/2012).

16. To help coordinate support to meet needs, see Alzheimer's Association, "Creating Your Care Team," www.alz.org.

17. Mom's neuropsychologist recommended this resource: The American Geriatrics Society 2012 Beers Criteria Update Expert Panel, "American Geriatrics Society updated Beers criteria for potentially inappropriate medication use in older adults," *Journal of the American Geriatrics Society*, 2012; 60:616–31.

18. See Melinda Smith, MA, et al., "Preventing Alzheimer's Disease and Dementia—or Slowing Its Progress," www.helpguide.org (updated 3/2021) for seven pillars recommended to improve brain health.

19. *Al-Anon's Twelve Steps & Twelve Traditions*, 25 (n. 12).

20. *Alateen's 4th Step Inventory* (Virginia Beach, VA: Al-Anon Family Group Headquarters, Inc., 1989).

21. Melody Beattie, *Codependent No More: How to Stop Controlling Others and Start Caring for Yourself* (San Francisco, CA: Harper/Hazelden, 1987), 173.

22. Hazelden, *Step Four: Getting Honest* (Center City, MN: Hazelden Foundation, 1992).

23. See Caregiver's Forum Message Board, "Alzheimer's Patient Worse Now Taking Prednisone," www.alzconnected.org (1/5/2012).

24. "Prednisone Tablet, Delayed Release (Enteric Coated)—Uses, Side Effects, and More," www.webmd.com.

25. See "Diverticulitis," www.webmd.com, reviewed since by Neha Pathak, MD (9/16/2021).

26. "Prednisone Tablet, Delayed Release (Enteric Coated) Precautions," www. webmd.com.

27. Daniel J. DeNoon, reviewed by Louise Chang, MD, "Pain a Problem in Alzheimer's Disease, Undertreated pain plagues Alzheimer's patients who hurt, but can't tell," www.webmd.com (9/22/2006).

28. Carole B. Larkin, "How to Take Care of a Dementia Patient in the Hospital," www.alzheimersreadingroom.com (12/6/2016).

29. Wilco P. Achterberg, et al., "Pain management in patients with dementia," www.ncbi.nlm.nih.gov (11/1/2013).

30. Amy M. Collins, associate ed., "Fecal Impaction and Dementia: Knowing What to Look for Could Save Lives," ajnoffthecharts.com.

31. "Can Milk of Magnesia Relieve Constipation?" www.healthline.com.

32. See Nancy L. Mace, MA, and Peter V. Rabins, MD, MPH, *The 36-Hour Day, A Family Guide to Caring for People Who Have Alzheimer's Disease, Related Dementias, and Memory Loss* (New York, NY: Grand Central Life & Style, 2011).

33. Heidi Godman, executive ed., *Harvard Health Letter*, "Regular exercise changes the brain to improve memory, thinking skills," www.health.harvard.edu (updated 11/29/2016).

34. See W. Gifford-Jones, MD, "Use it or lose it, Studies show that increased activity translates into greater brain power," www.pressreader.com (1/31/2017).

35. *Al-Anon's Twelve Steps & Twelve Traditions*, 31 (n. 12).

SPRINGING

36. For more tips on how to care for somebody with dementia, see Donna Schempp, LCSW, "Ten Real-Life Strategies for Dementia Caregiving," www.caregiver.org.

37. Alzheimer's Association, "Do not resuscitate (DNR)," www.alz.org.

38. For additional help making a daily plan to guide caregivers, promote independence, and adapt to change, see Alzheimer's Association, "Daily Care Plan," www.alz.org. See also Camille Peri, "Alzheimer's Disease: A Caregiver's Checklist for Daily Care," www.webmd.com.

39. Al-Anon Family Group Headquarters, Inc., *Al-Anon's Twelve Steps & Twelve Traditions* (Virginia Beach, VA: Al-Anon Family Group Headquarters, Inc., 1981), 39.

40. See Liz Neporent, "Strep Throat May Cause OCD, and 5 Other Surprising Facts," abcnews.go.com (January 29, 2013).

41. See Fiona MacDonald, "Scientists Identify a Virus and Two Bacteria That Could Be Causing Alzheimer's, 'We can't keep ignoring the evidence,'" www.sciencealert.com (3/11/2016).

42. See Priya Maheshwari and Guy D. Eslick, The University of Sydney, Penrith, NSW, Australia, "Bacterial Infection and Alzheimer's Disease: A Meta-Analysis," www.alzheimersanddementia.com (2014).

43. Lund University, "Gut bacteria may play a role in Alzheimer's disease," www.sciencedaily.com (2/10/2017).

44. James M. Ellison, MD, MPH, Swank Center for Memory Care and Geriatric Consultation, ChristianaCare, "Infections that Can Cause Dementia," www.brightfocus.org (11/14/16, updated 7/15/21).

45. Paula Spencer Scott, "Anticipatory Grief: How to Cope with the 'Living Death' of Alzheimer's," www.caring.com (updated 4/24/2017).

46. Sid Kirchheimer, reviewed by Brunilda Nazario, MD, "Caregiver Grief Triggers Mixed Emotions," www.webmd.com.

47. Alzheimer's Association, "Grief and Loss as Alzheimer's Progresses," www.alz.org.

48. Scott, "Anticipatory Grief: How to Cope" (n. 45).

49. DeNoon, "Pain a Problem in Alzheimer's Disease" (n. 27).

50. Alzheimer's Society, "Delirium," www.alzheimers.org.uk.

51. See Amanda Gardner, "Alzheimer's and Sleep Problems," www.webmd.com.

52. See "Munchausen Syndrome by Proxy," www.webmd.com (5/18/16).

53. Jennifer Wegerer, "The Connection Between UTIs and Dementia," www.alzheimers.net (6/26/2017).

54. Marlo Sollitto, "Urinary Tract Infections in the Elderly," www.agingcare.com (6/19/2017).

55. *Al-Anon's Twelve Steps & Twelve Traditions*, 45 (n. 39).

56. Alzheimer's Association, "New Alzheimer's Association Survey Reveals Dramatic Impact of Alzheimer's Disease on Families," www.alz.org (6/1/2017).

57. Scott, "How to Avoid Strained Sibling Relationships When a Parent Has Alzheimer's," www.caring.com (7/3/2017).

58. Connie Matthiessen, senior ed., "Love and Marriage (and Caregiving): Caring.com's Marriage Survey," www.caring.com (12/3/2016).

59. Alzheimer's Association, "New Alzheimer's Association Survey Reveals Dramatic Impact of Alzheimer's Disease on Families," stage.alz.org (6/1/2017).

60. See Connie Matthiessen, senior ed., "Marriage and Relationships: How Caregiving Couples Can Make It Work," www.caring.com (updated 5/16/2017).

61. *Al-Anon's Twelve Steps & Twelve Traditions*, 49 (n. 39).

62. *Al-Anon's Twelve Steps & Twelve Traditions*, 50 (n. 39).

63. John B. Adams, MD, and David A. Margolin, MD, "Management of Diverticular Hemorrhage," www.ncbi.nlm.nih.gov.

64. John P. Cunha, DO, FACOEP, and Bhupinder Anand, MD, "Gastrointestinal Bleeding," www.emedicinehealth.com (10/17/2016).

65. T.O. Kovacs, "Small Bowel Bleeding," www.ncbi.nlm.nih.gov (2005).

66. Maxwell Chait, MD, "Lower Gastrointestinal Bleeding in the Elderly," www.managedhealthcareconnect.com (9/5/2008).

67. Otto S. Lin, "Performing colonoscopy in elderly and very elderly patients: Risks, costs and benefits," www.ncbi.nlm.nih.gov (6/16/2014).

68. Deepak Gunjan, et al. "Small bowel bleeding: a comprehensive review," www.ncbi.nlm.nih.gov.

69. Mayo Clinic staff, "Capsule Endoscopy," www.mayoclinic.org (9/8/2015).

70. The American College of Gastroenterology, "Ulcers and Gastrointestinal Bleeding: Protecting Your Health—What you should know about the safe and appropriate use of common pain medications," www.illinoisgastro.com.

71. Catherine Salmon, PhD, and Katrin Schumann, *The Secret Power of Middle Children: How Middleborns Can Harness Their Unexpected and Remarkable Abilities* (New York, NY: Hudson Street Press, 2011), 265–66.

72. The Mayo Clinic, "Empty nest syndrome: Tips for coping," en.m.wikipedia.org (retrieved February 9, 2013).

73. F.T. Cohen, et al., "The marriage and family experience: Intimate relationships in a changing society," en.m.wikipedia.org (2011).

74. Dale Carnegie, *How to Win Friends & Influence People: The Only Book You Need to Lead You to Success* (New York, NY: Gallery Books, 1936), 70.

75. *Al-Anon's Twelve Steps & Twelve Traditions*, 57 (n. 39).

76. *Al-Anon's Twelve Steps & Twelve Traditions*, 60 (n. 39).

77. See Mark D. Coggins, "Tramadol Safety Concerns," Today's Geriatric Medicine Vol. 8 No. 4, www.todaysgeriatricmedicine.com, 6.

78. See Susan J. Jeffers, PhD, *Feel the Fear and Do It Anyway: Dynamic Techniques for Turning Fear, Indecision, and Anger into Power, Action, and Love* (New York, NY: Ballantine Books, 1987), 144.

SUMMERING

79. Al-Anon Family Group Headquarters, Inc., *Al-Anon's Twelve Steps & Twelve Traditions* (Virginia Beach, VA: Al-Anon Family Group Headquarters, Inc., 1981), 63.

80. *Al-Anon's Twelve Steps & Twelve Traditions*, 65 (n. 79).

81. See Skin Cancer Foundation, "Mohs Micrographic Surgery: An Overview," www.skincancer.org.

82. For more information on deep vein thrombosis, see Mayo Clinic staff, "Deep vein thrombosis (DVT)," www.mayoclinic.org. See also "Inferior Vena Cava Filter Placement and Removal," www.radiologyinfo.org.

83. See "If a tree falls in a forest," en.wikipedia.org.

84. *Al-Anon's Twelve Steps & Twelve Traditions*, 69 (n. 79).

85. *Al-Anon's Twelve Steps & Twelve Traditions*, 69 (n. 79).

86. Darcy Wakefield, *I Remember Running: The Year I Got Everything I Ever Wanted—and ALS* (New York, NY: Marlowe & Company, 2005), 113.

87. As our need for in-home help evolved, so did our management approach. Organizing finances above-table not only acknowledged the importance of Mom's caregivers, it also allowed them to collect unemployment insur-

ance after she died, while seeking new work. In the midst of caregiving for Mom myself, I appreciated the assistance of the payroll company we hired, as well as online resources like "In Home Care," www.alz.org; and Family Caregiver Alliance, "Hiring In-Home Help," www.caregiver.org. See also Erik Johnson, "How to start paying your caregiver on the books: Six steps to transition your nanny or senior caregiver from being paid under the table," www.care.com (7/16/2021).

88. See Alzheimer's Association, "Treatments for Sleep Changes," www.alz.org.

89. See Alzheimer's Association, "Risk Factors," www.alz.org.

90. Sandee LaMotte, "Can poor sleep lead to Alzheimer's or dementia?" www.cnn.com (8/23/2017).

91. *Al-Anon's Twelve Steps & Twelve Traditions*, 75 (n. 79).

92. Referred to as "The Big Book": William G., AA cofounder, *Alcoholics Anonymous: The Story of How Many Thousands of Men and Women Have Recovered from Alcoholism* (New York, NY: Alcoholics Anonymous World-Wide Services, Inc., 1976), 95.

93. National Institute of Health (NIH) National Institute on Aging (NIA), "Managing Money Problems in Alzheimer's Disease," www.nia.nih.gov (reviewed 5/18/2017).

94. Jason Samenow, "More than 1 million power outages in the Northeast after blockbuster fall storm," www.washingtonpost.com (10/30/2017).

95. See Don Miguel Ruiz, MD, with Janet Mills, *The Four Agreements: A Practical Guide to Personal Freedom, A Toltec Wisdom Book* (San Rafael, CA: Amber Allen Publishing, 1997), 29.

96. Jeffrey M. Schwartz, MD, and Beverly Beyette, *Brain Lock: Free Yourself from Obsessive-Compulsive Behavior, A Four-Step Treatment Method to Change Your Brain Chemistry* (New York, NY: Harper Perennial, 2016), 58.

97. Barbara Cooney, *Miss Rumphius* (Puffin Books, 1982).

98. *Al-Anon's Twelve Steps & Twelve Traditions*, 7 (n. 79).

99. Caroline Knapp, *Drinking: A Love Story* (New York, NY: The Dial Press, 1996), 14, 20.

100. See Daily Caring, "3 Ways to Reduce Caregiver Stress with Positive Self Talk," dailycaring.com; Daily Caring, "10 Ways Caregivers Can Take a Quick Break Right Now," dailycaring.com; and Daily Caring, "3 Ways to Manage Caregiver Stress and Prevent Burnout," dailycaring.com.

101. Daily Caring, "Stop Caregiver Stress from Killing You," dailycaring.com.

102. *Al-Anon's Twelve Steps & Twelve Traditions*, 13 (n. 79).

103. See Alzheimer's Association, "Parent's Guide, Helping Children and Teens Understand Alzheimer's Disease," www.alz.org.

104. See, e.g., Brenda Barron, "9 Tips for Managing Sandwich Generation Stress," www.care.com.

105. Aileen Fisher, illustrated by Stefano Vitale, *The Story of Easter* (Harper Collins Publishers, 1997).

106. Robert B. Santulli, MD, and Kesstan Blandin, PhD, *The Emotional Journey of the Alzheimer's Family* (Hanover, NH: Dartmouth College Press, 2015), 101.
107. See Sam Sellers, president of Dignity Enterprises, Inc., *Finding Freedom at Home: The Ultimate Guide to Home Care* (Little Rock, AR: Paperback Expert, 2013).
108. See Alzheimer's Association, "Medication Safety," www.alz.org.

FALLING
109. Atul Gawande, *Being Mortal: Medicine and What Matters in the End* (New York, NY: Metropolitan Books, 2014), 229.
110. Lisa Steele-Maley, Dean of the Chaplaincy Institute of Maine, *Arriving Here: Reflections from the Hearth and Trail* (USA: Lampryridae, LLC, 2020), 49. Stepping forward from caring for her father as dementia unfolded, Lisa anchors her ongoing experience of spiritual development in the natural changes that accompany the seasons of the year, a reminder to me that even when we consider the details of our own experiences unique, something greater connects us.
111. Alzheimer's Association, "End-of-Life Decisions, Honoring the Wishes of a Person with Alzheimer's Disease," www.alz.org.
112. The Family Caregiver Alliance, "Advanced Illness: CPR and DNR," www.caregiver.org (12/31/2004).
113. Kevin M. Dirksen, MDiv, MSC, HEC-C, and Neil S. Wenger, MD, MPH, "For elderly patients, CPR unlikely to be the right medicine," www.pressherald.com (3/19/2013). See also, Paul C. McLean, "CPR more often prolongs seniors' suffering than saves lives," www.theguardian.com (3/5/2013).
114. Michael Gordon, MD, MSC, FRCPC, "The Role of CPR in the Elderly," www.hmpgloballearningnetwork.com (4/19/2013).
115. Susan M. Matthews, PhD, "CPR Versus DNR for the Elderly Patient," www.lifemattersmedia.org (8/19/2016).
116. See, e.g., David Railton, "Herpes may account for 50 percent of Alzheimer's cases," www.medicalnewstoday.com (10/19/2018).
117. See, e.g., Catharine Paddock, PhD, "Study links severe gum disease to raised dementia risk," www.medicalnewstoday.com (3/20/2019).
118. See, e.g., Nicholas J. Justice, "The relationship between stress and Alzheimer's disease," www.ncbi.nlm.nih.gov (4/21/2018).
119. See, e.g., Harrison Wein, PhD, "Sleep deprivation increases Alzheimer's protein," www.nih.gov (4/24/2018); Claudia Wallis, "The Sleep–Dementia Connection," apple.news (4/16/2019); and Tara Bahrampour, "Interrupted Sleep may lead to Alzheimer's, new studies show," www.washingtonpost.com (7/18/2017).
120. Alzheimer's Association, "Grief and Loss as Alzheimer's Progresses," www.alz.org.

121. David Kessler, *Finding Meaning: The Sixth Stage of Grief* (New York, NY: Scribner, 2019), 10.
122. See "2019 National Senior Games Presented by Humana Boasts Record-High Athlete Attendance," nsga.com (June 10, 2019).
123. Maggie Oman Shannon, *The Way We Pray: Prayer Practices from Around the World* (Berkeley, CA: Conari Press, 2001), xv. This book, assigned as chaplaincy homework, offers all kinds of ways to connect with the Divine, which helped me as I cared for Mom.
124. Judy Flickinger, *Spirit Matters: How to Remain Fully Alive with a Life-Limiting Illness* (Mustang, OK: Tate Publishing & Enterprises, 2009), 167.
125. See Donna Authers, "How to Support a Loved One Who Is Dying," www.agingcare.com.
126. See Amanda Jellig, "1 year later: a look back at the worst wind-storm in Maine's history," wgme.com (10/28/2018).
127. See Charlie Lopresti, "Powerful nor'easter hits Maine, thousands without power," wgme.com (10/17/2019).
128. "Grief and the Holidays, dealing with the pain," grief.com.
129. Amy Morin, "How to Deal with Grief During the Holidays: The holidays can be the toughest time of the year," www.psychologytoday.com (12/21/2015).
130. Tish Harrison Warren, "Want to Get into the Christmas Spirit? Face the Darkness: How I fell in love with the season of Advent," www.nytimes.com (11/30/2019).
131. For more strategies on how to cope with the holidays while grieving, see Litsa Williams, "64 Tips for Coping with Grief at the Holidays," whatsyourgrief.com (12/3/2019). See also, Anthony Komaroff, MD, *Harvard Health Letter*, "Coping with grief and loss during the holidays," www.health.harvard.edu (updated 12/1/2017).
132. Lulu Wang, *The Farewell*, www.scriptslug.com, 69.
133. See "Your Rights Under HIPAA," www.hhs.gov.
134. See Kathleen Allen, LCSW, C-ASWCM, "Alzheimer's Disease: The Magic of Pets," www.brightfocus.org.
135. Anne-Marie Botek, "Canine Caregivers Improve the Lives of People with Alzheimer's Disease," www.agingcare.com.
136. For more on the benefits for patients and caregivers of interacting with animals of all sorts—service, pet, robotic, and stuffed, see Being Patient, "Good Dogs: Dementia Service Dogs Provide Patients, Caregivers with Improved Quality of Life," www.beingpatient.com (12/28/2018).
137. Tal Axelrod, "Maine issues stay-at-home order," thehill.com (3/31/20).
138. See CDC, "People who are at higher risk for severe illness," www.cdc.gov (3/26/2020).
139. See Tanner Jensen, "Dr. James Ellison: How to Keep People with Dementia Safe from Coronavirus," www.beingpatient.com (3/5/2020). See also,

Alzheimer's News Today, "Information About COVID-19 for Alzheimer's Disease Patients," alzheimersnewstoday.com (3/24/2020).

140. David B. Feldman, PhD, "Why the Five Stages of Grief Are Wrong: Lessons from the (non-)stages of grief," www.psychologytoday.com (7/7/2017).

141. Definition of *synchronicity*, www.lexico.com.

142. Edie Thys Morgan, "Losing My Mom to Alzheimer's, Then Finding Her Again: I wish someone had told me about the beauty that waited at the end of this journey," www.nytimes.com (5/9/2020).

143. R.M. Vaughan, "What to expect when your parent is dying," www.the-gloveandmail.com (1/1/2015, updated 5/12/2018).

144. Christina Gregory, PhD, "The Five Stages of Grief: An Examination of the Kubler-Ross Model," www.psycom.net (updated 9/23/2020).

145. Feldman, "Why the Five Stages of Grief Are Wrong" (n. 140).

146. Susan Howe, Interfaith Chaplain, "Reconnecting with Nature," a workshop provided by the Chaplaincy Institute of Maine (10/4/2020).

147. "How to Give Your Parent a Peaceful Passage: 9 Pieces of Bedside Wisdom," www.parentgiving.com.

148. Feldman, "Why the Five Stages of Grief Are Wrong" (n. 140).

149. "The Sixth Stage of Grief with David Kessler," www.onecommune.com (6/11/2020).

150. Carol Staudacher, *A Time to Grieve: Meditations for Healing after the Death of a Loved One* (New York, NY: HarperOne, 1994).

AFTERWORD

151. mirabai starr, *Wild Mercy: Living the Fierce and Tender Wisdom of the Women Mystics*, (Boulder, CO: sounds true, 2019), 202.

152. Sarah Shepley, Interfaith Minister, "The Wisdom of Trauma," a workshop provided by the Chaplaincy Institute of Maine (11/7/2021).

ABOUT ME

©Amy Wilton Photography

Raised in Maine, graduated from Dartmouth College and Harvard Law School, I had spent the better part of the last three decades parenting our three kids in Wisconsin. In 2016, in the midst of their leaving the nest, Mom moved in with us from Maine, leading to precious time and daily opportunities I'd never anticipated. I learned, in large part by trial and error, how to give care to an elder with Alzheimer's disease and other health challenges, while also walking with our kids into adulthood.

On June 6, 2021, a year and a half after Mom died, our nest empty for the first time, I was ordained an Interfaith Minister by the Chaplaincy Institute of Maine. I've come to believe that sharing my caregiving journey is one of the ways I am called to chaplain. I hope these reflections inspire insight and growth, humor and joy, and a sense of community that offers fuel in walking life's greatest challenges, which sometimes turn out to be our greatest blessings. I am grateful for how revisiting my real-time reflections has helped me process and heal.

Time is precious, especially when we are caring for others, so thank you for spending some of yours walking with us. Safe travels.